Finance and the World Economy in Weimar Cinema

Finance and the World Economy in Weimar Cinema

Owen Lyons

Routledge
Taylor & Francis Group
LONDON AND NEW YORK

The publication of this book was supported by a grant from Toronto Metropolitan University.

First published in 2023 by Amsterdam University Press Ltd.

Published 2025 by Routledge
4 Park Square, Milton Park, Abingdon, Oxon OX14 4RN
605 Third Avenue, New York, NY 10158

Routledge is an imprint of the Taylor & Francis Group, an informa business

ISBN: 9789463727136 (hbk)
ISBN: 9781041179443 (pbk)
ISBN: 9781003695684 (ebk)
NUR 670

Cover illustration: Entrance to the Berliner Börse, September 18, 1931. "After the collapse of DANAT Bank and the Nordwolle Group, the stock exchange has to close." Photo: Scherl for *Süddeutsche Zeitung.*

Cover design: Kok Korpsershoek

DOI 10.5117/9789463727136

Table of Contents

List of Illustrations

Acknowledgements

I would like to thank the series editors, Malte Hagener, Patricia Pisters, and Wanda Strauven, as well as commissioning editor, Maryse Elliot, for their guidance, and the anonymous reviewers for their insightful suggestions. Completion of this book was made possible by funding from the Social Sciences and Humanities Research Council of Canada. I would like to thank Michael Wedel at the Filmuniversität Babelsberg Konrad Wolf for supporting my research, Philipp Stiasny and Cordula Döhrer for their generosity and guidance of my research at the Filmarchiv des Bundesarchivs and the Deutsche Kinemathek in Berlin, and Karl Wratschko for his assistance at Filmarchiv Austria. Thanks also to Anton Kaes, Johannes von Moltke, and Eric Rentschler and for my invitation to the German Film Institute at the University of Michigan, Ann Arbor. I would like to thank all of the participants of those seminars for their invaluable insight, and especially Paul Dobryden, Barbara Hales, Mihaela Petrescu, Christian Rogowski, and Valerie Weinstein. Similarly, I would like to thank members of the Berkeley-Tübingen-Wien-Harvard research network, including Wolfgang Fichna, Kristin Kopp, Rob McFarland, and Gabe Trop for their suggestions on an early version of this book. Thanks to Quinn Slobodian for many inspiring conversations and for his comments on an early version of the first chapter of this book. I am grateful for having had the opportunity to present aspects of this project at various conferences and symposia, including Weimar 2020 at Western University, the Weimar Film Network at the University of Warwick, Carleton University, the German Historical Institute, German Studies Association, Society for Cinema and Media Studies, Modern Languages Association, Annual Screen Studies Conference, Film and Media Studies Association of Canada, and the European Network for Cinema and Media Studies (NECS). Thank you to my parents and family, as well as Erika Balsom, Scott Birdwise, Matthew Croombs, Marc Furstenau, Barbara Leckie, Támas Nagypál, and Paul Theberge. I am deeply indebted to Mitchell Frank and Barbara Gabriel for their mentorship and guidance. A special thank you goes to the late Thomas Elsaesser for his inspiration and generosity as a professor and his early review of this book project.

Finally, to Višnja, Julian and Zoe, thank you for the journey – both past and yet to come.

Introduction

> You will get a practical knowledge of the mechanisms and be obliged to follow the stock exchange reports from London, New York, Paris, Berlin and Vienna at first hand, and in this way the world market, in its reflex as money and stock market, will reveal itself to you. Economic, political and other reflections are just like those in the human eye, they pass through a condensing lens and thereafter appear upside down, standing on their heads. Only the nervous system which would put them on their feet again for representation is lacking. The money market man only sees the movement of industry and of the world market in the inverted reflection of the money and stock market and so effect becomes cause to him.
> – Friedrich Engels in correspondence with Conrad Schmidt, 1890.[1]

Writing shortly before the birth of the cinema, Friedrich Engels described how the mechanisms of the stock exchange represented the world market as inverted reflections, 'standing on their heads.' Using this explicitly optical metaphor – which also describes the precise relationship between image and subject in a camera obscura – Engels claimed that stock exchange reports were 'utterly useless for the course of industry' because the 'gentry' who relied on them 'tried to explain everything from crises on the money market, which were generally only symptoms.'[2] To Engels, the metaphor of an 'inverted reflection' represented the idea that though financial markets depend on underlying economies of goods and services, they are effectively only representations of these economies and often move independently from them. Further, this is a visual metaphor that relies on a conception of financial activity as a vast *labour of representation* that inverts cause and effect according to the logic of the 'nervous system' of the market itself. At the turn of the twentieth century, this optical metaphor was the subject of debate between those who embraced the idea of the market as a camera

1 Friedrich Engels, "Letter from Friedrich Engels to Conrad Schmidt in Berlin – Oct. 27, 1890," in *Marx and Engels Correspondence*, trans. Donna Torr (New York: International Publishers, 1968), 482.
2 Ibid.

Lyons, O., *Finance and the World Economy in Weimar Cinema*. Taylor & Francis Group, 2023.
DOI 10.5117/9789463727136_INTRO

that provided accurate 'snapshots' of the economy – in Joseph Schumpeter's words – as opposed to those who, like Engels, claimed that this optical and cinematic arrangement produced only a self-fulfilling illusion. For Engels, the image created by this arrangement reconfigured the relationship between capital and reality, becoming not merely a representation of the external world of the market, but rather, a force that caused ripples on the surface of that world to appear. In Engels's words, 'as soon as trading in money becomes separate from trade in commodities it has (under certain conditions imposed by production and commodity trade and within these limits) a development of its own, special laws and separate phases determined by its own nature.'[3] Engels finds the 'most striking example of this' in the American and English railways that are laid, 'not in the interests of production and communications but simply because of a rivalry which usually only had the object of facilitating the stock exchange dealings of the shareholding money traders.'[4] In the halls of the stock exchange, the image of the market was then interpreted and turned 'upright' on its feet through the 'nervous system' of the assembled traders on the floor.

The visual nature of the technologies of the stock exchange has only become truly obvious in the last several decades and with the advancement of screen-based technologies for watching and acting on the market. These technologies have developed from rudimentary charting and graphing in the nineteenth century to the sophisticated multi-screen visualizations of the modern-day Bloomberg Terminal and similar technologies. This phenomenon has become an object of a considerable body of scholarship from within the sociology of financial markets which has confirmed the scopic relationship that exists between the tools financial workers use and the market.[5] As an example of this, Karin Knorr-Cetina's work based on interviews with interbank currency traders in the late 1990s and early 2000s is truly illuminating. Asked what the market represented on the screen of his terminal 'is,' one trader responded 'Everything. Everything.' – these screens are 'a building site on which a whole economic and epistemological world is erected.'[6] Financial markets, of course, have not

3 Ibid., 483.

4 Ibid.

5 See Alex Preda, *Framing Finance: The Boundaries of Markets and Modern Capitalism* (Chicago: University of Chicago Press, 2009); Karin Knorr-Cetina and Alex Preda, eds., *The Sociology of Financial Markets* (Oxford: Oxford University Press, 2006).

6 Karin Knorr-Cetina, "How are Markets Global? The Architecture of a Flow World," in *The Sociology of Financial Markets*, ed. Karin Knorr-Cetina and Alex Preda (Oxford: Oxford University Press, 2006), 48.

always been represented on the screens of specialized hardware for their participants, however, as will be discussed in this study, the roots of this optical arrangement can be traced back to the invention of charts, indices and mathematical methods for coming to terms with speculation – the invention of which almost exactly corresponds with that of the birth of the cinema.

The research behind this book is bracketed by two financial crises – it was begun shortly after the crash of 2008 and emerges now in the midst of the uncertainty of a post-pandemic world and a crash and seeming recovery of global markets that have decoupled from any notion of the 'real' economy. As such, it has been informed by the ways in which fictions of finance have represented and shaped these two recent crises. Following the events of 2008, narratives began to emerge that attempted to come to terms, or in some cases explain, events that defied understanding outside of a narrow pool of specialists. The problem was too complex, but non-specialists turned to *other* screens to attempt to understand why their savings had disappeared and to catch a glimpse of the submerged contours of the interconnected leviathan of the global economy. After 2008 it became apparent that cinema would function as a method of explaining the complexity back to a bewildered audience. Films began to appear that distilled the complexity of market events into digestible narratives, such as Oliver Stone's sequel to his 1987 financial drama, *Wall Street: Money Never Sleeps* (2010). Oliver Stone's father had been a stock broker and the film was co-written by Allan Loeb, whose previous career at the Chicago Board of Trade seemed to lend the script an added level of elucidative power. These bona fides were duly noted in reviews of the film that easily accepted that it was *expected* to in some way explain the intricacies of the financial world. As Anthony Oliver Scott wrote in his review of the film for *The New York Times*:

> The real story of modern financial calamity is so enormous, so intricate and so confusing that any fictional distillation of it is likely to fall short and ring false, and even casual readers of 'The Big Short' by Michael Lewis or the business section of *The New York Times* will find factual nits to pick with the new 'Wall Street.' But there are also moments of astonishing insight, and a sweeping sense of moral drama that feels true in spite of inaccuracies and implausibilities.[7]

7 A. O. Scott, "Michael Douglas Returns in Oliver Stone's Sequel," *The New York Times*, September 23, 2010.

By 'inaccuracies and implausibilities' Scott suggests that the film be compared to the shaky and still emerging history of the 2008 crisis and, like other reviewers, he accepts that the film contains a 'teachable' moment, stating that: 'If the film were a college course, it would be Economics for Poets,' and indeed, a reformed Gordon Gekko – the infamous cultural icon birthed by the first *Wall Street* – delivers a long monologue on the state of the financial markets after 2008 from the podium in an actual lecture hall. But the lesson does not reveal the secrets of the market and, as Scott laments: 'To the question "What went wrong?" the film offers an answer that is both irrefutable and unsatisfying: human nature.'

Sitting in a darkened movie theatre in 2011 while the trailers rolled before a screening of J. C. Chandor's *Margin Call*, it became clear to me that the assembled audience – a packed house, most of whom were middle-aged or older – was in attendance as much to enjoy this spectacle of the recent financial crisis as they were to get some answers as to where all the money had gone. There was a feeling of anticipation – that the narrative of the film, and the dialogue taken directly from the jargon of financial markets, would explain what a credit default swap was or how the 'masters of the universe'[8] had so spectacularly let the whole house of cards come crashing down. But rather than dismiss these audiences and films as a somehow parallel phenomenon to the 'real' market, it is clear that – along with the talking heads on financial news networks and the screen-based terminals that traders used to 'see' it – these films are part of the hypermediated screen-based culture of modern financial markets. Like the frenetic antics of CNBC star Jim Cramer – host of *Mad Money*, a daily financial opinion show known for its cartoonish props and sound effects – these films were part of the distended armature of visual representations of the market that began with the charts and graphs of Louis Bachelier at the turn of the twentieth century and continue to surround us today on the market tickers and chyrons of massive video screens that stand at the urban financial centres of the world. These are the screens upon which the market becomes visible, or as Scott concludes his review, 'Oliver Stone is not the man to explain Wall Street, or to stoke public indignation at its crimes. But no one else could turn it into a show like "Wall Street."'

Images of today's exchanges differ in significant ways from earlier scenes of panicked traders and ticker tape on the floor. Exchanges are now virtual, placeless, and largely emptied of people. Today their participants connect

8 Now a commonly used label in financial discourse, the term originates in Tom Wolfe, *The Bonfire of the Vanities* (New York: Farrar, Straus Giroux, 1987).

from remote locations and are surrounded and engaged by a plethora of visual technologies. As such, marketplaces are now composite assemblages of digital imagery and concrete tectonic forms, while at the same time, their participants are increasingly involved in an image-making process of its own kind. This conflation of the realm of visual production and finance is no more clearly articulated today than in the case of the NASDAQ (National Association of Securities Dealers Automated Quotations). Established in 1971, America's first electronic market has never comprised an inhabitable physical space – it has no trading floor and its servers are remotely located in New Jersey. Nevertheless, the façade of the iconic NASDAQ MarketSite tower on Times Square announces its presence with a massive LED screen and, instead of a trading floor, its interior houses a television studio set from which financial networks broadcast daily market reports. Within this extended media terrain, financial fictions like *Margin Call* and *Wall Street: Money Never Sleeps* should be taken seriously as feeding back into the doubled reflection of the financial markets. Certainly, in the case of Oliver Stone's original *Wall Street* of 1987, the 'greed is good' monologue that was delivered by Michael Douglas as Gordon Gekko and secured him a Best Actor Oscar, became a mantra for the era of Reaganomics. Evoking the image of lost 'greatness' that still dominates American political discourse today, Gekko became an archetype of the Wall Street set – his slicked-back hair, pinstripes and trademark suspenders aped by countless breathless traders yelling on the floor of the exchange and eager to assume their imagined mantle of neoliberal hypermasculinity. Today, we clearly see this particular performance of masculinity, that was born in the excesses of the 1980s Wall Street style, at the highest levels of the American political establishment, but its central imaginary and cultural code recall much older constructions. Accordingly, questions concerning the construction of masculinity – or the bolstering of an imaginary image of masculinity in the face of the accelerated pressures of finance capital – will be examined extensively in this book.

This book shows that it is through these cultural codes and others, with all their inherent semiotic baggage, that the supposedly rational space of the market is filtered. Confronted with this conflation of visual regimes, I set out to recount a history of how this doubled reflection that comprises the image of financial markets came to be. Where and when did the market appear to audiences in its spectral and scopic form? Over the course of my research, it became apparent that, through a combination of factors that will be discussed at length, the appearance of the market on screen was experienced in the time of the Weimar Republic in a manner that was unparalleled. In a unique conflation of the legacy of German-language economic theory, with the particular circumstances of the German experience of money and finance in the 1920s, the contours of the world economy appeared on the screens of the Weimar Republic in a manner that not only made this abstract space visible as a mass effect, but that was intimately bound with the development of Weimar as the 'laboratory of modernity.' The well-known shocks of the hyperinflation of 1921–23 and the stock market crash of 1929 are only part of a much wider nexus of crisis inaugurated by a global money system, which was materially present in the fabric of Weimar institutions and individuals while, at the same time, the extent of its reach into every domain of public and private life was largely invisible. This crisis was instead refracted into a fraught scene of representations, as social critics and artists alike sought to find a new visual vocabulary to capture a phenomenon that destabilized the secure boundaries of the nation, challenged traditional categories of time and space, mobilized rapidly changing new technologies, and oscillated between frameworks of rational and irrational forces. As such, this book is an attempt to reveal how representations of finance capital and the world economy have been overlooked in histories of Weimar cinema even when examples of its presence can be found everywhere.

In a very tangible sense, and as was commented on at the time by the German sociologist and historian Karl Demeter, the history of the cinematic output of the Weimar Republic is coupled with the movements of the global market. He writes that:

> German cinematic geography – if I may use this expression – appears to offer a precise parallel to German economic geography in every detail. In other words, the expansion and the frequency of cinemas in any given region are dependent upon the expansion of capitalist production processes.[9]

Further, Demeter claims that it is 'no wonder' that the 'homo economicus characterizing our capitalist age and capitalist countries, concerned as he is with the rational economy, looks to film for the satisfaction of his spiritual needs.'[10] It is this turning to the cinema – by the masses of white-collar workers and others connected to the financial industry – that this study

9 Karl Demeter, "The Sociological Foundations of the Cinema Industry," trans. Michael Cowan, in *The Promise of Cinema: German Film Theory, 1907–1933*, ed. Anton Kaes, Nicholas Baer, and Michael Cowan (Berkeley: University of California Press, 2016), 174. Originally published as "Die soziologischen Grundlagen des Kinowesens," *Deutsche Rundschau* 52 (July 1926).

10 Ibid.

addresses. As Joseph Max Jacobi argued in 1917, the 'international language' of film was 'the most powerful propaganda tool for Germany's financial sector,' and 'there should be films explaining every part of the national economy."[11] I ask, when faced with the subsequent and accelerated financial shocks that marked the life of the republic, what images on screen did they seek out, and further, what was the explanatory power of these images?

At the same time that these white-collar workers looked to the content of the films discussed in this study to see the world of finance reflected, the rapid rise in the number of film studios in the Weimar Republic was being fed by the speculative fever that marked its early years. At this time, the film industry benefited greatly in the short term from the hyperinflation which drove an export boom by German film companies eager to sell their product for currencies other than the declining mark.[12] The largest of these companies was the publicly traded Universum-Film Aktiengesellschaft (UFA), which was formed on 18 December 1917. With an initial capitalization of 25 million marks, its board of directors was made up of 'a respectable cross section of the Wilhelmine haute bourgeoisie, with especially strong representation from Prusso-German financial and industrial capital'[13] and Emil Georg von Stauss, director of Deutsche Bank, as its chair. UFA would soon become the largest film company in Europe. The next largest film company, Decla Bioskop Aktiengesellschaft, was acquired by UFA in October 1921 as the premier film company rapidly expanded both its production and distribution capacity. A consortium of Bavarian banks stood behind the Emelka-Konzern, UFA's next-largest competitor, while the Deulig-Konzern was backed by capital from heavy industry in North Rhine-Westphalia, and Terra Film Aktiengesellschaft was largely backed by the Wiener, Levy & Co. banking house.[14] In the period between the end of the First World War and the stabilization of the mark in 1924, investment drove growth in the often high-performing companies[15] that controlled most German film distribution

11 Joseph Max Jacobi, "The Triumph of Film," trans. Alex H. Bush, in Kaes et al., *The Promise of Cinema*, 278. Originally published as "Der Triumph des Films," in *Der Kinematograph* 563 (October 10, 1917).

12 'At the height of the export boom (1921–23), it is estimated that only 30–40 per cent of the industry's costs were covered by the home market.' Julian Petley, *Capital and Culture: German Cinema 1933–45* (London: British Film Institute, 1979), 33.

13 Klaus Kreimeier, *The Ufa Story: A History of Germany's Greatest Film Company, 1918–1945* (Berkeley: University of California Press, 1999), 29.

14 Petley, *Capital and Culture*, 32.

15 UFA paid dividends of 30 per cent in 1921 and 700 per cent in 1922 which, though these figures must be adjusted for inflation, demonstrate the performance of its stock. Petley, *Capital and Culture*, 33.

between them. Weimar cinema was born of this speculative fever and here I will show how it reflected back an image of finance and speculation to its audience. Indeed, the majority of the films discussed here – and a large number of films that have come to define Weimar cinema – were born in the period of financial turmoil that is bookended by the inflation and the bankrupting of UFA by the box office failure of Fritz Lang's *Metropolis* (1927). The collapse of UFA led to its partial rescue by the American studios Paramount Pictures and Metro-Goldwyn-Mayer and then to the catastrophic takeover of the studio by the press mogul and reactionary politician Alfred Hugenberg. In this sense, Weimar cinema can be understood as having been shaped to a particularly large degree by the booms and busts of finance capital. It is no wonder then that, even beyond the examples discussed here, ruinous financial transactions are alluded to in a very large proportion of the films of the period.

Histories of the Weimar Republic and Weimar cinema have established the period as a 'laboratory of modernity' in their discussions of the ongoing crisis instigated by Germany's rapid transition to a modern social democracy.[16] However, the centrality of finance and speculation to the emergence of a modern subjectivity, and the role of finance in the everyday experience of the period, have been unsatisfactorily addressed – especially since financial speculation was the vital engine behind the brief period of artistic efflorescence that produced the canonical films of the period. Cultural histories that address financial crisis have, to this point, been primarily focused on the well-known episodes of the hyperinflation of 1921–23 and the onset of the Great Depression, and these two crises have come to serve as markers for the period as a whole.[17] However, in the focus on these two decisive moments of the Weimar Republic, the wider phenomenon of engagement with the financial sector, the emergence of an idea of an interconnected world economy, and the specific cultural codes that emerged from this sustained state of crisis of finance capital in German modernity have been overlooked.

Financial crisis was also central to the unification of Germany – the brief boom of the *Gründerjahre* (1871–73) was followed by a financial crash (and the onset of the global 'Long Depression') so severe that 'the sense of crisis

16 See Anton Kaes, Martin Jay, and Edward Dimendberg, eds., *The Weimar Republic Sourcebook* (Berkeley: University of California Press, 1995), xvii.

17 For a compelling discussion of the cultural resonances of the hyperinflation in Weimar culture see Bernd Widdig, *Culture and Inflation in Weimar Germany* (Berkeley: University of California Press, 2001).

lasted two full decades.'[18] As will be discussed in chapter 1, crises of finance capital of the nineteenth century shaped Germany's transition to modernity. As a result, their effects were deeply embedded in Germany's historical imaginary. Additionally, during the second half of the nineteenth century, the contours of what would come to be understood as an interconnected 'world economy' of 'financial flows' would increasingly loom into view and intrude on the emergent stabilizing conception of the nation itself.

Chapter 1, therefore, historicizes and contextualizes the sites of crisis that I outline here. It includes an examination of the crisis of *representation* that the world market provoked from the start. This crisis of representation, as we shall see, took three overlapping forms. Engels's notion of the world market as 'an inverted reflection' critiques the uneven distribution of wealth in the new flows of capital but also foregrounds the market in *visual* terms as a (mis)representation. Secondly, Marx himself persistently figured his critique of the international market in spectral terms that foreground both its elusiveness in traditional frameworks of representation and its perceived threat (already vampiric and Mabuse-like in nature). Finally, late nineteenth- and early twentieth-century critics recognized what has become even clearer in the meta-analyses of contemporary historians and sociologists of finance, namely, that the global market is *always-already a representation*, that is, it is dependent on modelling abstract relations, as well as on evolving technologies, which have been part of its story from the start. Of special interest for my own study is the way in which the development of technologies of communication in finance paralleled the development of the cinema in the late nineteenth century, as well as how economic theories of the world economy that originated from within the German context, emerged alongside the birth of the cinema. Thus, in this chapter I propose that the market itself should be seen as a labour of representation in its own right.

Chapter 1 also establishes a major claim of this study: that the stock market, and the extended spaces of finance capital in the urban environment, deserve to be considered as key spaces of modernity alongside more canonical examples such as the nineteenth-century shopping arcade, the railroad, the street, the hotel, the *Kaiserpanorama*, or the cinema.[19] In his

18 Joachim Radkau quoted in Michael Cowan, *Cult of the Will: Nervousness and German Modernity* (University Park, PA: Pennsylvania State University Press, 2008), 24.

19 A small sampling of the large body of scholarship on spaces of modernity includes the following: On the arcade and the shopping mall: Walter Benjamin and Rolf Tiedemann, *The Arcades Project* (Cambridge, MA: Harvard University Press, 1999); Anne Friedberg, *Window Shopping: Cinema and the Postmodern* (Berkeley: University of California Press, 1993). The

unfinished *Passagenwerk*, Walter Benjamin catalogues a material archive of the emergence of these modern spaces and practices.[20] For Benjamin and his exemplary modernist Baudelaire, the shops within the arcades reproduced the external world in commodity form – an image that has had lasting import for our understanding of the homogenizing effects of global capital. The arcades effectively 'collapsed space' by reproducing the world of commerce 'in miniature.' At the same time, the telegraph was beginning to represent the external world as price information in the halls of the stock exchange, reminding us that technologies fundamentally associated with the market operate as representational technologies.

What is less often discussed in Benjamin's work is the way in which the arcades linked the street with the spaces of high finance usually deemed to be cloistered away from everyday activity. Benjamin recognized not only the importance of new forms of movement and communication in the emergence of the railroads and the telegraph, but also the way that the specific forces of financial modernity manifested themselves in the connective tissue of the city. This occurred in the intersection of urban space with the spectral realm of high finance that would increasingly come to define the landscape of the city. For this reason, an examination of the development of these spatial practices in the German context is a key component of this study. In order to understand the complex codes and associations that are at the core of cultural representations of finance capital in Weimar cinema, it is highly illuminating to trace their development back to the nineteenth century. In examining everyday financial activity and speculation in late nineteenth- and early twentieth-century Germany, this book explores central historical debates specific to the German context that enrich our understanding of representations of finance and speculation in the Weimar Republic.

railroad: Wolfgang Schivelbusch, *The Railway Journey: The Industrialization of Time and Space in the 19th Century* (Berkeley: University of California Press, 1986); Stephen Kern, *The Culture of Time and Space, 1880–1918* (Cambridge, MA: Harvard University Press, 2003). The street: Edward Dimendberg, *Film Noir and the Spaces of Modernity* (Cambridge, MA: Harvard University Press, 2004). The hotel: Siegfried Kracauer, *The Mass Ornament: Weimar Essays*, ed. Thomas Y. Levin (Cambridge, MA: Harvard University Press, 1995). The *Kaiserpanorama*: Jonathan Crary, *Suspensions of Perception: Attention, Spectacle, and Modern Culture* (Cambridge, MA: MIT Press, 1999). The cinema: Thomas Elsaesser and Adam Barker, eds., *Early Cinema: Space, Frame, Narrative* (London: British Film Institute, 1990); Murray Pomerance, ed., *Cinema and Modernity* (New Brunswick, NJ: Rutgers University Press, 2006); Leo Charney and Vanessa R. Schwartz, eds., *Cinema and the Invention of Modern Life* (Berkeley: University of California Press, 1995).

20 See Susan Buck-Morss, *The Dialectics of Seeing: Walter Benjamin and the Arcades Project* (Cambridge, MA: MIT Press, 1989).

Chapter 2 introduces the one figure of Weimar cinema who embodies almost all of the key crises of finance capital and modernity: Dr. Mabuse. Among the canonical films of Weimar, Fritz Lang's *Dr. Mabuse der Spieler* ('Dr. Mabuse the Gambler,' 1922) was the most indispensable choice, as *the* film that operates as a veritable compendium of all the discourses that dominate the world market from its emergence in the mid-nineteenth century through to the Weimar period. Thus, I read *Dr. Mabuse* within the context of the contemporary scene of speculation and financial crisis. Given that the film opens with a sequence featuring an elaborate stock market manipulation, its representation of finance capital has been surprisingly overlooked in existing scholarship. I show that *Dr. Mabuse* connects crises of authority, identity, authenticity, and rationality back to the realm of finance capital. Many of the ideas developed in relation to *Dr. Mabuse* are thus key to the other films discussed in this study. In my reading, Mabuse emerges as a figure of the new international economic order that threatens notions of territory, border, and nation. At the same time, I argue that Mabuse, as a figure who has mastered the terrain of finance and modernity, can be read as a fantasy of empowerment and mobility to the emergent class of *Angestellten* ('white-collar workers' or 'salaried workers') as a film-going public. *Dr. Mabuse* is situated within a wider field of filmic representations of the figure of the *Raffke* and *Schieber*, two established stereotypes that caricatured the profiteers and the nouveau riche of the time. I suggest that these films be thought of together as a micro-genre consisting of what a reviewer at the time referred to *Börsenfilme* ('stock exchange films') that would have constituted the 'horizon of reception' for Weimar spectators. As Thomas Elsaesser has noted, the canon of Weimar cinema that we know today does not represent the experience of Weimar spectators.[21] By reconstructing the micro-genre of now lost *Börsenfilme* through their description in the trade press, I reveal the broader context of representations of finance and speculation that surrounded the release of Lang's film. Drawing on and extending Tom Gunning's work, I agree that, in its form and its construction of an 'image of the times,' *Dr. Mabuse* is an 'allegory of modernity.'[22] However, I add more specifically, that the film *produces* the distended abstract space of a newly emergent world economy.[23]

21 Thomas Elsaesser, *Weimar Cinema and after: Germany's Historical Imaginary* (London: Routledge, 2000), 18.

22 Tom Gunning, *The Films of Fritz Lang: Allegories of Vision and Modernity* (London: British Film Institute, 2000).

23 Henri Lefebvre, *The Production of Space* (Malden, MA: Blackwell, 1991).

Chapter 3 addresses the highly gendered space of financial markets. While participants on the official exchange were almost all male, financial activity and the 'irrationality' of the market itself was coded as female. In the first decades of the twentieth century, however, the clear separation of the public sphere of working men and the private sphere of women was increasingly challenged. During the First World War, German women's movements identified financial independence as a cornerstone of their demands for emancipation. This chapter begins by discussing Asta Nielsen and Edmund Edel's *Die Börsenkönigin* ('The Queen of the Stock Exchange,' 1916), a unique and iconoclastic film that defied established gender binaries through its depiction of a woman speculator. The film's depiction of this figure was doubly threatening: it challenged the already unstable separation of gender roles and *Geschlechtskarakter* ('the character of the sexes') and it mobilized a woman as an *agent* of exchange, rather than, in the established trope of Weimar cinema, as an *object-to-be-exchanged*. The crisis of the construction of gender in the domain of financial exchange introduced by this contradictory figure is symbolically 'resolved' in many later Weimar films, which relegate the conflation of women and exchange to the ubiquitous trope of the 'prostitute.' This chapter then turns to several key films that depict women as *objects* of exchange, such as *Die Austernprinzessin* ('The Oyster Princess,' 1919), and the forgotten *Fräulein Raffke* ('Raffke's Daughter,' 1923), before addressing G. W. Pabst's canonical *Die freudlose Gasse* ('The Joyless Street,' 1925). As with *Dr. Mabuse der Spieler*, the undercurrent of global financial markets runs through Pabst's film, and emerge, in my reading, through an allegory of economic activity.

Chapter 4 further develops this critical discussion of gender and finance, turning to the contested field of masculinity. I draw on the work of Sabine Hake, Patrice Petro, Klaus Theweleit, and Zygmunt Bauman, to fully articulate a concept briefly introduced in chapter 2.[24] I address the occurrence in many of the films in this study of 'moments of liquidity,' that is, filmic instances that combine formal visual effects of dissolution with financial themes. These key moments illustrate a crisis of masculinity posed by post-industrial labour and the destabilizing effect of global financial flows. I develop this concept through an analysis of F. W. Murnau's *Der letzte*

24 See Zygmunt Bauman, *Liquid Modernity* (Malden, MA: Wiley-Blackwell, 2000); Klaus Theweleit, *Male Fantasies*, vol. 1, *Women, Floods, Bodies, History*, trans. Stephen Conway, Erica Carter and Chris Turner (Minneapolis: University of Minnesota Press, 1989); Klaus Theweleit, *Male Fantasies*, vol. 2, *Male Bodies: Psychoanalyzing the White Terror* trans. Stephen Conway, Erica Carter and Chris Turner (Minneapolis: University of Minnesota Press, 1989).

Mann ('The Last Laugh,' 1924) and Marcel L'Herbier's *L'Argent* ('Money,' 1929). Distributed in Germany and featuring two of Weimar cinema's major stars, *L'Argent* addresses the idea of financial liquidity in both the form and content of its cinematic representation of the global market. In a related sense, I discuss the conflation of the image of women and water in *Die Büchse der Pandora* ('Pandora's Box,' 1929) and *Berlin: Die Sinfonie der Großstadt* ('Berlin: Symphony of a Great City,' 1927) in order to further examine the connection between finance, liquidity, and a crisis of gender. This chapter then turns to Gerhard Lamprecht's forgotten film *Hanseaten* (1925). This important yet unknown film, which has escaped inclusion in the Weimar film canon altogether, provides a key narrative of *stabilization* to this study. *Hanseaten* is also centrally concerned with questions of nautical commerce, the international, finance capital, and masculinity, but attempts to reconcile the tensions within these categories through its depiction of gender. Placing it in the context of Lamprecht's better-known *Die Verrufenen* ('Slums of Berlin'), of the same year, I argue that *Hanseaten* attempts to redeem and stabilize finance capitalism and masculinity in patriarchal, nationalistic, and *völkisch* terms that anticipate the 'reactionary modernism' that marked the end of the republic.[25]

Chapter 5 is primarily concerned with critical cinematic representations of capital and the crystallization of the image of the world economy as an image of the aggregate. Though they are the products of a wide spectrum of political ideologies, all these films represent the crisis of authenticity posed by finance capital. The chapter opens by analysing leftist attempts to envision the world market in cinematic and theatrical form. I discuss Sergei Eisenstein's plan to create a film using Karl Marx's *Das Kapital* as a 'script,' which would have employed a montage aesthetic in its depiction of capitalism as a global phenomenon. I then turn to Bertolt Brecht's unfinished play *Jae Fleischhacker in Chikago* ('Jae Fleischhacker in Chicago,' 1924), which attempted to dramatize the workings of the world grain market. I examine the fragments of Béla Balázs and Bertold Viertel's *K 13 513: Die Abenteuer eines Zehnmarkscheins* ('Adventures of a Ten Mark Note' or 'Uneasy Money,' 1926) and read Bertolt Brecht and Slatan Dudow's *Kuhle Wampe, oder: Wem gehört die Welt?* ('Kuhle Wampe, or: Who Owns the World?,' 1932) within the larger context of the popular visual convention of the *Querschnitt* ('cross-section'). I then trace the ways in which an initially radical montage aesthetic was said to have been emptied of its political content and normalized in Walter

25 Jeffrey Herf, *Reactionary Modernism: Technology, Culture, and Politics in Weimar and the Third Reich* (Cambridge: Cambridge University Press, 1984).

Ruttmann's *Berlin Sinfonie* (1927), and then further diluted by Ruttmann in the creation of a corporate vision of the world economy in *Melodie der Welt* ('Melody of the World,' 1929). This shift, and depoliticization, of the cinematic 'aggregate image' is discussed alongside parallel developments in the sphere of econometrics. I show how the manifestation of the aggregate in popular media mirrored the deployment of new statistical models for the creation of an image of the German economy as rational and predictable.

Financial crisis is central to this site of the 'crisis of classical modernity.'[26] It is perhaps unsurprising then that, once you begin to look, representations of finance and the economy can be found almost everywhere in Weimar popular culture. The 'world economy' that began to take shape in the mid-nineteenth century, but was not fully theorized in economic discourse until the 1930s, can be read as a scene of modernist crisis in Weimar cinema. Accordingly, I show how key films of the Weimar Republic stage the crisis of finance capital and, in many cases, attempt symbolically to stabilize it. I demonstrate that a constant oscillation between destabilization and re-stabilization is played out in these films, across fixed notions of subjectivity, nation, gender, and authenticity, central to the experience of modernity.

26 Detlev Peukert, *The Weimar Republic* (New York: Hill and Wang, 1993).

1. The Stock Exchange as a Space of Modernity and Labour of Representation

Abstract: Chapter 1 establishes central debates and cultural codes specific to the context of this study – in particular the close association of finance capital with anxieties surrounding France, Jews, and the importance of the historical separation of gambling from speculation. It lays the groundwork for the critical examination of these codes in Weimar cinema. This chapter also lays out two key claims: firstly, that stock exchanges have been overlooked as central spaces of modernity alongside more canonical examples such as the late nineteenth-century shopping arcade, the railroad, the street, and the cinema; and secondly, that financial markets are engaged in the creation of an image of the world – a labour of representation – the history of which parallels the development of the cinema itself.

Keywords: Speculation and Gambling, Finance Capital, Imperial Germany, Architecture and Urban Space, Modernity and Cinema, Nineteenth-Century Globalization

The Stock Exchange as a Space of Modernity

Introduction

Before moving to a discussion of the cinema of the Weimar Republic, the primary goal of this chapter will be to show how the stock exchange should be considered a central space of modernity within the ranks of other key spaces, such as the cinema and the arcade, that have been outlined in the introduction. In order to do this, I will begin in the nineteenth century and describe some of the salient architectural and historical features of German exchanges and, in particular, the ways in which the official exchanges

Lyons, O., *Finance and the World Economy in Weimar Cinema*. Taylor & Francis Group, 2023.
DOI 10.5117/9789463727136_CH01

interacted with both the unofficial *Winkelbörsen* ('bucket shops') and the space of the city, and Berlin in particular. I show how this architectural and spatial history intersects with cultural codes and practices surrounding gambling, speculation and the production of the boundaries of the nation itself. I will then discuss how, already in the nineteenth century, the spatial and cultural practice surrounding financial activity constituted a vast labour of representation – the creation of an image of the world economy and its inhabitants – to which the films under discussion in later chapters would become a part. This groundwork provides the essential cultural context in which the tropes and codes of the films and texts examined in later chapters become suddenly and vividly legible. In addressing these key developments of the nineteenth century, I also aim to recount a history of spaces and spatial practices that have been overlooked within the discourse of modernity and the city. Stock exchanges, and the semi-official spaces of finance that surround them, are under-discussed in the literature on modernity and the city and yet they present some of the first instances of both the experience of the press of the crowd and of the intersection of everyday life with the fragmentary space-time of modern communications technologies.

The Weimar Republic, and its capital, Berlin, may at first seem like an atypical site for a study such as this. The role of finance in Paris, New York, and London is well documented and forms an integral part of histories of these 'capitals of modernity,' but the role of finance in the development of modern German cities is less well known. Frankfurt's association with finance comes both from its long history as a financial centre, as well as from its current role as the leading German market. However, the period of Berlin's dominance as the country's premier exchange, from 1867 to 1945, is under-discussed with respect to the development of what would become the premier metropolis of Germany, and the *locus classicus* of European modernity in the early twentieth century.[1] It is helpful here then to review some of the salient points of the unlikely history of the emergence of Berlin as a financial centre.

Berlin's rise to prominence as a financial centre is one of the more unlikely outcomes of the shift of financial power within nineteenth-century Germany. Little more than a provincial backwater at the beginning of the century and situated far from the hubs of Western Europe, Berlin nevertheless

1 For a detailed history of Berlin's eclipse of Frankfurt as the premiere German financial centre of this period see Carl-Ludwig Holtfrerich, *Frankfurt as a Financial Centre: From Medieval Trade Fair to European Banking Centre* (Munich: Beck, 1999).

joined the ranks of the leading world financial centres in the four decades leading to the founding of the German Reich in 1871.[2] In addition, and within only a few decades, it also became the foremost industrial capital within continental Europe.[3] Thus, the grounds for Berlin's emergence as a centre of modernity in Europe must be understood within the context of this industrial and financial development, and an understanding of this history and the cultural significance of finance can shed new light on the cultural productions of the Weimar Republic itself. The effects of key crises and events that mark the nineteenth century still resonated in the culture of the Weimar Republic and, rather than turn for insight to the First World War, here I turn to these earlier examples of crisis and disruption from the nineteenth century that must be considered in order to gain a fluency in the popular codes surrounding finance and speculation in Germany. Thus, in what follows, several key historical developments and the perception of finance in the German public sphere will be highlighted and discussed.

The role of finance in Wilhelmine Germany has been understated, and it may surprise some to learn that the city of Berlin occupied a tertiary role as a global financial power in the late nineteenth and early twentieth centuries, after Paris and London, respectively. Assumptions that financial markets were less important to the development of the German economy than other countries, or about the 'backwardness' of the German economy of the nineteenth century, have, along with other pillars of the *Sonderweg* thesis, been overturned by revisionist scholarship.[4] Conventional wisdom had held that the German universal banks played an inordinately large role in the underwriting of German industry, and thus, that the turn to private capital was less important than it was in France or America. While the universal banks were certainly significant, this was not, as has been assumed, to the great detriment of securities markets.[5] Prior to the First

2 Hartmut Berghoff, "Der Berliner Kapitalmarkt im Aufbruch (1830–1870)," in *Geschichte des Finanzplatzes Berlin*, ed. Hans Pohl (Frankfurt: Knapp, 2002), 53.

3 Alexandra Richie, *Faust's Metropolis: A History of Berlin* (New York: Carroll & Graf, 1998), 152.

4 See Caroline Fohlin, *Finance Capitalism and Germany's Rise to Industrial Power*, Studies in Macroeconomic History (New York: Cambridge University Press, 2007) and John M. Kleeberg, "The Disconto-Gesellschaft and German Industrialization: A Critical Examination of the Career of a German Universal Bank, 1851–1914" (PhD diss., Oxford University, 1988).

5 See Alexander Gerschenkron, *Continuity in History, and Other Essays* (Cambridge, MA: Belknap Press of Harvard University Press, 1968). Caroline Fohlin takes issue with this assumption amongst German economic historians, outlining examples of what has been called the 'Gerschenkron hypothesis.' See Fohlin, *Finance Capitalism*, 43. Charles P. Kindleberger builds on Richard Tilly's questioning of Gerschenkron's assertion of Germany's 'backwardness' in financial

World War, most major German cities had active securities and commodities exchanges, which 'performed very well, even by contemporary American standards.'[6] The perception that securities markets were not important to the German economy before the First World War may have been a product of observations from after the Second World War in Germany, in which banks did play 'an unusually significant role in corporate finance, and securities markets lagged behind those of some other highly industrialized countries.'[7] As we shall see, the fluctuations of financial markets, both domestic and international, were in fact important to the emergence of a unified Germany in the nineteenth century, as well as an important factor in German modernity.

Many states within the German Confederation may have been initially resistant to the mechanisms of finance capital, but they were eventually adopted from practices in neighbouring countries like France and Belgium. For example, in the early nineteenth century, Prussian law actually restricted the founding of industrial concerns on the basis of the issuance of shares. These restrictions limited the total number of joint stock companies founded between 1815 and 1840 to a mere four.[8] However, beginning in the 1830s, the development of industry and the boom in railway building exceeded the capacity of private banks, which led to the emergence of the first joint-stock banks in the German Confederation and a newfound reliance on the issuance

development, 'holding rather that the mainsprings of German economic development in the second half of the nineteenth century lay neither in banks nor in planning by an efficient state bureaucracy, but in thousands of profit-oriented decisions by capitalist entrepreneurs operating throughout Prussia and especially in the Rhineland.' See Charles P. Kindleberger, *A Financial History of Western Europe* (London: Allen & Unwin, 1984), 128. Lehemann-Hasemeyer and Streb analyse the historical data to conclude that 'it might therefore be misleading to interpret nineteenth-century Germany's financial sector as the textbook example of a bank-based financial system. It is true that Germany had a well-developed banking sector with large universal banks, many small savings banks, and credit cooperatives. But the German economy could also rely on the large and efficient Berlin stock market with a market capitalization above the world average. [...] Germany's industrialization and innovation depended much more than previously assumed on the provision of equity capital.' Sibylle Lehmann-Hasemeyer and Jochen Streb, "The Berlin Stock Exchange in Imperial Germany: A Market for New Technology?," *The American Economic Review* 106, no. 11 (2016): 3574. They also underline their own assumptions in approaching this study – i.e., that the German financial system was somehow the exception to the rule in Europe and less reliant on the stock exchange, stating the 'surprising fact that in the period of the Second Industrial Revolution the Berlin stock exchange was already a well-functioning market for new technology,' ibid., 3558.

6 Fohlin, *Finance Capitalism*, 222.

7 Ibid.

8 Ilja Mieck, "Berlins Aufstieg zum ersten preußischen Finanzplatz bis zur Industrialisierung," in *Geschichte des Finanzplatzes Berlin*, ed. Hans Pohl (Frankfurt: Knapp, 2002), 49.

of shares on the open market.[9] The Belgian Société Générale de Bruxelles, formed in 1822, was the original model for the joint-stock bank. It was first copied in France, in the form of the 1852 Crédit Mobilier, and subsequently spread to Germany and the rest of Europe.[10] The new industrial banks were responsible for the financing of the mid-century boom in railway building and other infrastructure across what would eventually become Germany.[11] The creation of the joint-stock banks in the following decades was met with much resistance from members of the establishment and *Junkertum* ('nobility'), who preferred the control that a large state bank would have afforded them. The new banks were also met with some resistance by the banking establishment. James Mayer de Rothschild, for example, denounced their 'encouragement to speculation and gambling on margins.'[12] The disruptive potential of this new development was compounded by the fact it had taken place so quickly, in a few years as compared to the two hundred or so years over which it had occurred in Britain.

By the mid-nineteenth century, the new and freely moving capital was felt not only in the disruption of established hegemony, but also in the drastic decrease in the living quality of workers who were increasingly employed in the terrible and unsafe conditions of factories. The playwright and author Gerhart Hauptmann dramatized these conditions in his 1892 play, *Die Weber*, which depicted the uprising of the Silesian weavers in 1844 and their struggle against automation and the demands of market-driven overproduction. This event would become central to the narrative of the revolutionary left and critical representations of capitalism, appearing in Käthe Kollwitz's 1893–97 print series *The Weavers's Revolt* and again in a 1927 filmic adaptation directed by Frederic Zelnik and starring Paul Wegener. As David Harvey notes:

> Capitalism had matured by 1848 to a sufficient degree that even the blindest bourgeois apologist could see that financial conditions, reckless

9 Julia Bersch and Graciela L. Kaminsky, "Financial Globalization in the 19th Century: Germany as a Financial Center," September, 2008, http://home.gwu.edu/~graciela/HOME-PAGE/RESEARCH-WORK/WORKING-PAPERS/Germany-center.pdf.

10 On the influence of *Crédit Mobilier* on the founding of German credit banks, see J. Reisser, *The German Great Banks and Their Concentration in Connection with The Economic Development of Germany*, vol. 4, Publications of the U.S. National Monetary Commission (Washington: Government Printing Office, 1911), 49.

11 Ibid., 1–7.

12 Everett John Carter, "The Green Table: Gambling Casinos, Capitalist Culture, and Modernity in Nineteenth-Century Germany" (PhD diss., University of Illinois at Urbana-Champaign, 2002), 6.

> speculation (particularly with respect to the railways), and overproduction had something to do with the human tragedy that swept out of Britain in 1847 and quickly engulfed the whole of what was then the capitalist world. Most of Europe experienced the same crisis simultaneously, making it difficult to confine its interpretation solely within national narratives of government failure of this or that sort. This was a full-fledged crisis of capitalist overaccumulation, in which massive surpluses of capital and labour power lay side by side with apparently no way open to reunite them in profitable union.[13]

This revolt occurred at the same time as the frenzy of speculation that marked the midpoint of the nineteenth century. Karl Marx noted in 1851 with disapproval that 'the urge to dig new mines, erect new factories, build new railroads, and above all to invest in corporations and to speculate with stocks gripped all classes from peasants to the prince with the noble crown.'[14]

The material cause of this financial frenzy, specifically the laying of railroad track and the digging of mines, resulted in the first expression of the concept of an *economic* crisis. In his intellectual history of the evolution of the term 'crisis,' Reinhart Koselleck claims that it was in the decades between 1840 and 1860 that the economic use of the term came into its own, as separate from previous medical and juridical meanings. In the writings of Marx and Engels, for example, it was used predominantly in the economic sense after 1844. Koselleck points to the role of the crash that followed the California Gold Rush (1848–55) in creating the conditions for the first truly global economic crisis after 1856 that was locatable 'everywhere and nowhere' at the same time.[15] The global economic consequences of the gold find in the Sierra Nevada had been massive, spurring growth in shipping, changing migration patterns, boosting the buying power of countries whose gold reserves were greatly increased, and setting off a wave of worldwide speculation, the interconnected nature of which had never been seen before. In France, the influx of capital as a result of the gold rush promoted lending at a low interest rate and created the conditions for the invention of Crédit Mobilier, which would change the face of European finance, and serve as a model for the great German industrial banks.[16] In Germany, the gold rush

13 David Harvey, *Paris, Capital of Modernity* (New York: Routledge, 2003), 90.

14 Quoted in Kindleberger, *Western Europe*, 210.

15 R. Koselleck and M. W Richter, "Crisis," *Journal of the History of Ideas* 67, no. 2 (2006): 392–93.

16 Ralph J. Roske, "The World Impact of the California Gold Rush 1849-1857," *Arizona and the West* 5, no. 3 (October 1, 1963): 222.

contributed to a similar boom in credit institutions and an 'orgy of bank founding'[17] that accompanied the boom in *Aktiengesellschaften* ('joint-stock companies'), as well as a rise in financial speculation in the middle and upper classes.[18] This turbulent period's association with the Californian gold rush left a deep impression in the German popular imagination, and can be traced in the discourse surrounding the authenticity of gold as a basis of monetary as well as spiritual value.[19]

The invention of new systems of mass lending resulted in effects that could be seen in the very fabric of the modern metropolis itself and produced a 'revolution in space relations,' as urban land and real estate came under the pressure of newly created capital flows.[20] Disputes between bankers from established institutions, who had control of 'hard currency' in the form of gold, and those who gained access to new forms of credit institutions, altered the landscape of the financial world which, in turn, shaped the development of the modern city. This power shift was the subject of the epic battle between the bankers Gunderman and Saccard in Emile Zola's *L'Argent* (1890), and Marcel L'Herbier's 1925 filmic adaptation, which will be discussed in chapter 4.[21] Zola recognized that this arcane and specialized world of high finance drove the revolutionary and violent changes of the Haussmannization of Paris between 1853 and 1870, and specifically the creation of Paris's massive boulevards. Financial markets created the conditions by which 'the new streets were speculated in as one speculates in stocks and shares'[22] and 'the land itself, as well as the buildings upon it, became a form of fictitious capital.'[23] Consequently, these financial forces drove the development of new experiences and situations of modernity, and 'financial markets did more than make and lose money: they altered time space – and memory.'[24] Thus, developments in the credit system and changes in the structures of financial markets were closely connected to what would come to be regarded as the experience of modernity. What is

17 Roske, "Gold Rush," 225.

18 See Fohlin, *Finance Capitalism,* 224; Bersch and Kaminsky, "Globalization."

19 See Owen Lyons, "'Denn Gold ist Glück und Fluch dieser Welt:' Examining the Trope of Gold in 'Gold' (1934) and 'Der Kaiser von Kalifornien' (1936)," in *Continuity and Crisis in German Cinema 1928–36*, eds. Barbara Hales, Mihaela Petrescu, and Valerie Weinstein (Rochester: Camden House, 2016), 92–110.

20 Harvey, *Paris*, 120.

21 For a further discussion of the historical figures Zola based the central dispute of the novel (James Rothschild and Emil Pereire in 1851) see Harvey, *Paris*, 113.

22 G. Duchene in 1869, quoted in Harvey, *Paris*, 131.

23 Harvey, *Paris*, 131.

24 Matt K. Matsuda, *The Memory of the Modern* (New York: Oxford University Press, 1996), 50.

less well understood, however, are the specific spaces and spatial practices of the markets themselves and how they can be considered central to the discourse surrounding the emergent spaces of modernity in the modern metropolis. In what follows, some characteristics of the major German exchanges will be discussed in order to provide an overview of the different levels of access, and spatial practices, that characterized each market, as well as how these spaces functioned within the modern German cityscape.

The Official Spaces of Finance

The official exchanges of the major German cities are under-examined within the discourse on the emergent spaces of modernity. Here, I will describe some salient features of these spaces as well as cultural codes and practices that emerged from them since, as we shall see, an understanding of this financial landscape, and some of the particulars of regional exchanges, is essential to understanding the representation of financial activity in the cinema of the Weimar Republic.

As measured by capital exports and lending, in the nineteenth century, Germany was third in importance globally, after Britain and France.[25] Germany was somewhat distinct in the decentralized nature of its exchanges – a remnant of the history of the political geography of the German-speaking territories and the *Zollverein* ('Customs Union'). For example, in 1896 there were 25 active exchanges in Germany, some of which dealt chiefly in one commodity, such as coffee or cotton. Regulation of these exchanges was inconsistent when compared to the centralized financial systems in Britain or France, and opportunities for less than legal dealings were abundant in Germany.[26] In addition, the three largest of the German exchanges – Berlin, Frankfurt, and Hamburg – varied considerably in terms of access, protocols and architectural layout.

At the beginning of the nineteenth century, Frankfurt had long been a centre of commerce and had arisen to a place of central importance in European markets. It became known for the trading of government bonds and later for the issuance of international debt between governments. Frankfurt's international role was also bolstered by the success of Bankhaus Rothschild, one of the most significant political and financial forces of its time. From 1812 to 1915, it remained the 'biggest bank in the world [...] in terms of their combined capital' and the Rothschilds 'remained in a league

25 Bersch and Kaminsky, "Globalizaton," 4.

26 Carter, "Green Table," 249.

of their own until, at the earliest, the 1880s.'[27] Prior to unification (1871), Frankfurt maintained its more traditional role by insisting on a focus on government loans, however, Berlin began to thrive because it was ready for the new reality of industrial shares.[28] Frankfurt would slip to second place amongst the German exchanges, largely due to this shifting reality and political circumstances. Its decline in importance was compounded by the resistance of the financial elite in the city to the emergence of the joint-stock company and publicly traded shares, as well as to new financial technologies – whereas Berlin adopted these new technologies more quickly. For example, with the widespread adoption of the telegraph by 1850, James de Rothschild complained that 'the telegraph is ruining our business [...] anyone can get the news.'[29] This sentiment underscored how technological development marked a transfiguration of the boundary conditions of modern finance and reconfigured the spatial coordinates of an established power structure. While these new forms of communication formed an invisible backdrop to the actual spaces of the exchanges themselves, they were no less important than the physical barriers that determined access, privilege, and power. With the annexation of Frankfurt by Prussia in 1866 during the Austro-Prussian War, Frankfurt's role was diminished and Berlin emerged as the largest exchange by the time the German Empire was founded in 1871.[30] Hamburg, the third largest German financial centre in the late nineteenth century, would become as important as Frankfurt by the outbreak of the First World War.[31] Frankfurt's role as the leading German exchange would not be re-established until after the Second World War.

In his 1896 *Die Börse*, Max Weber provides one of the most detailed accounts of the spatial and social configuration of German exchanges at the turn of the twentieth century. Weber's book, published in the Göttingen Worker's Library series, was an explanatory text for a non-specialist, working-class audience and was designed to demystify the inner workings of financial exchanges.[32] It emerged at a time when, according to Friedrich

27 Niall Ferguson, *The House of Rothschild* (New York: Penguin, 1998), 15.

28 Youssef Cassis, *Capitals of Capital: A History of International Financial Centres, 1780–2005* (Cambridge: Cambridge University Press, 2006), 72.

29 Alex Nalbach, "'Poisoned at the Source'? Telegraphic News Services and Big Business in the Nineteenth Century," *The Business History Review* 77, no. 4 (December 1, 2003): 588.

30 Berghoff, "Der Berliner Kapitalmarkt," 55; Bersch and Kaminsky, "Globalization," 5.

31 See Rainer Gömmel "Entstehung und Entwicklung der Effektenbörsen im 19. Jahrhundert bis 1914," in *Deutsche Börsengeschichte*, ed. Hans Pohl (Frankfurt: Knapp Fritz GmbH, 1992).

32 According to Jerry Muller, this was 'a series published by a Protestant labor movement formed to improve the education and condition of the working class and to draw workers away

Engels, the stock exchange had become the focus of popular discontent with capitalism in general,[33] a discontent that was given official sanction by the institution of the restrictive *Börsengesetz* ('Stock Exchange Act') of 1896. This law was described at the time as the 'most elaborate attempt ever made to regulate speculative markets,'[34] and one of its main proposals – the restriction of the futures market in grain – will be returned to (particularly in chapter 5) as it had important ramifications for the popular conception of what role finance capital should play in the economy.

The terms of membership in official exchanges varied by nation. American and English exchanges, for example, required a large security deposit from members and had 'the character of closed clubs of professional exchange-traders.'[35] In Paris, access to the *parquet* ('floor') of the exchange itself was not restricted per se, but the right to trade was the strict purview of only sixty *agents de change* ('commissioned brokers') who were sanctioned in their role by the French government.[36] These brokers occupied 'a room, surrounded by barriers,' and it was this 'final link tying together buyer and seller, that [was] the monopoly of a privileged group of people.'[37] According to Weber, individual seats on the German exchanges were 'as in the churches in Germany – inheritable and cost very large sums,' and consequently, the exchange was 'organized as a monopoly of the rich.'[38]

During the late nineteenth century, Hamburg, the oldest exchange in Germany, was 'in essence a market with a roof over it' that 'the whole of the honourable male public' could attend.[39] The new Hamburg Handelskammer that Weber describes shared an inner courtyard with the Hamburg city hall and was a space through which 'seamen and foreign merchants' could move and conduct business, functioning more as a passageway than as a cloister. Like other exchanges of its time, its neo-classical construction and prominent location functioned as architectural markers of the power of finance within the urban landscape. The neo-classical style also lent the exchange the air of an ancient temple, concealing frenzied activities within.

from the atheism of the Social Democrats.' Jerry Z. Muller, *The Mind and the Market: Capitalism in Modern European Thought* (New York: Alfred A. Knopf, 2002), 238.

33 Muller, *Mind and the Market*, 233.

34 Henry Crosby Emery, "The Results of the German Exchange Act of 1896," *Political Science Quarterly* 13, no. 2 (June 1898): 286.

35 Max Weber, "Stock and Commodity Exchanges 'Die Börse' (1894)," *Theory and Society* 29, no. 3 (June 1, 2000): 326.

36 Ibid., 327.

37 Ibid., 328.

38 Ibid., 327.

39 Ibid., 328.

Figure 1. Eric Schilling, 'Der Welthandel' (World Trade), *Simplicissimus*, April 20, 1921. Caption: 'Warum kann der Kerl nicht mehr laufen? Wir haben ihm doch nur das deutsche Bein amputiert.' ('Why can't this guy walk anymore? We've only amputated the German leg.') Klassik Stiftung Weimar.

Inside, the foyer stairwell housed a well-known symbol of commerce – a statue of *Merkur* (Mercury/Hermes). The inner courtyard was adorned with reliefs of coats of arms from far flung cities, such as *Marseille, Singapur, Konstantinopel* – images that solidified the idea of Hamburg as a globally interconnected city. The association of trade with *Merkur* was a common feature of representations of finance both at this time and, as we shall see, throughout the Weimar Republic (Figure 1), and added to the air of prestige that the exchanges projected.[40]

40 The figure of *Merkur* appeared frequently in imagery associated with finance capital. It was also frequently used in the satirical magazine *Simplicissimus* and was a staple allegorical figure for trade and finance.

Because of the ability of laypersons as well as professional traders to enter into transactions on its floor, Weber described the Hamburger Börse as putting the 'principle of a "free market" into practice with thoroughgoing consistency.'[41] In its hall, Weber envisioned an idealized meeting of *homo faber*, whose hand has produced the goods or commodities for sale, and *homo economicus*, who merely sells them on at a profit. Here, he clearly outlines the opposition between 'productive' vs. 'non-productive' capital that will be returned to later in this chapter. The idea that these two types of people met within its halls was represented in the frieze that adorned the façade of the Handelskammer, which consists of pairings of *wissentschaftlichen* ('scientific') and *praktischen* ('practical') aspects of various industries, for example: geographer with helmsman, and engineer with smith. This connection is reflected in murals, friezes, and ornamentation of stock exchanges around the world.[42]

The period of 1890–1914 was one of rapid growth and, in Hamburg, the rise of the joint-stock companies, and what Rudolf Hilferding would refer to as 'organized capitalism,' posed a direct threat to the established merchant class, since they could raise much more capital than private firms under the guarantee of limited liability.[43] This shift in financial power was the setting of Thomas Mann's 1901 novel, *Buddenbrooks*, which depicted the decline of a family of wealthy grain merchants in Lübeck, another important Hanseatic city in the north of Germany, in the face of the ascendancy of Prussia and Berlin. Hamburg's long history and its importance in the international Hanseatic League meant that the new forces of finance capital had a different cultural resonance there. Any simple opposition of world trade and national protectionism is complicated by the fact that the Hanseatic cities were already considered to be part of an international network since the Middle Ages. Thus, the dynamic forces of finance capital would play out across a different register in the case of Hamburg – along the lines of private syndicalism vs. public shares – and the arrival of venture capital connected to railroad expansion was less of a radical rupture for the northern German city state. *Buddenbrooks* was to become a touchstone text for German fictional representations of finance in the twentieth century and the nuances of Hamburg's position will be returned to in chapter 4, through an analysis of Gerhardt Lamprecht's *Hanseaten*, of 1925.

41 Weber, "Die Börse," 329.

42 As another example, see the murals by Jan Toorop in the Beurs van Berlage, Amsterdam.

43 Niall Ferguson, *High Financier: The Lives and Time of Siegmund Warburg* (New York: Penguin, 2010), 11.

In contrast to Hamburg and Frankfurt, the Berliner Börse ('Berlin stock exchange') operated in a manner somewhere between the closed exchanges of Britain and America and the open floor of the Hamburg Handelskammer. Access to the Börse in the 1890s required recommendation by a member of the exchange, the purchase of a ticket, and being of 'native' (Prussian) descent.[44] The new Börse, completed in 1863, was designed by architect Friedrich Hitzig, a disciple of Karl Friedrich Schinkel. Similar to that of Hamburg, its interior was adorned with symbols of 'productive' capital, even if the activity that it housed was considered to be 'non-productive.' As with many exchanges, Hitzig's was constructed in the classical style, and its entrance was framed by an imposing Doric colonnade, as if to render solid and lend the weight of history to the radically disruptive activity that it contained. A bust of King Wilhelm I was exhibited inside the vestibule of white Carrara marble, and in the main hall large murals depicted scenes of farming, animal husbandry, and viticulture.[45]

The Börse was erected in a place of importance in the city, at the foot of the Friedrichsbrücke and the beginning of what is now Ann-Louisa Karsch-Strasse – a temple of finance across the Spree from the sacred space of the Berliner Dom, though its footprint was much larger.[46] It is important to emphasize the scale of the new Börse: its main 'sumptuous, columned hall,' built to accommodate 5,000 people, was the largest enclosed space in Berlin at the time. It was also an important site of exposure for the effects of urban modernity as daily activities on the floor were amongst the first experiences of mass gathering in the still relatively small city.[47] The Börse also contained galleries, which overlooked the activity on the main floor and which could be entered for a price. The building was thus designed with the accommodation of onlookers in mind.[48] As Hartmut Berghoff remarks, even if spectators 'did not understand the business activities of the brokers and traders, under the impression of the gigantic coulisse, they divined that something important was playing out before their eyes.'[49]

44 Weber, "Die Börse," 329.

45 Berghoff, "Der Berliner Kapitalmarkt," 100.

46 The nearby Bahnhof Börse on the S-Bahn was built in 1882 and is now known as Bahnhof Hackescher Markt. The building stood until it was destroyed in 1944 by allied bombardment. From 1941 to 1943 it housed the Judenreferat der Staatspolizeileitstelle Berlin (Department for Jewish Affairs of the Gestapo's Berlin Regional headquarters) that organized the deportation of over 50,000 Jews and housed a 'protective custody' prison.

47 Berghoff, "Der Berliner Kapitalmarkt," 71.

48 Ibid.

49 Ibid. Author's translation.

In Germany, the *Stand* ('estate/class') of exchange traders, though restricted, was not entirely composed of the wealthy, and it was not uncommon for traders operating on the 'smallest swings' in prices to rub shoulders with representatives of the largest banks, or for bankrupt merchants to be assigned the role of *Makler* ('broker') in order to 'work themselves back up.'[50] German exchanges developed a form of stock quotation that was quite different from the continuous publication of price data in the American and British systems. After the *Börsengesetz* of 1896, stock quotations were published from the exchange only twice or three times daily – often in coordination with the common practice of morning and evening editions of newspapers. Another distinct feature of official German exchanges was the position of the *vereidigte Makler* ('certified broker'), who were sworn in by the state and whose role was to certify stock quotations.[51] Participants at the Berliner Börse were not necessarily required to conduct business with these 'certified brokers' and could in fact access the various 'free' brokers. Berlin thus fell somewhere between Paris and London's rigid central control by very wealthy brokers, and Hamburg's openness in terms of access and participation. However, the transactions conducted by the *vereidigte Makler* were the only ones recorded and published for official price production.[52] While further specifics of the activities on the exchange floor at this time are beyond the scope of this study, these few details show something of the nature of the space itself. In particular, they show how the representational function of the exchange worked at an interpersonal level, as well as how the creation of an image (price) was negotiated through concentric circles of inclusion and exclusion.

Though Weber offered the Hamburg Handelskammer as an example of the free market at work, he in fact argued for the exclusion of non-professional traders from the markets, stating that 'the exchange is a monopoly of the rich, and nothing is more foolish than to disguise this fact by admitting propertyless, and therefore powerless, speculators.'[53] Weber considered the individual citizen as at risk of being taken advantage of by more experienced traders on the official exchange. Thus, privilege and inclusion were enacted through a matrix of expertise and social capital, as well as architectural boundaries and thresholds. Furthermore, opportunities for 'speculation' in

50 Weber, "Die Börse," 330.

51 Hans Hirschstein and Karl W. Scholz, "Commodity Exchanges in Germany," *Annals of the American Academy of Political and Social Science* 155 (May 1, 1931): 208–17, 209.

52 Weber, "Die Börse," 330.

53 Ibid., 334.

late nineteenth-century Germany were not limited to the official spaces of finance, and participation and access to the market, in secondary and tertiary form, could be achieved by a variety of means and along a sliding scale of relative legality. In the case of each of the main exchanges in Germany, concentric layers of access and exclusion were based around the official space of the stock exchange floor, but emanated into the non-sanctioned space of the city itself.

Where the Exchange Meets the City

> If you pass in front of the Stock Exchange at noon, you will see a long line composed of men from all walks of life who purchase shares of stock [in front of the exchange] which they sell off during the same session. That old white-haired fellow who offers a pinch of snuff to the guard passing by is the dean of these speculators [...] From the general look of the trading on the floor and off, and from the faces of the stockbrokers, he is able to divine, with a marvellous instinct, the rise or the fall of stocks.
>
> – Taxile Delord, "Les Petits Paris," in *Paris-Boursier* (Paris, 1854)[54]

The fragment above, collected by Walter Benjamin from the *Paris-Boursier* of 1854, details several important spatial and social characteristics of nineteenth-century exchanges. The exchange is described from the outside and by a passing observer not immediately involved in the fray. The throng is drawn from all walks of life, but does not have direct access to the exchange floor itself. Instead, they speculate through an intermediary – the 'old white-haired fellow,' who is 'able to divine' from the outside, the movement of prices in the faces of the stockbrokers on the floor itself. A mild transgression is suggested here; a semi-official, secondary market that allows limited access for the everyday public of Paris and is condoned through the votive offering of snuff to the passing guard. This market conducted its business away from the sanctioned space of the floor but within earshot of the crier, who receives second-hand information of dubious accuracy. The tension between 'inside' and 'outside' is vividly illuminated here and informs the spatial logic of the stock exchange to this day. This is also an essential depiction of the relationship between the exchange and the surrounding city. The market is ostensibly public and, since the mid-nineteenth century, has had its price movements published in non-specialized print media. In

54 Taxile Delord, "Les Petits Paris," in *Paris-Boursier* (Paris, 1854), 44–46. Quoted in Benjamin and Tiedemann, *Arcades Project*, 782. Convolute [g3,1].

short, what is described here is an early example of the complex layering of representation and visibility, and corresponding interplay of levels of access to privileged information, that defined the space of the stock exchange. The constant access to and withholding of information forms a basic division between inside and outside knowledge, a characteristic of financial activity to this day.

Markets at this time were ostensibly public, in that any *man* could enter them, but participation was closely guarded by levels of membership and rites of initiation. On a material level, the separation of the official exchanges from their surroundings was replicated in the formal arrangement of the architecture of the exchanges themselves. New York City's 'Wall Street,' then in 'New Amsterdam,' for example, was named after an actual barricade erected by Peter Stuyvesant in 1653, ostensibly to sequester Dutch settlers from the indigenous Lenape inhabitants.[55] Most European exchanges replicated a similar, if less defensive, formal division in their architectural layout, presenting an imposing and orderly façade that separated the halls of the official exchange from the street. They also borrowed from the architectural language of classicism to lend the exchange an air of solemnity and gravitas. Access to information, and subsequently profit, was orchestrated through the negotiation of an elaborate series of boundaries that were at turns physical, social, and symbolic in nature. This logic set up a dialogic relationship between exclusion and display, which would increasingly frame the activity of markets as an elaborate labour of representation – a central claim of this book that will be addressed later in this chapter.

In nineteenth-century European exchanges, access to the floor was contingent on a combination of privilege and wealth, the conditions of which varied according to time and place. The official exchanges, however, were not the only point of access to the space of global finance. In the 1860s, the Bourse de Paris ('Paris stock exchange') itself contained a supplemental area known as the *coulisse*, the 'space in a stock exchange set apart for unofficial business.'[56] The *coulisse* 'guaranteed the ongoing life of the Stock Exchange,' in that 'there was never a closing time; there was almost never a night.'[57] In this space, literally the 'wings' or 'back stage' of the market, non-commissioned brokers were reluctantly tolerated, due to their sheer numbers,

55 Charles R. Geisst, *Wall Street: A History: From Its Beginnings to the Fall of Enron* (Oxford: Oxford University Press, 2004), 10.

56 Benjamin and Tiedemann, *Arcades Project*, 959 (footnote 3).

57 Julius Rodenberg, *Paris bei Sonnenschein und Lampenlicht* (Leipzig, 1867). Quoted in Benjamin and Tiedemann, *Arcades Project*, 38. Convolute [A2, 11].

and the official activity of the exchange blurred with the everyday.[58] The strict and expensive membership terms of the Bourse were offset by this unofficial and unregulated periphery. According to sources assembled by Benjamin, this 'backstage' area was supplemented by even more layers of access in the form of the *petite-coulisse,* which catered to 'the business of the petite-bourgeoisie,' and even the *contre-petite-coulisse*, which handled 'the capital of the proletariat.'[59]

Significantly, Benjamin produced direct evidence of a connection between these unofficial exchanges and the most important space of interest for his own inquiry into the emergent spaces of modernity of the nineteenth century, the Passage de l'Opéra: 'When Café Tortoni finally closed its doors, the column of stock jobbers would head across the adjacent boulevards and meander up and down there, collecting in front of the Passage de l'Opéra.'[60] What emerges is an image of concentric zones of inclusion extending from the core of the official Bourse – an arrangement of spaces that, at its outer extremes, overlapped with and fed off the abstraction of mediated and fictional representations in the cinema and popular press. The abstract space of international finance was woven into the fabric of the city through the complex interplay of the official and fixed architecture of the exchange, as well as the fluid and ephemeral configurations of this 'backstage.' And these unofficial spaces of economic activity – which themselves wove 'fictions' only loosely based on official market information – were another layer of reflection in the *mise en abyme* relationship of price information, the world economy, and reality.

Such unofficial spaces have historically functioned in the modern European and American city as fluid boundary zones between the everyday traffic of the street and the enclosed activities of the financial exchanges. Unofficial exchanges, the *coulisse* in Paris, the bucket shop in London and New York, or the *Winkelbörse* in the German context, were often configured in a similar manner to the official exchange, but the activity they fostered involved the purchasing of tokens that merely tracked the movement of actual commodities and securities.[61] Off-market betting provided no direct

58 Weber, "Die Börse," 338 (footnote 32).

59 Taxile Delord, *Paris-Boursier*, 1854. Quoted in Benjamin and Tiedemann, *Arcades Project*, 782.

60 Julius Rodenberg, *Paris bei Sonnenschein und Lampenlicht* (Leipzig, 1867). Quoted in Benjamin and Tiedemann, *Arcades Project*, 38. Convolute [A2,11].

61 For a further discussion of this in the American and British context see Ann Fabian, *Card Sharps and Bucket Shops: Gambling in Nineteenth-Century America* (New York: Routledge, 1999) and David Hochfelder, "'Where the Common People Could Speculate': The Ticker, Bucket

link in the form of a corresponding trade on an official exchange, functioning rather as a shadow market where 'fictitious' representations of the real market allowed people of limited means to speculate.[62] Interestingly, there were cases in which widespread public betting on unofficial exchanges had a direct effect on official markets, even though no 'real' commodities changed hands, such as in the panic of 1907 in New York.[63] Side bets were sometimes even made by individuals who had access to the official exchange, as a form of hedging or trading around official regulations, and still had an effect on the popular sentiment of the market environment. As a result, the public did not always differentiate between the *Winkelbörse* and 'legitimate' speculation on the exchange. Both involved a level of semiotic detachment from the underlying referent that was only distinguishable to the buyer through a language of official codes. As such, we can read the elaborate architecture of the official exchanges as a conscious effort to differentiate them from, and perform their authority over, unofficial spaces that were in many cases their direct competitors for the money of small investors.

Unofficial trading often had an indirect effect on the official markets because of shifts in 'market sentiment.' In Frankfurt, the *Effekten-Societät* ('private stock clubs'), though allowed by the state, performed the same role as the *Winkelbörse* and operated after hours for a select elite, while in Hamburg, the *Abendbörse* ('evening exchange') developed in this role.[64] Bucket shops in Germany appear at least as early as the 1820s in Frankfurt.[65] In Berlin, these peripheral spaces were found around the Behrenstrasse, the 'new financial district,' which still runs parallel and one block south of Unter den Linden today.[66] The *Winkelbörsen* were described as 'gatherings or clubs' of traders and merchants in unregulated spaces. These traders could in some cases be 'fined or arrested' for taking part in illegal trading according to reforms and laws that were put in place in Prussia in the 1850s.[67]

Aside from these secondary spaces of financial exchange, the activity of finance capital permeated the everyday life of the city through the semi-public space of café culture. In 1890s Berlin, after the daily close

Shops, and the Origins of Popular Participation in Financial Markets, 1880–1920," *The Journal of American History* 93, no. 2 (2006): 335–58.

62 Hochfelder, "Where the Common People Could Speculate," 336.

63 Also known as the 'Knickerbocker Crisis.'

64 Bruno Mayer, *Die Effectenbörsen und ihre Geschäfte* (Vienna: A. Hölder, 1899), 10.

65 See C.J. Eisenlohr, *Ueber die Errichtung allgemeiner Komm-Scuhulden-Tilgungs-Kassen für einzelne Kreise und ganze Länder* (Karlsruhe: C.C. Müllerschen, 1818), 72.

66 Richie, *Faust*, 148.

67 Mayer, *Effectenbörsen*, 10.

of the Börse, 'decided movement toward the west [was] apparent' in the centre of Berlin, as the bankers and financiers made their way from the Burgstrasse, along Unter den Linden, towards their houses located in the Tiergarten area.[68] These stately and ostentatious villas were the realm of the *Geldaristokratie* ('moneyed aristocracy') that emerged as a distinct group throughout the nineteenth century in Berlin, and which combined the established members of the upper class with a large influx of bankers and other financial workers who immigrated to Berlin.[69] On their way to these villas, they would congregate at establishments near or on the Kranzlerecke ('Kranzler Corner'), named for the Café Kranzler, a famous Berlin *Konditorei* ('café' or 'confectionery'), that stood at the corner of Friedrichstrasse and Unter den Linden from 1825 until its destruction in 1944. The Kranzlerecke would remain a meeting point for 'international society' long into the Weimar Republic and, according to Billy Wilder, was a destination for the 'beau monde who stay in the hotels on the boulevard of Unter den Linden.'[70] Walter Benjamin directly compared the traffic and interaction at Kranzlerecke of Berlin with Paris's *Passage de l'Opéra*.[71] In the 1840s the *Rampe* ('street level terrace') of Café Kranzler was the meeting point of the 'crème de la plus noble sociéte,' the Café Josty was the hangout for soldiers, the Café Stehely the haunt of the officer class, professors, and artists, while the Café Courtin was the domain of brokers and other regular financial sector workers.[72] Berlin's plethora of newspapers were on display at all of these cafés, which functioned as reading rooms and conversation spaces where brokers would pore over the prices of the day. Over time, however, the strict divisions of social class would give way to the much larger spaces of the 1870s, such as the Café Bauer, located one block away from Berlin's most famous arcade, the Kaisergalerie. Café Bauer was 'able to accommodate on its first floor alone as many guests as all of the [older] Konditoreien of Berlin together' and its clientele were 'from all classes of

68 Paul Lindau, "Unter den Linden," in *Great Streets of the World* (London: Osgoode, McIlvaine, 1892). Reproduced in Iain Boyd Whyte and David Frisby, eds., *Metropolis Berlin: 1880–1940* (Berkeley: University of California Press, 2012), 177.

69 Berghoff, "Der Berliner Kapitalmarkt," 94.

70 Billy Wilder, "Berlin Rendezvous," *Berliner Börsen Courier*, November 13, 1927; reprinted in Billy Wilder, *Der Prinz von Wales geht auf Urlaub: Berliner Reportagen, Feuilletons und Kritiken der zwanziger Jahre* (Berlin: Fannei & Walz, 1996), 55–56. Reproduced in Whyte and Frisby, *Metropolis Berlin*, 533.

71 'In its importance for the affairs of the coulisse, the Passage de l'Opera is comparable to the Kranzlerecke.' Benjamin and Tiedemann, *Arcades Project*, 38. Convolute, [A2,a3].

72 Berghoff, "Der Berliner Kapitalmarkt," 94.

society.'[73] In the café culture of Berlin, the financial world was on display and, due to the relaxation of social codes, those in the specialized worlds of finance mixed with other members of Berlin society. It was also here that the bread and butter of financial transaction, that is, the gathering of information, meshed seamlessly with the activity of the emergent and prolific Berlin media and press. Berlin café culture constituted another layer of access to the distended everyday space of the financial market, located in the centre of the city. The enclosure of markets separated specialized market activity from the public sphere at the same time that it promoted secondary forms of observation and indirect ways of understanding the market as a thing-in-itself.[74] These off-market spaces were part of the extended threshold between the official space of the world market and the everyday spaces of the modern metropolis. In Weimar Berlin, cafés and other spaces performed an important function as the backdrop for the interplay of the worlds of finance and media, a backdrop on which imagery and information that made up the labour of representation of the financial markets played out. Off-market spaces provided a backstage to the official exchanges and blurred the boundaries between the abstract space of finance and the streetscape of the modern city.

The Stock Exchange as a Labour of Representation

The Image of the World Market

Communications technologies have always been at the core of the disruptive power of financial markets. Financial markets not only relied upon communications technologies, but also drove innovation as exchanges competed to remain at the cutting edge of information gathering technologies. In the nineteenth century, four dominant newswire services were founded across Europe – Havas in France, Reuters in Britain, the Associated Press in the United States, and Wolffs Telegraphisches Bureau in Germany. It is important to note that all four were first and foremost financial news services before they were used for more general content. In fact, financial news and price quotations drove the development of these services. Reuters, for example,

73 Heinrich Albert, "Die Arbeiterhäuser des Berliner Spar- und Bauvereins," *Zeitschrift für Architektur und Ingenieurwesen, Wochen-Ausgabe* 44, no. 2 (January 14, 1898). Reproduced in Whyte and Frisby, *Metropolis Berlin*, 178.

74 Preda, *Framing Finance*, 19.

was established in 1850 by German entrepreneur Paul Julius Reuter, who set up a 'submarine telegraph' office in London in 1851, a month before the connection of the Dover to Calais cable.[75] Reuter's initial success lay not in his gathering and proliferation of the news per se, but in his ability to secure access to the opening and closing prices for both the London Stock Exchange and the Paris Bourse, which he provided twice a day, for a fee.[76]

Similarly, Dr. Bernhard Wolff founded Wolffs Telegraphisches Bureau in 1848, in conjunction with the launch of his own newspaper the National-Zeitung. On November 28, 1849, the National-Zeitung for the first time published the previous day's stock and commodities prices in its morning edition. Since usage of the telegraph was prohibitively expensive, in the beginning Wolff focused entirely on financial news and it was not until 1855 that Wolff began selling 'political and general news' through his telegraphic service.[77] Price quotations were not just essential to the newswire services, they were their main source of revenue at the time.[78] Wolffs was not as successful as some of the larger services and in 1865 he was forced to appeal to Kaiser Wilhelm I to maintain the 'Prussian' character of the newswire service after a hostile takeover bid by Havas and Reuters. Wilhelm obliged and a holding company run by Gerson Bleichröder was formed to support the service. One result of this alliance was a closer aligning of the newswire's content with the official Prussian line.[79] Bleichröder, like other financiers who actively sought ownership and control of wire services across Europe, realized the power inherent in this new technology and used Wolffs to his financial and political advantage. Market information was relatively hard to come by and the barriers were high in this information-starved period. As a result, information was often unreliable and 'planted' stories, used to manipulate prices, were all too common.[80] Access to information was increasingly recognized as key to financial success and, as a result, efforts were made to control information through the creation of media cartels.

At the same time, new methods from statistics were applied to the raw data that began to be recorded from the markets. This was partly an attempt to avoid the pitfalls of manipulated financial journalism, but

75 Donald Read, *The Power of News: The History of Reuters, 1849–1989* (Oxford: Oxford University Press, 1992), 11.

76 Ibid., 17.

77 Nalbach, "Poisoned," 581.

78 Ibid., 583.

79 Ibid., 585.

80 Even though they operated in very difference circumstances, this was a common criticism of all four major newswire services. For an extensive overview of this see Nalbach, "Poisoned."

it also performed the ideological work needed to stabilize and manage the threat of unpredictability in markets.[81] It was in these attempts and through the emergence of financial technologies such as the graph and the index that the world market began to be written into existence. Because of the increased speed of transaction afforded by telegraphy, clearer and more precise methods for the collection and display of market information became necessary. Telegraph engineers were closely involved in the development of price recording and display technologies,[82] as in the case of Edward A. Calahan of the American Telegraph Company, who invented the stock ticker in 1867.[83] The ticker allowed time series to be constructed and visualized, and led to the now ubiquitous use of stock graphs – known as 'chartism'– to show and analyse price movement over time.

By the turn of the twentieth century, chart analysis had become a staple fixture of brokerages. The chart was understood to show the 'bird's eye view of the market' to its participants; a process of revelation and representation that simultaneously reconfigured the parameters of its object, and another case of what Alex Preda has called the process of 'appresentation' at work in financial markets.[84] In other words, as technologies and techniques for representing the market were developed, the images and contours that they produced increasingly *became* the market itself – a situation in which representations came to stand in for the underlying reality that they were intended to describe. With each improvement and iteration of the technologies used for price production, the contours of this world became increasingly well defined. The ticker reconfigured the space of the market, as it allowed access to price information while not requiring presence on the market floor, thus breaching the physical boundary space of the exchanges.[85] This form of representation and recording of price information laid the groundwork for what would later emerge as the 'efficient market hypothesis,' which continues to be an integral part of the ideology of finance today. It holds that the price of an asset reflects all available information about its value or that prices 'always reflect the

81 See Ian Hacking, *The Taming of Chance* (Cambridge: Cambridge University Press, 1990).

82 Preda, *Framing Finance*, 23.

83 The London Stock Exchange also began using the ticker in 1867. See Geisst, *Wall Street*, 67.

84 Preda, *Framing Finance*, 165.

85 In practice this was more complicated than is suggested by this image. For example, at the New York Stock Exchange, the introduction of the ticker introduced a new form of competition in which market actors would pay to position themselves closer to it in order to maintain a slight edge for their runners. See Geisst, *Wall Street*, 67.

true value of the thing being traded.'[86] An early form of this hypothesis emerged in 1900 in the doctoral dissertation of the French mathematician Louis Bachelier, entitled *Théorie de la speculation*. Bachelier's work would be taken up most famously by Eugene Fama in 1970, and it is now a central, if contentious, concept within economics. The hypothesis (in its 'strong form'), that all available information is reflected in an unbiased manner in the price of a commodity, relies on a fundamental assumption of instantaneity and simultaneity that could only be afforded by the communication technologies that arose at the turn of the twentieth century. That price information could be relied upon as 'simultaneously' available and agreed upon by market participants, was essential to the idea that markets were a 'reflection' of the world.

This was perhaps an elegant mathematical model, but it did little to approximate the real workings of the market. In Berlin in the latter half of the nineteenth century, any appeal to the notion of simultaneous transmission of information was complicated by a hybrid system of communication lines that added complexity to communications. The Haupttelegraphenamt ('central telegraph service') was located in the banking district on Französische Strasse, while the new Börse stood a kilometre away, past the Berliner Dom and over the river Spree. The city centre was crisscrossed not only by couriers running this route, but also by an elaborate and expensive *Rohrpost* ('pneumatic post') system that bridged the gap.[87] Because of the friction introduced by this elaborate system, any material advantage in speed could easily be translated into an advantage in informational and time based arbitrage, or 'front running.' But instantaneity still remained a powerful idea or projection of the desired form that this reflected image might take. Indeed, it is the network effect of instantaneity that forms the basis of any clear image of a cohesive market in its entirety – one in which an event on one stock exchange could be observed in other remote exchange at relatively the same time.

In Germany, evidence of the stock ticker (*Börsenfernschreiber* or *Ferndrucker*) does not appear until the end of the nineteenth century,[88] and

86 James Owen Weatherall, *The Physics of Wall Street: A Brief History of Predicting the Unpredictable* (Boston: Houghton Mifflin Harcourt, 2013), 16.

87 Berghoff, "Der Berliner Kapitalmarkt," 81.

88 The Bielefeld *Berlin und die Berliner* of 1905 described the *Ferndrucker*: 'Seit kurzem und vorläufig noch in bescheidenem Maß ist in Berlin auch diese technische Neuerung eingerichtet, welche durch dauerhafte und zuverlässigere Weitergabe dem Fernsprecher vorzuziehen ist, wenn man Zeit, Geld und Geduld hat.' *Berlin und die Berliner* (Whitefish, Montana: Kessinger Publishing, 2010), 454.

its usage was somewhat limited compared to other countries due to the German practice of only publicly releasing prices twice per day, rather than continuously.[89] At the same time, and somewhat counterintuitively, the concept of the world market and 'world economy' as a tangible image, was more developed in the German-speaking world than elsewhere.[90] The term *Weltwirtschaft* ('world economy') began to be used around 1900 by German-speaking economists and did not enter other European languages until after the First World War.[91] As Quinn Slobodian has shown, a debate about 'how to see the world economy' raged from the 1870s until 1914 between the historical economists who 'favoured empirical methods of statistics and sociology' and the marginalist economists who 'rejected panoramic descriptions of the world economy for a narrow focus on price movements.'[92] The former 'used trade and production numbers and cartography to make visible what they called the "world economic organism" in the late nineteenth century,' focusing on 'cross-border trade and the extension of telegraph and rail networks.'[93] In the marginalist camp, Joseph Schumpeter argued that 'at commodities and stock exchanges [...] one could literally see world prices being produced from moment to moment.'[94] In 1908, he 'offered the metaphor of the camera to argue that [...] through the observation of price, "we are taking, so to speak, a snapshot of the economy (*eine Momentphotographie der Volkswirtschaft*)."'[95] For Joseph Schumpeter, the 'snapshot' metaphor was literally extended to a cinematographic model of the world market. If price-point snapshots derived from graphs and formulated as indices were to be relied upon as accurate portraits of the condition of the world economy

89 Hirschstein and Scholz, "Commodity Exchanges," 208–17.

90 'It was only in 1879 that all goods crossing the borders of the new German Empire were systematically registered, classified and valued.' Adam Tooze, *Statistics and the German State, 1900–1945: The Making of Modern Economic Knowledge*, (New York: Cambridge University Press, 2001), 5.

91 Quinn Slobodian, "How to See the World Economy: Statistics, Maps, and Schumpeter's Camera in the First Age of Globalization," *Journal of Global History* 10, no. 2 (2015): 308.

92 Ibid., 308–9.

93 Ibid.

94 Ibid., 309.

95 Ibid., 327. Slobodian continues: 'The camera metaphor was not incidental for Schumpeter. He elaborated on it in three separate sections of the 1908 work, and referenced "images" and the "static apparatus" to describe his methodology throughout the book. In his later work, he would refer explicitly to the importance of "vision" as the worldview with which economists approached their intellectual problem. The metaphor resonated with other economists, too. Commentators, including Oskar Lange and Franz Oppenheimer, praised it and adopted it from Schumpeter. It is still used today to describe the method of comparative statics, on which Schumpeter expanded in his future work on evolution and economic development.'

at any given moment (as they still are today in the form of indices like the Dow Jones Industrial Average, which was first calculated in 1896), the movement of price data in time approximated the world as a moving image.

Schumpeter's use of this cinematic metaphor is partially attributable to the milieu of visual toys and proto-cinematic devices of the end of the nineteenth century in which his ideas took shape. That the regular intervals of the ticker, which standardized the time of the stock market and quantized the irregular emissions of price, could be compared directly to the cinematic apparatus was no coincidence. In the United States, Thomas Edison developed the patent for his Universal Stock Ticker – filed as a 'Chemical Stock Quotation Telegraph' – in 1885, three years before he began filing patents related to the development of the Kinetoscope and five years before the Kinetograph (an early motion picture camera). In fact, some of the very mechanisms that produced the quantized time of market price data were employed towards the creation of the cinematic illusion itself.[96] Thus, the invention of this method of visualization of the emergent world market was born of precisely the same technologies for recording movement and reconstituting it as a moving cinematic image.

For neoclassical economists like Schumpeter, markets functioned as barometers for the health of the world economy, a perspective in economic thinking that places markets above other considerations, such as social and psychologic factors, and remains central to neoliberal thought today. As Slobodian writes, 'when the concept of the world market eclipsed the world economy, the state disappeared and individuals appeared to encounter one another as buyers and sellers unmediated in a shared global space.'[97] The 'financialized' worldview that emerges in the course of the twentieth century is reliant, in the first instance, on the construction of the world according to this cinematographic metaphor, as a series of discrete events on a measurable timeline. This development coincided historically with the standardization of time in Germany and other countries in the 1890s around the problem of coordinating railroad timetables.[98] The notion that a 'snapshot' of market activity could be taken at any given time – although

96 Erik Born and Tara Hottman describe Edison's use of a Maltese Cross mechanism to advance and print on the ticker tape, the same mechanism that was essential for the development of film camera and the quantization of cinematic time. See "In Praise of the Ticker," (paper presented at the annual meeting of the Forschungsnetzwerk Berkeley, Tübingen, Wien, Harvard "Spekulation," University of North Carolina, Chapel Hill, NC, May 24, 2013).

97 Slobodian, "World Economy," 331.

98 Stephen Kern, *The Culture of Time and Space, 1880–1918* (Cambridge, MA: Harvard University Press, 2003), 12.

fraught with inconsistency in terms of actual implementation – had powerful consequences for the terrain of modernity. While train travel and other forms of modern transportation have been widely acknowledged as contributing to the collapse of distance, and the 'elimination' of space so central to theories of modernity, it was within the communications technologies of finance that the spatial conditions of modernity were most clearly articulated. Around the same time as these metaphors of the world market appeared, the *chronophotograph* of Étienne-Jules Marey and the motion studies of Eadweard Muybridge reduced motion to a discrete series of points in time on a two-dimensional photographic surface – thus piling discrete sections of space onto a single moment in time. But it was the visualizations of the financial world that were the most direct in their application of this central metaphor of modernity – the elimination of space – to a practical end. This suggests that we should take Jonathan Crary's claim literally that the 'deletion of space' in Muybridge's work 'announced a vision compatible with the smooth surface of a global marketplace and its new pathways of exchange.'[99]

Increases in the availability of price information that were made possible by technologies like the ticker led to a vast reconfiguration of the nature of market activity. In this new arrangement, time became the all-important factor – time became money – and exchanges engaged in a technological arms race to acquire even the most minimal of advantages over their competitors – a race that continues today in the form of high-frequency algorithmic trading. As Matt Matsuda has claimed, in its relationship to time, the stock exchange became a 'non-lieu de mémoire'– a place in which the past was constantly and relentlessly erased to make way for the future.[100] In Paris, this destruction of the spaces of the past was quite literal in the 1870s, as a wave of market-driven land speculation swept away the Paris Commune, and paved Hausmann's new boulevards over the old streets.[101] In Berlin (and Vienna), a post-unification building boom occurred at the same time that was financed by the *Maklerbanken* ('real-estate brokers or banks') and *Baubanken* ('construction banks').[102] This boom also produced many of the *Mietskaserne* ('blocks of flats') that still define the Berlin streetscape.

With the adoption of these communication technologies, the old space-based practice of arbitrage – the act of identifying a price differential

99 Jonathan Crary, *Suspensions of Perception: Attention, Spectacle, and Modern Culture* (Cambridge, MA: MIT Press, 2001), 142.

100 Matsuda, *Memory*, 14.

101 See Matsuda, *Memory*; Harvey, *Paris*.

102 Kindleberger, *Financial History*, 125.

between two locations and accordingly buying low in one and selling high in the other at a profit – began to be replaced by time-based practices such as the futures contract. As Jonathan Levy clarifies: 'within the span of one lifetime the telegraph had made it so that merchants knew prices in markets at the port of destination before they shipped their goods. The only "blind venture" now left was a futures transaction across time' – capital had entered its temporal phase.[103] Historically, the futures contract has been one of the least understood and most maligned of the many derivatives that arose as financial abstraction and complexity increased into the twentieth century. Futures contracts in commodities such as grain and coffee seemed to stand in stark contrast, in their abstraction, to the perceived utility and use value of the underlying commodities that they were tied to.

After unification, futures trading that was increasingly facilitated by advances in communications technology became an object of popular debate and a political issue in Germany.[104] Futures trading (*Termingeschäft* or *Zeitgeschäft*) was regarded as a threat on several levels and took on an ideological significance that outstripped its actual importance as a practice. Suspicion of futures trading partly arose due to the fact that it involved speculation in the most tangible of commodities – *Lebensmittel* ('foodstuffs') and other basic fungible commodities. In this sense, it brought the professions that were the least associated with speculation and non-productive capital into direct contact with the market – particularly in the example of the farmer. This conflict exposed a central tension of the modern economy and undercut romantic notions of the farmer as attached to the land, producing goods of 'real' value. In practice, however, agricultural producers needed to establish a future price for their crops before planting as an insurance against the unpredictable whims of the weather and other hazards. While agrarian elites argued that futures markets depressed the price of commodities, speculators and bankers argued that they decreased risk for all involved, and provided liquidity.[105] Because of what a futures 'contract' allows – the ability to buy and sell contracts that purportedly represented actual commodities while never physically exchanging (or even intending to exchange) anything – they were seen as a threat to the 'contractual basis, and thus the moral order, of civil society.'[106] Commodities futures in foodstuffs were particularly prone to

103 Jonathan Levy, *Freaks of Fortune: The Emerging World of Capitalism and Risk in America* (Cambridge: Harvard University Press, 2012), 240.

104 See Max Weber, *Börsenwesen: Schriften und Reden 1893–1898*, eds. Knut Borchardt and Cornelia Meyer-Stoll (Tübingen: J.C.B. Mohr (Paul Siebeck), 1999), 18.

105 Slobodian, "World Economy," 34.

106 Carter, "Green Table," 252.

negative portrayals in popular media, since they provided the most concise juxtaposition of highly abstracted financial instruments with goods that had immediately apparent use value. For example, in 1909, D.W. Griffith demonized speculation in wheat futures in his film *A Corner in Wheat*, by using parallel montage to juxtapose the activities of ruthless speculators with a family of farmers starving because of the fluctuations caused in the price of wheat. A similarly negative portrayal of futures contracts in Bertolt Brecht's *Kuhle Wampe* (1932), in which characters discuss how millions of tons of coffee are being destroyed to drive up its price on the international market, will be returned to in chapter 5. Both films seize on the accessibility, to a general audience, of the concept of speculating in basic goods in order to drive home their critique of inequity and capitalism, respectively.

Instead of providing stability, trading in derivatives exacerbated monopoly conditions and fed the practice of 'cornering,' which was highly disruptive. In order to protect against drastic price swings in basic goods, most countries with advanced markets enacted some form of regulation concerning futures in the last decades of the nineteenth century. Germany's 1896 *Börsengesetz*, however, was the most comprehensive and prohibitive, effectively banning futures trading for decades to come.[107] The unofficial and largely unregulated exchanges also became the target of anti-speculative sentiment and there were attempts to ban them outright after the passing of the *Börsengesetz*.[108] This was in part due to the fact that unofficial exchanges had been partially responsible for the popularization of futures trading for the wider public.[109] Beyond the obvious lack of transparency, as well as the high potential for swindles on the part of owners who controlled both the bets of their patrons and the flow of information, unofficial exchanges presented another, perhaps deeper existential threat to the official exchanges. The *Winkelbörse* cast speculative activity back into the realm of gambling and threatened the notion that exchanges had a useful and productive function, that of determining the *price* of a commodity.

Germany was unique at this time in terms of the extent that laws governing futures trading were implemented. These new regulations permitted only 'producers or users of grain or flour, merchants, or registered cooperatives dealing in such products or making loans against them' to participate in

107 A previous attempt had been made to ban futures contracts in 1860 but did not succeed. Berghoff, "Der Berliner Kapitalmarkt," 73.

108 Lance Davis, Larry Neal, and Eugene N. White, "How It All Began: The Rise of Listing Requirements on the London, Berlin, Paris, and New York Stock Exchanges," *The International Journal of Accounting* 38, no. 2 (Summer 2003): 131.

109 Levy, *Freaks*, 26.

legal transactions under the 'Berlin contract.'[110] In practice, illegal, or at least non-state sanctioned, futures trading did continue, but accounts and transactions were not 'legally protected.'[111] The implementation of these restrictions may partially explain the stark differentiation between concepts of 'productive' and 'non-productive' capital in the German financial imaginary – a dichotomy that is of central importance to cultural representations of finance. The popularization of futures exchanges also pushed the quality of market activity to new levels of abstraction and reconfigured the space of world trade. These consequences are key to our understanding of how disruptive futures exchanges were. Futures trading eliminated the need for the physical transfer of goods as the basis for changes in supply and demand, and consequently in price, across international markets. This led not only to more rapid swings in the price of basic goods, but also to unforeseen effects of international events – a change in the price of a commodity in a market as distant as South America, for example – that could have direct consequences on markets at home.[112] In this sense, futures posed much more of an existential than an economic threat in Germany, as they represented a form of border crossing and loss of imaginary sovereignty that clashed with romantic ideals and nationalist notions of soil, terrain and *Heimat* ('homeland').

'Productive' vs. 'Non-Productive' Capital

The emergence of the German bourgeoisie at the end of the nineteenth century constituted a massive demographic and societal shift. Members of the middle class could, under the Prussian system, obtain non-hereditary titles, which were coveted well into the 1890s,[113] and, increasingly, this new demographic owned shares. In terms of the popular engagement with financial instruments, Germany lagged behind Britain where it is estimated that 'financial assets represented 39 per cent of all assets owned by individuals,' rising to 64 per cent in 1913.[114] In Britain, this number included 'mortgages, bank deposits, trade credit, and government and corporate debt,' and a sampling of the shareholders of 6,120 joint stock companies listed in Britain in 1901 reveals some 3.3 million names.[115] By comparison,

110 Hirschstein and Scholz, "Commodity Exchanges," 210–11.

111 Ibid., 210.

112 Muller, *Mind and the Market*, 236.

113 Richie, *Faust*, 150.

114 Preda, *Framing Finance*, 7.

115 Ranald C. Michie, *The London Stock Exchange: A History* (Oxford: Oxford University Press, 1999), 72.

Max Weber reported that in Germany in 1896, approximately 1.5 to 2 million individuals 'received dividends' from financial assets.[116] While not providing a comprehensive picture, these numbers give an idea of the relative scale of the investment in securities at this time for the populations of the two countries (about 33 million[117] in the United Kingdom and 56 million[118] in Germany) at the turn of the twentieth century. However, these numbers also do not take into account participation in the *Winkelbörsen* ('bucket shops'), unofficial exchanges that were places of off-market betting, which would have accounted for a significant portion of speculative activity. Hard statistics on everyday participation in the market are somewhat difficult to come by prior to 1871, but evidence of the culture surrounding finance remains in the form of secondary reflections such as financial literature, popular representations in the press, and in instructional pamphlets.[119] These pamphlets borrowed analytical language from engineering, medicine, meteorology, and other hard sciences in a conscious effort to legitimize and provide a rational groundwork for financial activity.[120]

It was not long, however, until the appearance of new forms of capital accumulation within the financial sector that were increasingly abstracted forms of accumulation more closely associated with 'use value,' gradually came under scrutiny and attack. Though the rise of finance fuelled the technological advancements of the *Gründerzeit*, the role of finance was often disavowed and those who were associated with it were often treated as unwelcome house guests. Though finance capital was centrally connected to all elements of Germany's economy, and in many cases was essential for its function, various forms of economic activity were increasingly categorized as either 'productive' or 'non-productive' – in German the dichotomy crystalizes around the binary opposition of *raffendes Kapital* vs. *schaffendes Kapital* ('non-productive' or 'money-grubbing' vs. 'productive' capital). This fraught binary construction positions activities such as banking and trading securities as fundamentally opposed to industry, craft, and particularly agriculture. As has already been discussed, nowhere was this clearer than in the market for futures contracts for commodities with immediate and tangible value, particularly foodstuffs. In the cultural climate of late nineteenth-century Germany and Austria, these terms

116 Weber, "Die Börse," 268.

117 According to the United Kingdom 1901 census.

118 According to the German census of 1900.

119 Preda, *Framing Finance*, 23.

120 Ibid., 90.

also carried an additional anti-Jewish implication that was born out of a fundamental disavowal of Jews as integrated members of German society and of the role of finance capital in the birth of the modern German state. In reading the filmic depictions of finance and speculation of the Weimar Republic, it is essential to understand the centrality of this disavowal of the importance of finance capital in the mythology of the German nation. For it is through an understanding of the relationship between capital, nation, and the construction of a national 'other' that we can unpack the complex mobilization of this discourse in key films, such as Fritz Lang's *Dr. Mabuse der Spieler.*

During the 1860s and 1870s, the demonization of 'non-productive' capitalism was also part of mainstream discourse that attempted to define the amorphous term 'liberalism' in a variety of ways.[121] However, Jews were not the only national 'other' upon which the negative aspects of capitalism were cast. For example, the German establishment 'National Liberal' movement was cautious of the perceived disruptive power of international finance to the fledgling idea of a German nation. This disavowal of undesirable aspects of capital echoed Prussian King Frederick William IV's 1853 protest that the new investment banks presented 'a disgusting example of French speculative fever and corruption,'[122] – a complaint that the ills of capital must originate from an extra-territorial source, which was, as we shall see, often France. Compare this to Engels's moral condemnation of all forms of both speculation *and* profit making:

> The speculator always counts on disasters, particularly on bad harvests. [...] immorality's culminating point is speculation on the Stock Exchange, where history, and with it mankind, is demoted to a means of gratifying the avarice of the calculating or gambling speculator. And let not the honest 'respectable' merchant rise above the gambling on the Stock Exchange with a Pharisaic 'I thank thee, O Lord...,' etc. He is as bad as the speculators in stocks and shares. He speculates just as much as they do. He has to: competition compels him to. And his trading activity therefore implies the same immorality as theirs. The truth of the relation of competition is the relation of consumption to productivity.[123]

121 Ritchie Robertson, *The 'Jewish Question' in German Literature, 1749–1939: Emancipation and Its Discontents* (Oxford: Oxford University Press, 1999), 77–151.

122 Richie, *Faust*, 149.

123 Friedrich Engels, "Outlines of a Critique of Political Economy," in *The Young Hegelians, an Anthology*, ed. Lawrence S. Stepelevich (Cambridge: Cambridge University Press, 1983), 293.

While proponents of market liberalism were suspicious of finance capital, they hesitated to follow Engels's logic to its conclusion and instead attacked only the aspects that they recognized as disruptive to the emergent fixed idea of the German nation. Economic nationalism was thought of as a viable course of action in the face of the new global economic order of the nineteenth century.[124] However, the contradiction between the nationalist ideal and the international force of finance capital would have to be overcome, and the legitimization of finance along nationalist lines would manifest in complex ways. Much debate in the nineteenth century would focus on separating the notion of outright 'gambling' from acceptable forms of financial 'speculation' that could be given a seal of scientific validity, and this debate also coincided with a corresponding differentiation between forms of 'non-productive' and 'productive' capital.

The German victory in the Franco-Prussian War in 1870 provided the fledgling empire, in the form of French war indemnities, with the largest single cash infusion in the world up to this time.[125] When combined in 1870 with a loosening of restrictions on the formation of joint-stock companies, this prompted hundreds of companies to incorporate and drove a wave of industrial development.[126] After the subsequent *Gründerkrach* ('crash of the founders') of 1873, however, anti-Jewish sentiment increased strongly and combined with protestations against speculation. It is important to underline the internal contradiction here. This era of entrepreneurial expansion in the mid to late nineteenth century is so important to Germany's history that it is referred to as the *Gründerzeit* ('time of the founders'). However, instead of acknowledging the vital role of finance capital in making this boom possible, after the crash that immediately followed, blame for all the ill effects of rapid expansion was shifted onto 'speculators' who were deemed to be part of the 'non-productive' economy.

One of the most visible victims of the popular and openly anti-Jewish wrath that followed the crash was the industrialist and railway baron Bethel Henry Strousberg, known as the *Eisenbahnkönig* ('railway king'), who lost his fortune in the crash and was remanded to debtors's prison in Russia. Popular perception held that 'Jewish banking and industrial families had not suffered in the crash' and that Jews had been the cause of the crisis in

124 See Eric Helleiner, "Economic Nationalism as a Challenge to Economic Liberalism? Lessons from the 19th Century," *International Studies Quarterly* 46, no. 3 (2002): 307–29.
125 Kindleberger, *Western Europe*, 156.
126 Fohlin, *Finance Capitalism*, 224.

the market.[127] As Marcel Stoetzler has argued, anti-Semitism was at the centre of German debates on nationhood, provoked largely by agitations of the prominent National Liberal parliamentarian Heinrich von Treitschke. In fact the term 'anti-Semitism' emerged in its modern incarnation at this time.[128] The so-called *Berliner Antisemitismusstreit* ('Berlin anti-Semitism Dispute') held Jews to be at the centre of the tension between economic liberalism and nationalist unity, as nationalism's demand to 'enforce some extent of cultural homogeneity' clashed with the 'twin processes of Jewish emancipation and assimilation.'[129] Critiques of capitalism, as Leigh Claire La Berge points out, 'often pair racist or anti-Semitic, nationalist sentiments with anticapitalist sentiments' as a critique of the 'abstraction' of modernity itself, since 'Jews became associated with the abstract dimension of capital through their participation in financial activities.'[130] Anti-Semitism was also focused and organized into a political lobby in groups like the Bund der Landwirte (Agrarian League), which lionized the powerful romantic imagery of the farmer, connected to the land and labour, in contrast to the ravages of, purportedly Jewish, speculation on the open market. Again, the importance of futures contracts should be noted as the Bund was influential in the implementation of the *Börsengesetz* ('Stock Exchange Act') of 1896 and its attempt to protect agriculture from speculation. The rise of anti-Semitism at this time was rife with internal contradictions, and the association of Jews with the destructive aspects of finance capital was driven by unreasonable and irrational assumptions that would remain in the popular consciousness. In post-unification nineteenth-century Germany, Jews were negatively associated with the 'non-productive' labour of financial markets in rhetoric stemming from across the political spectrum. Finance was seen as parasitical to the 'real' sectors of the economy, especially with respect to its role in commodities markets. In Germany, the definition of productive vs. non-productive capital was closely tied to ideas of national identity itself, and the abject reality of dealing with money was assigned to the German Jewish 'other.'

127 Richie, *Faust*, 244.

128 Marcel Stoetzler, *The State, the Nation, and the Jews: Liberalism and the Antisemitism Dispute in Bismarck's Germany* (Lincoln: University of Nebraska Press, 2008), 4.

129 The term *Berliner Antisemitismusstreit* is attributed to Walter Boehlich who assembled a volume of its key texts in 1965. See Stoetzler, *Antisemitism*, 4–8.

130 Leigh Claire La Berge, "The Rules of Abstraction Methods and Discourses of Finance," *Radical History Review* 2014, no. 118 (December 21, 2014): 101. La Berge draws on Moishe Postone, "Anti-Semitism and National Socialism: Notes on the German Reaction to 'Holocaust,'" *New German Critique* 19, no. 1 (1980): 97–115.

Thus, the idea of 'productive' vs. 'non-productive' capital emerged as an ill-defined binary at this time, a popular distinction that attempted to hold together the central contradiction of an economy that relied on markets to function but that deeply distrusted those who made money off them. As we shall see, this distinction, if not the contradiction inherent in it, loomed large in the popular imaginary of the Weimar Republic and its cultural productions.

Gambling and the Financial Imaginary in Germany

In addition to the importance placed on the separation of the 'productive' from the 'non-productive,' the history of the separation of the concepts of 'gambling' and 'speculation' during the *Gründerzeit* (the years of economic and industrial expansion around the time of the unification of Germany in 1871) is also central to our understanding of the cultural codes employed to depict finance in the films of the Weimar Republic. As in other countries, legitimate forms of financial activity would gradually be extricated from association with gambling and games of chance, but it was the specifics of this process – and the liminal spaces along the German border in which it occurred – that make the German context unique. As will be shown here, the separation of 'gambling' from 'speculation' was closely tied to the mythology of the German nation state, as well as its territorial conflict with France. Around the time of German unification in 1871, the definition of legitimate and non-legitimate forms of economic activity was directly tied to the emerging identity of the fledgling nation state and played out in the casinos on the French border. Ideas born out of this time about the nature of gambling and speculation would continue to inform popular attitudes up to and throughout the Weimar Republic.

Growing participation in financial markets amongst the German middle and upper classes familiarized an increasing number of people with financial markets in the early nineteenth century. At the same time, the popular understanding of financial markets remained closely associated with the discourse surrounding gambling. In the first half of the nineteenth century, 'playing' the market was still regarded as akin to gambling in a casino, and superstitious associations and supposed pseudo-scientific 'systems' meant to tame the laws of chance were transposed from the blackjack table to the stock exchange. Gambling and speculation grew in popularity at this time and were considered closely related phenomena. All across Europe, casinos that had previously been the exclusive purview of the aristocracy were developed into popular gaming centres and resorts, which catered to a wider range of social classes.[131] In the 1820s, Baden-Baden, Wiesbaden, and Bad Homburg began to 'organize an entire tourist system around the experience and profits of gambling,'[132] whose patrons were largely drawn from the 'middle and lower-classes.'[133] This development was later boosted by the abolition of gambling in France in 1836,[134] which led to the relocation of French entrepreneurs, including managers from the casinos in the famed Parisian Palais-Royal, across the German border into the Rhineland. This was an important development as gambling would come to be negatively portrayed as a French import to Germany.

A new disposition in the figure of the nineteenth-century gambler in France was noted by Walter Benjamin:

> The lack of consequences that defines the character of the isolated experience [*Erlebnis*] found drastic expression in gambling. During the feudal age, the latter was essentially a privilege of the feudal class, which did not participate directly in the production process. What is new is that in the nineteenth century the bourgeois gambles. It was above all the Napoleonic armies that, on their campaigns, became the agents of gambling for the bourgeoisie.[135]

The nineteenth century also saw the appearance of the public racetrack, the slot machine, and, towards the end of the century, the casino, as a collection of rooms solely devoted to gambling, a form that would be most familiar to the citizens of Weimar-era Berlin.[136] Recognizing the importance of gambling to his theory of modernity, Benjamin paid particular attention to casinos and other spaces in which gambling took place. These spaces allowed pre-modern magical thinking and superstition to collide with the

131 Gerda Reith, *The Age of Chance: Gambling in Western Culture* (London; New York: Routledge, 1999), 74.
132 Carter, "Green Table," 2.
133 Reith, *Chance*, 74.
134 'Dubech and d'Espezel "*Histoire du Paris*" (Paris, 1926) noted that this closing, on December 31, 1836 in Paris, provoked a "small riot" and was the "mortal blow to the Palais-Royal, already dethroned since 1830 by the boulevard.' Quoted in Benjamin and Tiedemann, *Arcades Project*, 494. Convolute [O2a,3].
135 Benjamin and Tiedemann, *Arcades Project*, 512. Convolute [O12a,1]. His own note.
136 'It is in this period that the recognisably modern forms of the casino, the public racetrack and the mechanised slot-machine first appeared. In place of the huge sums wagered by the individuals of the seventeenth-century aristocracy came more democratic games for many players organised around modest stakes which allowed for prolonged rather than excessive play.' Reith, *Chance*, 74.

trappings of economic activity and the rational realms of statistics and actuarial science. Benjamin's observations on the importance of the spaces of gambling for the experience of modernity are further supported in the work of E. J. Carter, who asserts that 'casinos were places where Europeans encountered a rapidly modernizing world' and that 'patrons of the roulette tables were feeling out a new relationship with the phenomena of risk, money, credit, and the changing economic structure of space and time.'[137] Following this line of reasoning, I will discuss how the close relationship between gambling and speculation during this time is particularly illuminating to the experience of modernization in Germany, to questions of subjectivity and identity, and to the conceptual ossification of the categories nation and territory.

Gambling and financial speculation were inseparable practices in most market economies at the beginning of the nineteenth century. For example, after the War of 1812, American financial exchanges competed directly with lotteries, such as the M. Allen Company of New York, as methods of raising capital. Lotteries were used to underwrite business ventures, and they were an early vehicle for the popularization of financial products to everyday consumers.[138] Similar practices were adopted in Germany, as in the case of Gerson Bleichröder's father, Samuel, who, in 1803, opened both a *Wechselstube* ('currency exchange bureau') and a *Lotterie Geschäft* ('lottery business') that issued tickets for the raising of state funds for such expenses as 'army widows and disabled soldiers.'[139] In the mind of the average citizen, there was little to distinguish the mechanics of 'playing' the lottery, the market, or the roulette table. Over the course of the nineteenth century, the German popular understanding of the relationship between gambling and speculation would gradually be redefined as one of opposition. The particulars of this development are of great import to the historical understanding of 'speculation' in the German context, for it is in this formative period, leading to the unification of Germany, that much of the accepted knowledge, biases and popular sentiment evident in the Weimar Republic, would arise and become crystalized.

As Carter shows, the Rhineland casinos played a role in bringing 'structures and functions of capitalism into the public sphere' and in 'authorizing speculation and risk-taking in a manner hitherto unknown among European

137 E. J. Carter, "Breaking the Bank: Gambling Casinos, Finance Capitalism, and German Unification," *Central European History* 39, no. 02 (2006): 186.

138 Geisst, *Wall Street*, 21.

139 Stern, *Gold and Iron*, 26.

societies.'[140] It is no coincidence that the heyday of the world-renowned pleasure and gambling centres, such as Baden-Baden, Bad Homburg, and Wiesbaden – immortalized in 1887 in Dostoevsky's *The Gambler* as the composite location 'Roulettenburg' – corresponds almost exactly with the popularization of financial markets in Germany. The parallel history of the rise and fall of gambling in Germany at this time deserves closer scrutiny, as it enriches and explains much of the sentiment around financial transactions and the new role of money and credit in German society. It was also an especially rich source of material for fictional representations.

In the 1830s, the Rhineland casinos were the premier casinos in the world and Baden-Baden was the largest and most famous resort town in Europe.[141] They would continue to feature heavily in popular discourse and were regarded as spaces of modern cosmopolitanism that brought the educated bourgeoisie into contact with the old aristocracy. Of course, the impenetrability of birth privileges remained in place, but the (limited) intermingling of classes was disruptive to the old order. This, combined with the added variable that chance introduced into this equation, meant that these casinos functioned as microcosms of a liberal market-based society, as aristocrats and common people could stand next to each other while making or losing fortunes at the gaming table. In this sense, gambling, like other relations of monetary exchange, was concurrent with a new form of social interaction between people that transcended the established order to a certain degree.[142]

In addition to being located on the French border, the Rhineland casinos were almost exclusively French-owned and operated; they were even staffed by French *croupiers*. German visitors and commentators correspondingly took note and protested at the extra-territoriality of these sites, where French was sometimes the only language spoken and in which they felt like strangers on German soil.[143] In addition, the ostentation of wealthy, often noble, French visitors to the casinos began to attract the ire of moralists in Germany.[144] A common refrain developed around the casinos concerning this 'morally corrupting' French influence. As will be shown, the stereotypes of French decadence that developed in the mid-nineteenth century remained ingrained in the German popular imaginary into the years of the Weimar

140 Carter, "Green Table," 3.

141 Ibid., 30.

142 For a further discussion of this in the American context see Levy, *Freaks*.

143 Carter, "Green Table," 261.

144 Ibid., 260.

Republic. With the founding of the German Empire, Bismarck, who would later be instrumental in the abolition of gambling, echoed this sentiment. He was the first to conjure the image of the 'gambling ship' in relation to the territory of the nation, an image which would recur in the Weimar Republic. He joked that 'in a boat without a national flag a mile from the shore, Prussia and Germany do not exist, and there anyone can gamble as much as he likes.'[145] This deep association of water, instability, and speculation, as threats to the stability of the German state remained in the German psyche, and is a reoccurring theme of this study. The evocation of a ship lost at sea also drew upon a deep-seated symbolic logic at work at the heart of the spa-casinos – sites of water, gambling and financial flow. These *Weltbade* ('world-class spas'), as the more famous were known, were situated along the Rhine, a river central to the German historical imaginary in the works of Heinrich Heine, Felix Mendelsohn, and Goethe. This imaginary was being actively reinforced at the time, perhaps most memorably by Richard Wagner, in whose *Der Ring des Nibelungen* (1848–74), the river figured prominently as the hiding place of the *Rheingold*, an object of value that transcended economic exchange. Over-identification of the Rhineland with all that was German was also a historical side effect of the Rhineland provinces having been, until only a few decades before, part of the French Empire under Napoleon I. Thus, much was at stake in the symbolic economy of the casino, which would reach the apex of its influence when the Rhineland itself transitioned from a frontier to a demarcated national border at the time of unification. As Carter has shown, casinos, which functioned as sites of fluidity in terms of national identity and class, were casualties of rising nationalism which led to calls for their abolition. The Franco-Prussian War and the establishment of defensible borders between France and Germany effectively solidified the shifting terrain on which the casinos were located, and on which they were no longer welcome. After the war, a popular joke held that the French 'had lost everything in 30 and 40' – a pun that conflated the name of a popular French card game *trente-et-quarante* and the sum of the two numbers (70) – as in the fateful year 1870.[146]

As a parallel example, Urs Stäheli has convincingly argued that in nineteenth-century America, with more and more participation in financial markets, there was a need to separate speculation from gambling in order for speculation to be regarded as a 'legitimate' activity and a basic component of a market economy. Stäheli claims that 'the gambler is identified as a potential

145 Quoted in ibid., 59.
146 Ibid., 267.

speculator – but as a speculator who has not yet been formed as an economic subject through techniques of discipline and knowledge.'[147] In other words, speculation began to be differentiated from gambling through claims that it was a rational, knowledge-producing activity that was (ostensibly) scientific in nature. Similarly, the legitimization of speculation in Germany is in fact tangibly linked to the history of the great gambling concerns and, in particular, to the pseudo-scientific methods, techniques, and systems that sprung up around the popular notion of beating the odds or 'breaking the bank.' As has been discussed, the rising popularity of gambling in Germany corresponded with the growing familiarity of the German populace with money as living currency – an object of instability and fluidity. It also corresponded with the growing popular familiarity with laws of probability and chance. In its basic conformity to statistical thinking, gambling not only changed 'the experience of play forever,' but was also 'particularly suited to the imperatives of commercial organization.'[148] Though the science of statistics would only be adopted as an economic tool later in the century,[149] statistical thinking found increasing purchase amongst gamblers in the casino by the mid-nineteenth century, although its application was far from scientific. Gamblers developed systems that often combined a degree of statistical thinking with irrational superstitions and hunches. Amongst the less scientific of these systems was that of Fyodor Dostoevsky, who believed that, if a level of 'cold-bloodedly, calm, and calculating' detachment could be maintained, there would be 'no possibility of losing.'[150] Others went much farther in the creation of elaborate and dubious systems that promised sure-fire returns. Chief among the promoters of such ideas were the publishers of the *Deutsche-Kalifornien* series of pamphlets, which presented its readers with a mixture of pseudo-scientific techniques and advice concerning the character of other players.[151] Relying on the veneer of statistical theory, and often accompanied by the trappings of scientific argument in the form of charts and graphs, these pamphlets – the name of which reminded the reader of the globally connected economy – promoted new ways of thinking about how to profit in an environment of chance occurrences. They also had direct ramifications for individuals engaged in similar speculative activities on the market. The *Deutsche-Kalifornien* were

147 Urs Stäheli, *Spectacular Speculation: Thrills, the Economy, and Popular Discourse* (Stanford, CA: Stanford University Press, 2013), 11.

148 Reith, *Chance*, 80.

149 See Tooze, *Statistics*.

150 Carter, "Breaking the Bank," 187.

151 Ibid., 195.

also a quintessential example of a particular mode of thinking that applied readily to the market. This form thinking belied the emergent idea of the rational actions of a *homo economicus* and instead combined statistical analysis and the laws of probability with a romantic appeal to the will and individual power of the gambler.[152]

German casinos provided a venue and mechanism for experimentation with systems of prediction and attempts to formalize profit-making schemes, and their heyday from 1840 to 1870 paralleled the popularization of financial markets.[153] Prior to the onset of the rapid industrial growth of the 1840s, Germans had been conservative in matters of personal finance. However, between 1851 and 1857, just before the 'first wave of globalization,'[154] 119 *Aktiengesellschaften* were formed and the demand for credit that these companies created was soon turned toward the resources of the *Besitzbürgertum* ('propertied bourgeoisie'). Significantly, in 1853, the *Frankfurter Zeitung* began to list stock prices, and by 1858 reports of a 'gambling fever in shares' emerged that applied to 'all classes of the population.'[155] The share itself became a 'status symbol' and a 'fashionable object' in Berlin, and the world of finance entered into the popular consciousness.[156] By the 1860s, 'even the most conservative elements in Prussia had come to see that industrial expansion had outgrown the smaller banks and would best be served by joint stock companies.'[157] Among these could be found the Wiesbaden casino, which incorporated in the 1850s and sold shares throughout Germany and France.[158] It is essential to understand the history of this initial close association between, and then eventual separation of, gambling and speculation as it is at the core of popular ideas about what

152 Ibid., 193.

153 Ibid.

154 The period between the mid-nineteenth century and the Franco-Prussian War. See Kevin H. O'Rourke and Jeffrey G. Williamson, *Globalization and History: The Evolution of a Nineteenth-Century Atlantic Economy* (Cambridge, MA: MIT Press, 1999); Hans Pohl, *Aufbruch der Weltwirtschaft: Geschichte der Weltwirtschaft von der Mitte des 19. Jahrhunderts bis zum Ersten Weltkrieg* (Stuttgart: F. Steiner Verlag, 1989); Cornelius Torp, *The Challenges of Globalization: Economy and Politics in Germany, 1860–1914*, English-language edition (New York: Berghahn Books, 2014).

155 By 1858, David Hansemann could claim, 'The gambling fever in shares is more and more affecting almost all classes of the population.' See Martin Kitchen, *The Political Economy of Germany 1815–1914* (London: Croom Helm, 1978), 87.

156 See Richie, *Faust*, 150; Helmut Böhme, *An Introduction to the Social and Economic History of Germany: Politics and Economic Change in the Nineteenth and Twentieth Centuries* (Oxford: B. Blackwell, 1978), 37.

157 Richie, *Faust*, 149.

158 Carter, "Breaking the Bank," 191.

constitutes legitimate forms of financial activity in the Weimar Republic (and even today).

Price Production as Worldview

The parallel development of gambling and the popularization of financial speculation presented a conceptual problem for those who believed that finance had a legitimate role to play in a modern economy. As such, gambling and speculation were conceptually separated, often on moral grounds, as we have seen. A second line of reasoning held that speculation was necessary to the smooth functioning of a financial market, since it provided more opportunities for trades to occur and with less friction, something that could be considered as distinct from mere 'gambling.' This conceptual separation of 'legitimate' speculation from other non-desirable forms of future-focused wagering was reified in binary terms across various European languages. The opposition of the German *Spiel* ('game/play/gamble') vs. *Wette* (literally 'bet,' but in the usage of the time connoting 'speculate') found parallel articulation in the English stock 'jobbers' vs. 'brokers' or the French '*agiotage*' ('illegal speculation' or 'manipulation') vs. '*investment*' ('investment').[159] In Urs Stäheli's historical account of this conceptual separation in the American context, proponents of the legitimacy of speculation refuted claims that it was unproductive, parasitic, and as morally reprehensible as gambling by identifying and defending what they saw as the indispensable value of speculation to the market economy. Stock exchanges were imbued with a 'useful' function, in order to legitimize them amongst other forms of labour. Specifically, their value was defined in the function of 'price production' for goods and commodities on the open market. Price production, defined as instantaneous determination of the value of a commodity, was a 'product unique to the stock market.'[160] The argument is an early variant of that which supports the role of 'market makers' today. These provide a constant

159 It is worth revisiting the specifics of this subtle point. As E. J. Carter writes: 'A significant debate took place in the mid-nineteenth century on the juridical and moral distinction between gambling ('*Spiel*') and betting ('*Wette*'), which had considerable implications for the murky relationship between casinos and stock markets. [...] In *Über den begrifflichen Unterschied von Spiel und Wette* ['On the conceptual difference between gambling and betting' (1869)], A. Krügelstein [...] contended the bet is a (usually verbal) contract drawn up over a conflict of opinion, with the expectation that the party in the wrong will perform some service for the other party. Gambling, by contrast, is a matter of profit and loss which is determined solely by chance [...] By stressing the contractual nature of the bet, of course, he implicitly separated stock speculation from pure gambling.' Carter, "Green Table," 246.

160 Stäheli, *Speculation*, 45–46.

flow of liquidity for trading that guarantees the possibility of buying and selling. Speculators, who might only 'own' a commodity, such as wheat, for a matter of minutes or seconds before selling it for a profit or loss within a trading day, were deemed necessary in the determination of the price of a commodity at any given moment. Without these transactions, it was argued, the price of a commodity would vary too widely from one market to the next.

In its capacity of 'producing' a price, the market itself took on the 'visionary' role implied in the Latin root of the term 'speculation': *speculari* – to examine, explore, watch, or observe. As markets opened for an increasing number of commodities, the act of speculation effectively inscribed a map of the world as a vast terrain of known quantities. Alongside the social and political ramifications of this increasing and early form of 'financialization,' there were also important ontological consequences, since the very nature of objects traded on the exchange was defined by this discourse. For example, wheat, in order to be traded rapidly, did not in fact change hands directly, but rather, it was *the idea* of a standard bushel of wheat that was agreed upon in the act of buying and selling. As such, the parties involved in the exchange defined the ideal qualities of wheat – something akin to wheat as a Platonic form or idea. The precondition of the admission of commodities to this realm of abstraction was their fundamental *fungibility*, or their suitability to being exchanged – one unit of a commodity for *any other*, regardless of origin.

In their production of prices for all manner of tradeable commodities, markets increasingly redefined the outside world in visual terms and, as such, the labour of the stock exchange became a labour of representation. Objects, commodities, people, places, events: all were reduced by the discursive networks of the telegraph-based financial services to points of data. At the Parisian exchange, as Matt Matsuda notes, 'events were a screen, a backdrop in front of which the real "business" of the world now went on.'[161] A similar cinematic metaphor was used by Edward Dies in his 1925 novel *The Wheat Pit*, which likened the interior of the actual exchange to a 'film studio,' where the clerks resembled 'camera men preparing to film some spectacular event.'[162] Indeed, pushing this metaphor further, and given the theatrical architectural arrangement and the murals and friezes that adorned the halls of the exchanges, the entire arrangement resembles a kind of camera obscura, exposing an image of the world through the medium, or 'emulsion,' of price information.

161 Matsuda, *Memory*, 45.
162 Stäheli, *Speculation*, 70.

Historically, stock exchanges have been ahead of the curve in their adoption (or creation) of new communications technologies and, as such, have always existed as both locatable 'places' within the fabric of the urban metropolis, as well as gateways to the distributed space of the global market. Accordingly, the historical development of the stock exchange, beginning with the adoption of the widespread use of the electric telegraph in the mid-nineteenth century, has been characterized by the steady undermining of its physical presence and the increasing importance of its non-corporeal, or spectral existence as a space. During the years of the Weimar Republic, the neoclassical façade of Germany's largest exchange, in Berlin, projected an unchanging image of a fixed order, however, the communications technologies of the market, and the calculus of chance and contingency that would enable the accelerated capital flows of the twentieth century, had already breached its walls. While the arcade, according to Benjamin, produced the 'world in miniature' form as commodity,[163] and the railway collapsed space as well as led to the standardization of time, the stock exchange can be thought of as a technology that creates an *image* of the external world – coded through the emergent language of charts and graphs, which quantized time and space into a series of financial events.

The history of German modernity, and the roots of its particular relationship to finance, the global, and processes of financialization, would come to inform much of its political and cultural landscape in the twentieth century. Here I have provided a backdrop for the chapters that follow, in which questions of how the particular events of the brief history outlined here would inform and recur in cultural productions into and after the years of the Weimar Republic. The relationship of finance to questions of threshold and boundary, to corporeal and non-corporeal forces, to vision and how the world was constructed as an image of *Verkehr* ('trade' or 'transaction'), and to modernity itself, will be explored through the reappearance of these key themes and discourses in the cinema of the Weimar Republic.

163 Walter Benjamin quoted in Buck-Morss, *Dialectics of Seeing*, 3.

2. Dr. Mabuse and His Doubles

Abstract: Chapter 2 introduces Fritz Lang's *Dr. Mabuse der Spieler* (1922) as the quintessential film that embodies all of the key crises of finance capital and modernity. It examines how the film connects crises of authority, identity, authenticity, and rationality back to the realm of finance capital. Dr. Mabuse both threatens fixed notions of territory, colonies, border, and nation while also embodying a fantasy of empowerment and mobility for the emergent class of *Angestellten* ('white-collar workers') as a film-going public. The film is situated in the context of the figures of the *Raffke* and *Schieber*, two established stereotypes of the profiteers and nouveau riche of the time, and as part of a micro-genre of *Börsenfilme* ('stock-exchange films') of the time of the hyperinflation.

Keywords: Dr. Mabuse, Fritz Lang, Fictions of Finance, Hyperinflation, German Colonies, Salaried Masses

Dr. Mabuse the Speculator

Introduction

Fritz Lang's two-part *Dr. Mabuse der Spieler: Ein Bild der Zeit* was released in April and May 1922, during a period in which the Berlin stock exchange was closed for all but one day per week due to the overwhelming demand of speculators. The 'flight from the mark' that characterized the hyperinflation at this time blurred the boundary between speculation and investment, and made speculation in currencies a common practice.[1] This chapter situates Lang's canonical two-part film, the full title of which is *Dr. Mabuse der Spieler: Der Große Spieler: Ein Bild der Zeit* (released on April 27, 1922) and *Inferno: Ein Spiel von Menschen Unserer Zeit* (released on May 26, 1922),[2]

1 See Gerald D. Feldman, *The Great Disorder: Politics, Economics, and Society in the German Inflation, 1914–1924* (New York: Oxford University Press, 1993), 390.

2 The two films are a single extended narrative and will be referred to throughout as *Dr. Mabuse* or *Dr. Mabuse der Spieler.*

Lyons, O., *Finance and the World Economy in Weimar Cinema*. Taylor & Francis Group, 2023.
DOI 10.5117/9789463727136_CH02

within this historical context. Here, I take my cue from Siegfried Kracauer in discussing the film-going audience of the period, who were members of the class of *Angestellten*, the numbers of which increased exponentially after the war. In so doing, I attempt to identify and draw attention to the overlooked cultural and historical signifiers that would have resonated with this class of workers, a workforce that, in Berlin, included members of the rapidly expanding financial sector. I also reconsider the ways in which this key film reflects and amplifies a worldview that resonated with the daily professional engagement of these workers with the money economy and financial markets. While I support the view that *Dr. Mabuse der Spieler* is a key document of European modernity, I seek to lend more specificity to this claim by reframing the film as a remarkably prescient treatment of one of the most panicked and transformative scenes of modernity in general: the emerging of awareness of the global money economy that challenged not only all the traditional categories of time and space but also heightened anxieties around both the nation and the subject.

Dr. Mabuse is a text of central importance to both Weimar cinema as well as the argument put forward in this book. It is a path-breaking film of the period for its mobilization of tropes that would continue to be used in the depiction of finance, speculation, and the emergent image of the world economy, not only in the accelerated crisis of the ensuing decades in Germany, but with an afterlife that extends to today. As such, the film is shown to not merely represent but also actively construct the emerging discourse of this central space of modernity; the new scene of global capital, whose transformative flows would evoke all the key markers of the crisis of modernity around notions of subjectivity, nation, reason, gender, and authenticity. This chapter also demonstrates the centrality of the preoccupation with finance capital in the popular imaginary of the Weimar Republic by reclaiming a number of now lost Weimar-era films that invoke many of the same themes and stereotypes as *Dr. Mabuse*. These films constitute an *Erwartungshorizont* ('horizon of expectations')[3] within which *Dr. Mabuse* would have been received. In keeping with re-evaluations of the relationship between well-known canonical examples of auteurist art cinema, and *popular* Weimar cinema, these films are here introduced as a lost intertextual field in which *Dr. Mabuse* gains new contextual resonance.[4]

3 Hans Robert Jauss, *Toward an Aesthetic of Reception* (Minneapolis: University of Minnesota Press, 1982).

4 For examples of the recovery of this field of popular, or otherwise overlooked films of the period see Christian Rogowski, ed., *The Many Faces of Weimar Cinema: Rediscovering Germany's Filmic Legacy* (Rochester, NY: Camden House, 2010).

Figure 2. Norbert Jacques and his wife (Margerite Samuely) on a boat during a journey from Australia to Peru. *Berliner Illustrierte Zeitung*, Ullstein Verlag, no. 39, September 25, 1921. Photographer unknown. Ullstein Bild.

The source material for the film, Norbert Jacques's novel *Dr. Mabuse der Spieler*, was serialized in the *Berliner Illustrirte Zeitung* between September 1921 and January 1922 (Figure 2). At the time, the *BIZ* had one of the largest circulations of any magazine in Germany.[5] It was owned by the

5 Bernhard Fulda, *Press and Politics in the Weimar Republic* (Oxford: Oxford University Press, 2009), 18.

highly successful Ullstein publishing house, which was one of the big three publishers in Germany along with Mosse and Scherl. Ullstein was a 'Berlin-based Jewish enterprise supporting the left-liberal Democratic Party, which – despite this support – had ceased to exist by the end of 1930,'[6] and that 'came to be regarded as a pillar of the Weimar state like the Bauhaus, the Reichstag, and Stresemann.'[7]

In the film, Mabuse is largely confined to his urban setting while in the novel he is significantly more mobile, travelling from the back-room gambling dens to the Bodensee, while his henchmen cross Germany into Switzerland. Mabuse's mobility in the novel is drawn from the biography of its globetrotting and prolific Luxembourger author, who completed some thirty books and many articles during his lifetime. In the novel, this mobility is also explicitly tied to German colonial holdings in the South Seas, where Mabuse both runs a colony and owns slaves. His stated motivation, dropped from the film script, was to establish his rule over a colony in Brazil called 'Eitopomar,' and the novel can be read as a symptomatic fantasy of colonial domination in the wake of Germany's loss of all its colonies after the war. Erik Butler points to other key differences between the novel and the film, claiming that the former 'looks back to literary tradition' while the film 'embraces the modern,' and that these two different depictions of the villain are in 'different league[s].'[8] While it is certainly true that the novel and film present Mabuse in different lights, given the close proximity of the release of the novel to the film, as well as the wild success of both, I treat the figure of Dr. Mabuse as something akin to what today would be called a transmedia phenomenon. It is highly likely that audiences of the film would have already been familiar with Jacques's version in the *BIZ*. Awareness of the novel was widespread as it was Jacques's most successful, selling roughly 100,000 copies in its first year, and selling half a million copies in the following decade through translations into six languages.[9] In its serialized form, it is estimated that it had an audience of over one million. The *BIZ* had not seen such a demand for copy since its establishment in 1894.[10]

6 Fulda, *Press and Politics*, 2.

7 Ibid., 2.

8 Erik Butler, "Dr. Mabuse: Terror and Deception of the Image," *The German Quarterly* 78, no. 4 (October 1, 2005): 485.

9 Norbert Jacques and Günter Scholdt, *Dr. Mabuse, Der Spieler: Roman, Film, Dokumente* (St. Ingbert: W.J. Röhrig, 1987), 131.

10 Jacques and Scholdt, *Mabuse*, 131.

Print was the dominant medium of the time[11] and Jacques's novel was part of the wave of mass-marketed *Ullsteinbücher* that appeared in the German-speaking world in the first two decades of the twentieth century. Depending on who you asked, these were seen as either democratizing access to the written word or degrading the German literary tradition.[12] Austrian novelist Robert Musil associated this form with the capital markets directly when he quipped: 'Do not say "ullsteinisierung" (Ullsteinization). Say industrialization, the time of high capital. Even in literature we are progressing from craftsmanship to mechanization.'[13] As such, *Dr. Mabuse* appeared fully integrated within the other news items, reports, and stock quotations that constituted the financial media of the time, but also as a product of this form. When combined with the reach of newspaper distribution networks and publicity, this created the impression that Mabuse was suddenly 'everywhere.' Jacques's novel was closely integrated into the rhythms of the financial news networks that formed the basis upon which general news and forms of information were transmitted. Accordingly, the novel and the film were conversant with the cultural codes of this financial news network and served to reify popular and recurring stereotypes of the financial sphere that can be found throughout Weimar culture.

The Figure of the *Raffke* and *Schieber*

In his comprehensive history of the inflation years, Gerald D. Feldman dubs 1922 the 'year of Mabuse.'[14] Feldman argues that inflationary policies adopted during the time of the war economy in 1914 mark the beginning of the breakdown of society that culminated in 1924. Feldman notes two periods of intense speculation that punctuate the years leading up to

11 '[T]hroughout the 1920s newspapers were the predominant medium of mass communication in Germany. Radio broadcasting would come later, with 3.5 million registered listeners by 1930.' Fulda, *Press and Politics*, 3.

12 Balder Ottern, a former colleague of Jacques, states: '[Jacques] schreibt den zauberhaft schönen Roman "Funchal," wachte eines Morgens auf und war berühmt! Das er dann auf das Niveau seines Welterfolges, "Dr. Mabuse" herabstieg, daß er vom Dichter zum Filmbuchautor sank, einen Achtzehn-Zylinder-Mercedes fuhr und gute Literatur für einen sinnlosen Sport erklärte, war das Verhängnis seines zu frühen Erfolgs. Je höher die Honorare sausten, umso tiefer tauchte der Poet.' Quoted in Jacques and Scholdt, *Mabuse*, 134.

13 'Nicht sagen die Ullsteinisierung. Sage die Industrialisierung, Zeit des Hochkapitals. Auch in der Dichtung geht man vom Handwerk zur Maschine über.' Robert Musil in 1930, quoted in Jacques and Scholdt, *Mabuse*, 134. Author's translation.

14 Gerald D. Feldman, *The Great Disorder: Politics, Economics, and Society in the German Inflation, 1914–1924* (New York: Oxford University Press, 1997), 513.

the hyperinflation – 1918 and 1922. According to Reichsbank president Rudolf von Havenstein, this explosion of speculation was the result of the participation of 'an army of bank employees which form consortia reaching down to the female secretaries' and that these two periods of 'speculative fever' were both a rational response to 'profit increases of a number of enterprises' as well as caused by the perception of 'the great personal gains of the war profiteers.'[15] After the First World War, these profiteers, the *Schieber* or *Kriegsgewinnler* ('profiteer' or 'war profiteer'), emerged from the misery of the defeat as a class of new-money entrepreneurs. Selling essential items at inflated prices, these profiteers had access to black market goods (often of low quality). Simultaneously hated due to their wealth, but also needed due to their ability to grease the wheels of a barely functional consumer economy, they were the subjects of countless articles and films of the time.

In addition to the figure of the *Kriegsgewinnler* or *Schieber*, the related figure of the *Raffke* is to be found throughout Weimar-era cinema, often in a supporting role.[16] In fictional portrayals, the *Raffke* is not always interchangeable with the *Schieber*. He is often more elegant than the *Schieber*, clad in chic evening wear, although he is assumed to be as much a member of the uncouth nouveau riche as the former. The term *Raffke* is period slang and refers to the act of gathering money (*zussamenraffen des Geldes*) and, in reference to a (typically) male figure, translates roughly as 'a money-grubber' or 'a rake.' Fritz Lang, himself, claimed that Mabuse was 'ein Raffke,' and that the term was a 'prototype of the times,' coined in Berlin to describe the newly rich.[17] The *Raffke*, as a type, is most clearly delineated in the Kurt Tucholsky song 'Raffke,' sung in a contemporary Berliner slang:

15 Havenstein quoted in Feldman, *Disorder*, 49.

16 See Philipp Stiasny, "Das Kino und die Inflation," in *Erzählte Wirtschaftssachen. Ökonomie und Ökonomisierung in der Literatur und im Film der Weimarer Republik*, ed. Walter Delabar, Michael Grisko (Bielefeld: Aisthesis, 2013), 35–44.

17 'Die Zeit nach dem Ersten Weltkrieg war für Deutschland eine Zeit der tiefsten Verzweiflung, der Hysterie, des Zynismus, des ungezügelten Lasters. Entsetzliche Armut war neben ganz großem und neuen Reichtum, Berlin prägte damals ein Wort: Raffke, vom Zusammenraffen des Geldes. "Raffke," so nannte man den Neureichen. Dr. Mabuse ist der Prototyp dieser Zeit. Er ist ein Spieler. Er spielt Karten, er spielt Roulette, und er spielt mit Menschen. Er spielt mit ihren Schicksalen. Er glaubt nicht an tiefe Gefühle. Er sagt zu einer Frau, die er liebt: "Es gibt keine Liebe, es gibt nur Begehren." Und er spielt mit dem Leben dieser Menschen, und er spielt mit dem Tod.' Fritz Lang from an interview with Erwin Leiser for West German television in 1968. See Erwin Leiser, *Zum Beispiel: Fritz Lang*, Documentary, Short, (1968). Included in DVD extras: *The Testament of Dr. Mabuse*. DVD, dir. Fritz Lang Crime, (1933: Criterion, 2004).

Ick bin die allerneuste Zeiterscheinung,
Sie treffen mir an alle Orte an –
Ick pfeife uff die öffentliche Meinung,
Weil ick als Raffke mir det leisten kann.
Ick bin die feinste von die feinen Nummern,
Ick steh schon in die Illustrierte drin;
Denn ob Jeschäfte oder Sekt und Hummern:
Ick knie mir rin, ick knie mir richtig rin!
[…][18]

I am the latest trend,
You meet me everywhere –
I laugh at public opinion,
Because as a *Raffke*, I can afford it.
I am the finest of the finest stock,
Magazines – you'll find my picture in;
Whether business or champagne and lobster:
I dig in, I really dig in!

Here Tucholsky refers to the elevated presence of the *Raffke* in popular media, suggesting that his stature is in no small part due to his appearance 'in the illustrated magazines,' which amplified his presence in the popular imaginary.[19] Tucholsky makes clear that the *Raffke* is a figure who has become rich beyond the expectations of the class he was born into. He is, however, not only an object of derision for the masses, but also a threat to the established order – thumbing his nose at convention. As such, the figure of the *Raffke* or *Schieber* is more complex than his fat-cat image might initially suggest, and his breaking of conventions embodied key desires of the time. Roland Schacht drew attention to some of the intricacies of this figure in a satirical article entitled 'In Defense of the *Schieber*,' in 1922:

> Just think of the nonsense which the economists, those big shots, talked during the war. Intellectual activity? We cannot all be intellectually active. And are you not doing business with your intellectual activity? And for that matter, who is buying your special luxury editions, your folios of paintings, who is going to your concerts and theatre? Exclusively we *Schieber*. Do we not have intellectual and artistic interests? From whom would you cultivated people, who tolerated the war and its miserable management, live today, if we were not buying up your stuff. We are an economic blessing. We are the new men who are replacing the dried up *routiniers*, the people with the worn-out traditions. […] We are not

18 Author's translation. See appendix for the full text of the song.

19 For a discussion of related cabaret songs, see Peter Jelavich, *Berlin Cabaret* (Cambridge, MA: Harvard University Press, 1996), 140.

> anti-Semites and we do our shopping at Wertheim. We are the children of the people, who are making it. We are the true revolutionaries. *Schieber*? We are Germany's future.[20]

Filmic representations of the war profiteer that are extant today include Ernst Lubitsch's comedic *Die Austernprinzessin* (1919), which depicts the family life and marriage of the daughter of an American oyster magnate, and is discussed in chapter 3. Less well known is Reinhold Schünzel's *Alles für Geld* ('Anything for Money,' 1923), which opens with the following intertitle (English in the American version):

> The World War left in its wake social and industrial chaos. Princes became paupers, and Governments changed overnight. Old standards went down and new ones raised their heads – Out of this maelstrom emerged a new financial colossus – an uncultured, good natured, obscure butcher, who had developed into a money wizard and wrapped his flabby fingers around the packing industry – S. J. Rupp, the Beef King.

Rupp is played by Emil Jannings and the name is a play on the term *ruppig*, meaning 'rough' or 'gruff.'[21] It is also a thinly veiled reference to the Krupp family empire, one of the largest industrial concerns in Europe at the time. Krupp was the backbone of German industry and also a mainstay of the German war machine in the First World War. The film begins as a positive portrayal of a wealthy man who has not forgotten his roots in poverty and has enough of a sense of humour about his new position in life to hire a former count as his secretary. This class reversal is driven home by the film's portrayal of an aristocratic family that has fallen on hard times. In the end, greed seems to get the better even of good-natured Rupp, and the film devolves into an oedipal conflict that sees the beef baron accidentally have his son killed in a botched attempt to rig the results of an auto race that he is gambling on. *Alles für Geld* is significant for its portrayal of the *Schieber* character as representative of both social mobility and the erosion of the established order, but ultimately it resorts to the familiar narrative of greed-induced downfall.

While the figure of the *Schieber* or *Raffke* was a concrete reality during these years, his exaggerated media presence served to crystalize a variety of

20 Roland Schacht "Verteidigung des Schiebers," *Die Weltbühne* 18 (Dec. 14, 1922), quoted in Feldman, *Disorder*, 554.

21 Philipp Stiasny, *Das Kino Und Der Krieg: Deutschland 1914–1929* (Munich: Edition Text + Kritik, 2009), 12.

social and economic problems into a stereotype, and he became synonymous in the popular imaginary with the decay and corruption of the Weimar system. *Dr. Mabuse*'s 'image of its time' can only be fully understood within the larger context of these figures of the post-war period. In what follows, I will attempt to recover the field of representations across other Weimar-era films in order to show how *Dr. Mabuse* was not symptomatic of modernity *tout court*, but rather of a specific stage of crisis in modernity linked to the destabilizing flows of finance capital, the world market, and to the realignment of social categories through seismic shifts in power relations and wealth. Films like *Dr. Mabuse* cast back an inverted reflection of the new reality of a new financial order to their spectators – many of whom were members of the newly formed white-collar classes that worked in this world.

The Little Bank Tellers Go to the Movies

The effects of the inflation years were especially noticeable for the class of salaried white-collar workers in whom Siegfried Kracauer saw the most acute sense of 'spiritual homelessness' develop. Many of these workers were employed in fields directly or peripherally connected to the activity of the exchanges and had more direct access to financial information as well as to the social circles of the market. Speculation was a fact of everyday life for them and it is estimated that, in 1921, a significant percentage of the consumption of shoes and clothing was funded by speculation, especially by bank employees amongst other white-collar workers.[22] Kracauer lamented that while these workers's conditions of existence had more in common with the working class, they consistently identified politically with better-off members of society. Kracauer also notes that they made up a significant proportion of Weimar film audiences. In his 1926 essay 'Cult of Distraction: On Berlin's Picture Palaces,' Kracauer saw in the salaried class a '*homogenous cosmopolitan audience* in which everyone has the same response [*eines Sinnes ist*], from the bank director to the sales clerk, from the diva to the stenographer.'[23]

To give a sense of the growth of the financial sector at this time, consider that in 1913, the total number of employees at Deutsche Bank was 9,587, whereas in 1923 it was 37,000.[24] Between 1914 and 1924, the number of visitors

22 Richard Merton, quoted in Feldman, *Disorder*, 253.

23 Siegfried Kracauer, quoted in Inka Mülder-Bach, introduction to *The Salaried Masses: Duty and Distraction in Weimar Germany*, by Siegfried Kracauer (London: Verso, 1998), 12.

24 Harold James, "Strukturwandel in Kriegs- und Krisenzeiten 1914–1945," in *Geschichte des Finanzplatzes Berlin*, ed. Hans Pohl (Frankfurt: Knapp, 2002), 161.

to the Berliner Börse doubled, and the number of traders increased from 2,330 to 5,200, in part driven by the trading of German war bonds (*'Kriegsanleihe'*), which were essential to the popularization of financial instruments amongst the general public.[25] In Berlin, 9,168 people were employed by banks in 1907 and, at the high point of the inflation, this number reached 100,000. By the time of the next employment census in 1925, the number had fallen to 55,221, while the count of Deutsche Bank employees had decreased drastically to 14,000 by 1926.[26] Between 1919 and 1924, 867 new banks opened in Germany, 293 of which were in Berlin.[27] It was within this sector that many of Joseph Goebbels's generation (born at the turn of the century) were employed after the war. Goebbels himself (b. 1897) found one of his first jobs, after completing his PhD in 1921, as an employee (*'Bankangestellte'*) of the Dresdner Bank.[28] In the summer of that year, the sharp fall in the value of the mark sparked an orgy of stock market speculation that caused a threefold increase in the index of share prices. Clerks were unable to keep up with paperwork and there was chaos on the floor of the Berlin stock exchange. The result was the banning of guests from the floor for all but two days of the week (by November it was reduced to only one).[29] In addition to those employed by the financial sector, currency trading was also rampant, with everyday citizens trying to get rid of worthless marks in any way that they could. Joseph Addison, a diplomat stationed at the British embassy in Berlin, noted on September 20, 1921 that:

> Millions of persons in this country are, I think accurately, reported to be buying foreign currencies in anticipation of fresh tax burdens, and to be hoarding foreign bank notes [...] I hardly know a single German of either sex who is not speculating in foreign currencies, such as Austrian crowns, Polish marks and even Kerensky roubles. In as much as a fall in the value of the mark is inevitably accompanied by a rise in the quotation of industrial shares, speculators are supposed to be operating systematically to depreciate the mark with a view to reaping the benefit of higher quotations in the share market.[30]

25 Frank Zschaler, "Erzwungene Reorientierung im Zeichen der deutschen Teilung (1945–1990)," in *Geschichte des Finanzplatzes Berlin*, ed. Hans Pohl (Frankfurt: Knapp, 2002), 230–34.

26 Ibid.

27 James, "Strukturwandel," 160.

28 Ibid., 161.

29 Feldman, *Disorder*, 390.

30 Adam Fergusson, *When Money Dies: The Nightmare of the Weimar Collapse* (London: Kimber, 1975), 47.

Representations of foreign currency exchange, or *Valuta* as it was called, appeared in the illustrated press of the time in a variety of forms, most frequently in the guise of a woman, an association that will be returned to in the next chapter.

Black markets in foreign exchange that sprung up at this time blurred the boundary between the official and unofficial economy. They also redefined access to the spaces of the exchange within the city of Berlin. Joseph Roth describes one such scene:

> An instalment seller is only viable in a time of stable currency. The great Inflation drove all the instalment sellers out of their sorry business. They became money changers. A money changer fared little better. When he bought Romanian leis, the rate went down. When he sold, it rose. When the dollar was high in Berlin and the mark was high in Vienna, he went to Berlin to buy marks. He returned to Vienna to buy dollars with the high mark. Then he took his dollars to Berlin to buy yet more marks. But no locomotive can keep pace with a falling mark. By the time he was back in Vienna, he had half of what he set out with.[31]

Roth reveals the daily struggle to exchange *Valuta* in a manner that undercuts the image of the wealthy money changer at this time, and also provides a valuable description of how small-scale financial transactions were locally bound to place – a far cry from the increasingly connected world of the stock exchange. He continues:

> In order to make money the currency dealer would have to be in telephone contact with money markets all over the world. However, all he was in contact with was the black market where he was. Both the harmful effects and the connections of the black market have been greatly exaggerated. Blacker by far than the black market was the official exchange – innocent, whiter than white, and enjoying police protection. The black market was the dirty competition to an institution that was itself dirty.[32]

Driven by speculation and venture capital, many films of this period reflected the widespread permeation of market forces in Weimar society. Furthermore, as has been discussed more generally of Weimar culture, these

31 Joseph Roth and Elie Wiesel, *Wandering Jews*, trans. Michael Hofmann (New York: W. W. Norton, 2001), 62.
32 Roth, *Wandering*, 62.

films performed the two-fold function of both representing this reality while simultaneously contributing to its formation. Writing about the popular cinema of the Weimar Republic, Siegfried Kracauer reminds us that 'stupid and unreal film fantasies are the *daydreams of society*, in which its actual reality comes to the fore and its otherwise repressed wishes take on form.'[33] As Thomas Elsaesser notes, this was not a one-way relationship. Kracauer understood that identification with mass-media depictions was a form of self-alienation. Yet, he complicated this Marxist critique by suggesting that spectators 'unconsciously and yet lucidly, recognize their own subjectivity in the alienated, double mirrored representations,' and 'may be dreaming, but they are "not duped."'[34] *Dr. Mabuse* should be understood as a film in which this new class of workers could recognize itself and identify in various ways with the film's central figure.

A re-evaluation of *Dr. Mabuse* and the recovery of the film's contextual resonance as a document of the forces of finance capital require a reconstruction of available materials from the time. Accordingly, I have assembled evidence of a number of now lost films from the early years of the republic here in the form of synopses and reviews of relevant films. These materials reveal the intertextual field in which *Dr. Mabuse* would have been received, as well as the prevalence of plots based on financial manoeuvres and financial tropes in general. Of note in these films is the frequent use of the stock exchange as a backdrop to the action and the incorporation of market activity as a key element of their narratives. Contemporary reviews create a far from complete picture but are suggestive of the content of these films and are a testament to their prevalence. They include the following lost films.[35]

Schieber (Manfred Noa, 1920) contains elements that foreshadow *Dr. Mabuse der Spieler*. One reviewer calls it 'a timely film: a product of current images of love, and of a crime story. We see *Schieber*, marriage brokers, gambling clubs and thugs, and in general everything that is usually found in police reports or the court reporting section of a newspaper,' and states further that 'the *Schieber* has a brutal, ruthless criminal nature' and takes advantage of a woman who 'becomes his mindless dupe' and 'gives him her money, house, everything.'[36] The writer of *Planetenschieber* ('Planet Swindler,'

33 Siegfried Kracauer, *The Mass Ornament: Weimar Essays*, ed. Thomas Y. Levin (Cambridge, MA: Harvard University Press, 1995), 24.

34 Thomas Elsaesser, *Weimar Cinema and after: Germany's Historical Imaginary* (London: Routledge, 2000), 34.

35 Thanks to Philipp Stiasny for his guidance in compiling this list of films.

36 *Film-Kurier*, February 5, 1921. This review lists the scriptwriter as Edmund Edel, who directed *Die Börsenkönigin* (1916), which will be discussed in chapter 3. Author's translation.

Reinhard Bruck, 1920) 'dubs his creation a "grotesque storm of images in six whirlwinds."' One review of *Planetenschieber* runs as follows: 'a *Schieber* of the first degree, to whom 220 million is merely a penny, stages Armageddon in order to game the stock exchange. [...] Every possible caricature swirls around. All the types of our time are represented, and all the jokes and sayings.'[37] Again, the importance of the stock exchange narrative is noted, as well as how a collection of types describes an 'image of the time' similar to that in *Dr. Mabuse*. A review of *Der Schieberkönig* ('The Swindler King,' Hubert Möst, 1920) describes the film as portraying 'a stock exchange scheme. A fraudster claims to have discovered a gold mine and names it the "Lucky Mine"' – identical in name to the mine in *Die Börsenkönigin* of 1918, which is discussed in chapter 3. It continues: 'the "Lucky Mine" corporation is founded, and after the shares have risen astronomically, the fraud is discovered and the company collapses.'[38] These and other examples further demonstrate the importance of the figure of the *Schieber* or *Raffke* at this time.[39]

Das Geld auf der Strasse ('The Money in the Street,' Reinhold Schünzel, 1922) also demonstrates the prevalence of financial themes and the figure of the imposter. A *Film-Kurier* review describes a *Hochstapler* ('imposter') who 'uses a bank owner's fondness for his daughter to gain access to the stock exchange' where he 'speculates with the money of regular pensioners in gold stocks – and loses.'[40] Another 'imposter' film, *Kauft Mariett-Aktien* ('Buying Mariett Shares,' Alexander von Antalffy, 1922), takes a more comedic approach. It depicts a wealthy Dutchman, van der Burgh, who 'falls in love with the wife of a Russian capitalist.' Van der Burgh 'follows the Russian to London where he seeks to invest in the newly founded *Mariett-Aktiengesellschaft* ('Marriett Joint Stock Company'), but van der Burgh discovers that Mariett is a fraud, and schemes through a series of very funny pranks to gain control of the situation for himself and take what he can.'[41] Another comedy, *Bräutigam auf Aktien* ('Bridegroom on Shares,' Viggo Larsen, 1918), mocks the idea of commercial debt through its depiction of the nobly titled Hans von Reininger, who is completely indebted and contemplating suicide. His 'tailors, cobblers,

37 "Planetenschieber," *Film-Kurier*, February 7, 1921. Author's translation.

38 "Der Schieberkönig," *Film-Kurier*, July 5, 1920. Author's translation.

39 Further examples in the *Film-Kurier* index include: *So 'n Schieber* (1920), *Kriegsgewinnler Schiebermann* (1921), *Millionenschieber* (Rudolf Walter-Fein, 1921), *Raffkes Reise nach Hildesheim* (Gerhard Dammann, 1922), *Raffke fährt Auto* (Gerhard Dammann, 1922). See CineGraph, Hamburgisches Centrum für Filmforschung, *Film-Kurier Index* (Hamburg: Hamburgisches Centrum für Filmforschung, 1993).

40 "Das Geld auf der Strasse," *Film-Kurier*, February 3, 1922. Author's translation.

41 "Kauft Mariett-Aktien," *Film-Kurier*, December 4, 1922. Author's translation.

and moneylenders' decide that he can only pay his debts through a wealthy marriage, thus offering him up to the market.[42]

In the crime drama, *Gesindel* ('Rabble,' Martin Berger, 1921), a distinction between industrial and finance capital is made clear in the synopsis which describes an unscrupulous stock market magnate, 'in tune with modern times,' who takes advantage of an old industrialist 'who fails to recognize the modern era.'[43] The film depicts class conflict between the owners of a factory and its workers against a backdrop of speculation. In *Der schwarze Montag* ('Black Monday,' Robert Dietrich, 1922), one reviewer uses the term *Börsenfilm* ('stock exchange film') to suggest a micro-genre of the time, noting that 'the trade papers spoke of a stock exchange film, a bold statement for the couple of mediocre stock market scenes that appear in the last act of this film.' The programme for the film described is as 'a "*Film des Gegenwart*" ('film of the times')' and one reviewer reported that it portrays an oil baron 'Mr. North' who, while shipwrecked, throws the remaining water for him and his fellow sufferers overboard. He confesses his crime in a note that he places in a bottle, but is unexpectedly rescued. A love affair develops between Mr. North and Ethel Wilkinson. In the final scenes, their love is tied to the recovery of 'Ethel-Wilkinson-Shares' on the stock market.[44] Another crime drama, *City Bank* (Robert Scholz, 1921), is described as a 'detective film' in which a 'criminal who leads a double life' falls in love with the daughter of a banker, who herself is in love with an employee of her father (a cashier). The criminal draws the banker's daughter into his schemes which unjustly cast suspicion on the innocent cashier.[45]

As popular representations of finance, the stock exchange, and the historically new category of the world market, these films provided more than mere entertainment to their viewers. They contributed to the formation of a newly 'financialized' worldview. The term 'financialization,' though it may seem anachronistic to the 1920s, is nevertheless applicable to this period in which the forces of finance and speculation touched upon every aspect of society. Though now used more commonly to describe the shaping of policy according to the logic of financial markets after the 1970s, I am using this term here to describe the heightened use of financial instruments as a method of creating wealth (or even merely

42 See *Paimann's Filmlisten: Wochenschrift für Lichtbild-Kritik*, no. 153, 1918/19.

43 "Gesindel," *Film-Kurier*, January 25, 1920.

44 "Der schwarze Montag," *Film-Kurier*, February 16, 1922.

45 "City Bank," *Film-Kurier*, January 24, 1921.

subsistence) in the place of wages or the making and selling of goods during the Weimar years. My use of the term here is in keeping with Rudolf Hilferding's own definition of 'finance capital' in *Das Finanzkapital* (1910) as the 'financialization' of capitalist production – an extension or evolution of the Marxist definition into the 'latest phase' of capitalist production in which 'institutions of the financial system penetrated and dominated the economy as a whole.'[46]

The 'double reflection' of Weimar cinema is at work here in creating this financialized world view. As Thomas Elsaesser writes:

> The twice reversed structure here posited between fairy-tale fantasy, narrative motifs, social structure, class relations and gender gives a good indication of the kind of *mise-en-abyme* of social observation, political formation and popular entertainment that the films in the Caligari tradition were engaged in, distilling those uncanny moments of a recognition that may indicate the oblique ways in which film spectators organise and experience their (psychic and social) reality in the cinema.[47]

When read as part of the public-sphere discourse on the modern subject's relation to the world economy, these films construct rather than merely reflect a particular worldview through their repetition of cultural codes and depictions of key stereotypes. They familiarize audiences with the discourse of finance capital and, at the same time, provide their own visual material with which to illustrate its otherwise invisible mechanisms – material that then feeds back into the financial imaginary. We should ask then: how did *Dr. Mabuse* hail its newly minted financialized spectators and what codes and associations did it provide by way of illustration? For one, Dr. Mabuse is today usually understood as a 'gambler,' and this association will be unpacked in terms of its historical resonance in due course. However, I believe the figure of Mabuse served a more immediate function in the Weimar imaginary, as a character who had mastered the contingency of the market rather than the roulette wheel.

46 Hilferding's expansion of Marx's definition of capital responds to the changes within capitalist production in the half-century between Marx's foundational texts and his own. During this time, 'a greater concentration and centralization of industrial and banking capital and, more deeply, the transition from free competition capitalism to monopoly capitalism, especially in Germany and the United States' had taken place. See Matari Pierre Manigat, "Finance Capital and Financialization: A Comparative Reading of Marx and Hilferding," *OEconomia*, no. 10–4 (December 1, 2020): 687–710.

47 Elsaesser, *Weimar Cinema*, 98–99.

Dr. Mabuse: Gambler or Speculator?

In Jacques's novel, the occult and spectral aspects of Mabuse's mobility, so linked to technology in the film, are more clearly tied to the release of his id and bacchanalian displays. For example, a brief scene in the film in which Mabuse and his henchmen drink themselves into a stupor is given added resonance when we refer to the original in the novel. Jacques's version helps to explain Mabuse's strange combination of clockwork precision and reckless abandon. For Jacques, Mabuse's release of energy in the form of intoxication is central to his worldview and the projection of his will. Consider the following passage:

> He had to drink. He drank and sparked his strong evil intellect (*Geist*). Intoxication locked him into a castle, as if in *A Thousand and One Nights*, and separated his will from all distractions so that his imagination turned to great plans.
> No one understood this. The alcohol was to him a storyteller, it was the current that carried in itself the essence of life and offered it to him from the depths. He bathed in it, as if in the love for a woman, floating unmoored, breaking new paths continuously. It dissolved all laws and left him alone and unrestrained, limitlessly expanding beyond all limits (*Grenzen*)... His own system, his own world and sun.[48]

In the novel, perhaps more clearly than in the film, though it too includes a scene in which Mabuse and his gang drink themselves into a stupor, intoxication gives Mabuse access to the realm of the fluid – to liquidity and dissolution. Jacques describes Mabuse's condition here as one of complete surrender. His subjectivity distended over borders in time and space, he becomes a completely decentred entity. Mabuse exists in a liminal state during this episode, a condition that has been interpreted in various ways.

Bernd Widdig compares the rush of intoxication with the thrill of gambling, drawing from Walter Benjamin's description of *Schwellenerfahrungen* – 'the moment of a threshold experience.'[49] Benjamin describes this as akin to the '*rites de passage*' and 'ceremonies' that are less and less a part of modern life, and claims that 'falling asleep' and 'waking up' are a few of the only experiences of *Schwellenerfahrung* still available to us. In his

48 Jacques and Scholdt, *Mabuse*, 35. Author's translation.

49 Bernd Widdig, *Culture and Inflation in Weimar Germany* (Berkeley: University of California Press, 2001), 129.

reading of the film, Widdig directly relates the experience of inflation to the 'essence of gambling,' which 'allows the player, in a literal sense, to remain liquid'[50] and 'intensifies the up and down of inflation to an extreme.'[51] *Schwellenerfahrungen* are characterized by a 'presence of mind or spirit [*Geistesgegenwart*]' that 'signifies the focus of all human faculties on the single moment' and an 'encounter with fate' that is 'not compatible with the notion of a logically ordered life.'[52] In Widdig's analysis, Mabuse's status as a master-gambler, who is able to dictate the course of the game through the omnipotence of his thoughts, is at the centre of the popular fascination with him at this particular time. Mabuse is able to control the chaos of what was experienced every day, in Benjamin's description of gambling, as a 'series of shocks.' For Widdig, this unlinking of the experience of time as contingent from one moment to the next, through the unmooring of a system of monetary value, is directly tied to the destruction of moral value. His study of the culture of inflation draws a direct line of causation between it and the darkness that followed the Weimar Republic, and he sees the effects of the inflation in 'National Socialism's contempt for the basic foundations of civil society and the unscrupulous casualness with which the Nazis broke agreements, promises, and even international treatises as the direct outgrowth of the cynical nature of the inflationary process.'[53] While there is something to this claim, I believe that Mabuse's connection to the 'liquid' realm of dissolution should be read in financial terms as demonstrative of a new form of subjectivity formed by finance capital.

Widespread engagement with speculation on the currency exchanges might suggest a degree of gambling mania – the popular image of the republic as a gambling ship – but the engagement of individuals in the process of converting value from one moment to the next, in its various forms, be they goods, currency, or services, suggests an engagement with time that can be more accurately described as *speculating* rather than gambling. Unlike gambling, this speculation was not a choice, but rather, forced on the Weimar public as a means of survival. As such, it seems to be in an entirely different category of urgency if compared to the 'thrill' associated with the act of gambling that Widdig describes and, as a new experience, it meant that what was once a niche behaviour of specialists – for example, currency trading – became a mass phenomenon.

50 Ibid.
51 Ibid., 128.
52 Ibid., 130.
53 Ibid., 226.

As outlined in chapter 2, the legitimization of speculation within German society relied on its gradual conceptual separation from gambling. There is a categorical difference between the two actions as well. If we return to the ideal type of the gambler that Walter Benjamin outlines, we see that his formulation was accompanied by two others:

> Rather than pass the time, one must invite it in. To pass the time (to kill time, expel it): the gambler. Time spills from his every pore. To store time as a battery stores energy: the flâneur. Finally, the third type: he who waits. He takes in the time and renders it up in altered form – that of expectation.[54]

'Those who wait' was the precise term used by Kracauer to describe the 'scholars, businessmen, doctors, lawyers, students, and intellectuals of all sorts [who] spend most of their days in the loneliness of large cities.'[55] This is a more accurate description of the relationship with time that speculation demands; it is not merely a relationship with the present, as demonstrated in the addictive lure of gambling for some, but rather a condition that 'blurs the boundaries between past, present, and future'[56] and demands a constant adjustment to risk. In an increasingly financialized society (then as now), speculation as an act of hedging against risk, whether in financial or social relations, is separated from the excessive risk-taking of the gambler, and incorporated into the fabric of everyday life. United States Supreme Court Justice Oliver Wendell Holmes Jr. clearly identified the role of speculation in society when in 1905 he stated that: 'speculation [...] by competent men is the self-adjustment of society to the probable. Its value is well known as a means of avoiding catastrophes, equalizing prices, and providing for periods of want.'[57] Mabuse's obsession with punctuality and his overt statement that 'there is no such thing as luck – only the will to gain power' suggest for its audience that the money economy is not random, and its powers can be harnessed and controlled. Though he is supposedly a master gambler, his real power lies in the way in which he corrupts rules and fights against the established order for his own gain. In the aforementioned scene of intoxication near the beginning of the second film, Mabuse exclaims that he

54 Walter Benjamin and Rolf Tiedemann, *The Arcades Project* (Cambridge, MA: Harvard University Press, 1999), 107. Convolute [D3,4].

55 Kracauer, *Ornament*, 129.

56 Urs Stäheli, *Spectacular Speculation: Thrills, the Economy, and Popular Discourse* (Stanford, California: Stanford University Press, 2013), 49.

57 Ibid.

wishes to become 'a giant – a titan, churning up laws and gods like withered leaves!!' Mabuse's actions are more like the power of unregulated capital than the random chance of gambling, and he sees his only obstacle as the established order of the state. Mabuse is a figure of chaos, in the guise of the revolutionary, but also in the sense of the forces of the 'free market' pushing back against state control and recklessly destabilizing society.

It seems more accurate to describe the inflation as a period in which the rules of the game itself were constantly changing – that the game itself was rigged – a situation that denies the regularity and repeatability of the gambling round. As Gerald D. Feldman writes of *Dr. Mabuse*:

> These films reproduced the psychological and moral currents of their time, thus helping us to explain why they 'spoke' to contemporaries. They do not, of course, explain why everything had become a 'gamble' or even explain what the 'game' actually was. They do tell us much about popular perceptions – the appeal of the notion that the truth could be revealed by looking through the keyholes or listening at the doors of the mighty and the tendency to attribute the growing inflationary chaos either to human folly and incompetence or to superhuman and demonic machinations.[58]

Dr. Mabuse, we should recall, never plays a game that he does not himself somehow control, and his plans are *never* based on luck. In fact, he is the master of contingency, coupling events that would otherwise not be connected in time and space together with unseen structure. Lotte Eisner called Mabuse 'a kind of tireless Proteus, constantly changing his appearance,' a description that perfectly sums up the expectation placed on the emergent class of white-collar workers at this time. As Zygmunt Bauman suggests, they needed to remain 'liquid.'[59] In financial terms, 'liquid' describes assets that are easily exchangeable (the foremost being money itself) in contrast to those that are less so, and bound to physical location (such as real estate). As such, we should question the reading of Mabuse as merely an embodiment of the effects of the inflation or as an allegorical figure for modernity. Instead, I would suggest that he serves as the perfect protean figure to this emergent class of financial workers. He is able to transcend and master all of their daily obstacles, while laughing off quaint restrictions on mobility and financial liquidity, and disobeying regulations and laws. In order to

58 Feldman, *Disorder*, 513.

59 See Zygmunt Bauman, *Liquid Modernity* (Malden, MA: Polity Press, 2000).

discover how this might be the case, it is important to review some of the ways in which the figure of Mabuse has been interpreted.

Dr. Mabuse: Tyrant, Anti-Semitic Stereotype, or Weimar Anti-Hero?

One of the most lasting and influential interpretations of the figure of Dr. Mabuse appears in Siegfried Kracauer's classic 1947 commentary on Weimar cinema, *From Caligari to Hitler*. Kracauer included *Dr. Mabuse der Spieler* in his list of 'tyrant films,'[60] and concluded that 'the film succeeds in making of Mabuse an omnipresent threat which cannot be localized, and thus reflects society under a tyrannical regime – that kind of society in which one fears everybody because anybody may be the tyrant's ear or arm.'[61] Kracauer's quick dismissal of *Dr. Mabuse* in his reflections on the film after the Second World War and his eagerness to make the film conform to his thesis on 'the procession of tyrants' (which he argues inevitably presaged the rise of the Third Reich) has always seemed to me at odds with the astuteness of his Weimar-era essays. By placing the film in the company of other 'tyrant films' of the time, Kracauer overlooks interpretations of Mabuse as a figure that combined all of the anti-Semitic associations between Jews, finance, conspiracy, and world domination. His reading of Mabuse as an authoritarian figure that anticipated German society's embrace of fascism is particularly strange given the clear association of Mabuse with anti-Semitic stereotypes, specifically the image of the 'wandering Jew,' vividly suggests Georg Simmel's formulation of 'the stranger' – that figure that paradoxically embodies both the near and the far. In fact, Jacques himself was the subject of attacks that painted him along these lines. Jacques claimed in 1928 that he was attacked as a 'seducer of youth,' and 'corrupter of people' and that his name, which he claims can be 'traced back for centuries to good Catholic peasants in Northern France,' was besmirched as possibly being 'Jewish.'[62] In the book, Mabuse's stateless presence and his displacement from his former land situate him in the role of Simmel's stranger, the cosmopolitan trader who is 'no owner of soil' and who is outside the boundaries of nation. In the film, his undisguised role is that of a psychoanalyst, another profession stereotypically associated with Jews, while another of his alter egos, the

60 Siegfried Kracauer, *From Caligari to Hitler: A Psychological History of the German Film* (Princeton, NJ: Princeton University Press, 2004), 81. Kracauer identifies 1922 as a year in which three important tyrant films emerge: *Nosferatu* (F.W. Murnau), *Vanina* (Arthur von Gerlach), and *Dr. Mabuse*.

61 Kracauer, *Caligari*, 83.

62 See Jacques and Scholdt, *Mabuse*, 170.

one-armed hypnotist and conjurer Sandor Weltmann, plays into the notion that psychoanalysis itself was closely aligned with the occult – a conflation of two realms that were negatively associated with Jews.

In contrast to Kracauer's take on the film, consider this review of the film from the right-wing *Völkischer Kurier*:

> Who is not reminded of the 'Elders of Zion'? This is the image of the Eternal Jew [...] marching through the ages, always focused on one goal: the conquest of the world, even if it means entire nations must perish! [...] In so far as the film shows the typical image of the criminal Jew, it is exceptionally valuable to us. In the first section, the rendering of the activity of the stock exchange especially stands out, and [this scene] was accomplished par excellence.[63]

This reactionary review specifically refers to *The Protocols of the Elders of Zion*, a highly influential piece of fabricated anti-Semitic propaganda that purported to outline a Jewish plan for global domination that consisted, amongst other fabrications, of control of the world economy and the media. This reading should not be overlooked, and it was also not the first time that Lang had trafficked in these associations and stereotypes in his work.

Scenes in Lang's largely overlooked film of the previous year, *Vier um die Frau* (1921), can also be read as clearly anti-Semitic and *Dr. Mabuse* reuses several key tropes from this film. In fact, *Vier um die Frau* anticipates *Dr. Mabuse* in several ways. It opens with the intertitle 'during a pause on the exchange' that may have been the seed idea for the opening sequence of *Dr. Mabuse*. In fact, the ellipsis alluded to by this opening title is never resolved in the plot of the film, inserting the entirety of the film's narrative *in medias res* into the ongoing activity of the market. This opening title is followed by the entrance of 'Yquem the broker,' elegantly dressed with cape and *Zylinder* ('top hat'). Like Mabuse, Yquem is also part of a scheme involving forged banknotes, and he also dons a disguise in part of the film. Although the official stock exchange is never directly shown in the film, a parallel 'diamond exchange' appears, in which Yquem attempts to procure a counterfeit ring for his wife. Another character, the *Raffke* of the film, William Kraft, tries

63 "Dr. Mabuse, der Spieler," *Völkischer Kurier*, September 9, 1925. Quoted in Jacques and Scholdt, *Mabuse*, 149–50. The document was a hoax that first appeared at the turn of the twentieth century in Russia. It was completely discredited by *The Times* (of London) in 1921. Nonetheless, it was promoted as factual by reactionaries in Germany, and distributed widely by Henry Ford in the United States.

to have a fake ring made based on the exact specifications of one he wishes to steal, in order to swap it with the original. In this diamond exchange scene near the beginning of the film, we see a textbook example of a Jewish stereotype in the bearded, bespectacled, hunchbacked diamond seller.

Lang creates a very similar scene in *Dr. Mabuse* in the four-shot narrative of the war profiteer 'Schramm.' This 'mini-film' is *Dr. Mabuse*'s most direct representation of the figure of the *Schieber* and depicts a timeline of Schramm's rise from poverty to wealth. A *Film-Kurier* review of the time went so far as to call this character even more 'true to life' (*lebenswahrer*) than Mabuse himself.[64] He begins as a street pedlar ('1912') and is then shown as sitting out the war years as a clerk, dwarfed by piles of paper ('1913–1918'). At the end of the war ('1919'), he is shown examining a precious stone while his counterpart in the deal, who is clearly coded as Jewish, attempts to hide what he is doing, indicating that he is engaged in some form of illegal trade. The final scene shows Schramm counting money while smoking a cigar in an ornate room while the intertitle is decorated with laurel leaves and reads '1922… (*Handwerk hat goldenen Boden!*).' This idiom, which can best be translated by the English expression 'a trade in hand finds gold in every land' (literally: learn a trade and you will be wealthy wherever you go) is clearly being used cynically here as Schramm's trajectory from pedlar to clerk to ill-gotten riches makes a mockery of the gospel that hard work pays off (Figure 3). To a reactionary audience, the figure of the *Schieber* or *Raffke* is representative of non-productive and parasitic capital, thumbing his nose at 'hard work.'

To those engaged on a daily basis with finance and speculation, there is another interpretation that is possible. Lotte Eisner points out that Mabuse is not simply a 'tyrant' as he was always 'consumed by the desire to rule by money (whereas Dr. Caligari's thirst for power always remained abstract).'[65] Unlike Caligari or Graf Orlok (in Murnau's *Nosferatu*), whose motivations are monstrous and unknown, Mabuse's motivations and his own measure of his success stem entirely from his control of money. Eisner points out that:

> Dr. Mabuse suffers a nervous breakdown every time he loses at the tables; he gets drunk when he thinks he is winning. In a word, he is a human being and not a monster.[66]

64 *Film-Kurier*, April 4, 1922.

65 Lotte H. Eisner, *The Haunted Screen: Expressionism in the German Cinema and the Influence of Max Reinhardt* (Berkeley: University of California Press, 2008), 240.

66 Ibid.

Figure 3. The Schramm 'mini-film' in *Dr. Mabuse der Spieler* (Fritz Lang, 1922). Photo: Friedrich-Wilhelm Murnau Stiftung.

If Mabuse is to be thought of at all as a figure of mastery or authority, it should be clear this power stems directly from his control of the financial realm. And, indeed, it is in the scenes that revolve around financial activity that the film presents Mabuse at his most dominant. For example, at the end of the opening stock market caper, Mabuse's face is depicted superimposed over the now empty trading floor, an image that reinforces the power of his spectral presence and suggests the machinations of a single all-powerful individual. Mabuse's cryptic exclamation towards the end of the film – 'I feel as if I am a state within a state, with which I am at war!' – can be interpreted in a variety of ways. It may suggest that the figure of Mabuse combines a collection of Jewish stereotypes into one character and aligns them against the state, embodied in the figure of Wenk. But it is also possible to interpret Mabuse's exclamation here as a cry against the controlling power of state regulation and its interference in his pursuit of unfettered profit – indeed, these two interpretations are perhaps not mutually exclusive. Specifically, Mabuse may also have reminded those watching the film of prominent members of German society. To a reactionary audience, he could have evoked the figure of Walther Rathenau, for example, who inherited the vast AEG electrical engineering fortune, which made him, similar to Mabuse, a master of technology. A liberal, Jewish internationalist, he served as the foreign minister and was assassinated by right-wing paramilitary radicals in 1922 shortly after negotiating the treaty of Rapallo that released Russia and Germany from territorial and financial claims left over from the war. For nationalist conservatives of the Weimar Republic, Rathenau was a source of anxiety, such as the fear of internationalism – what Rathenau referred to as *Großwirtschaft* (the 'great economy')[67] – of opening borders to trade and immigration, and of the acceleration of Germany's association with America (*Amerikanismus*).

Mabuse may also have called to mind the powerful industrialist Hugo Stinnes, whose reach and influence, before his untimely death in 1924, was unmatched in Germany. Stinnes and other industrialists were frequently represented in the popular press as the 'one-per-centers' of their time, and there are some uncanny resemblances between the machinations of Stinnes at the height of his power and Mabuse. Stinnes, the most prominent of all the *Schieber*, who earned the moniker of 'King of the Inflation,' drummed up a strike by workers in order to secure his hold over the industrial Ruhr region in 1918. Additionally, he destabilized the German economy through his access to foreign currency, and, similar to Mabuse's counterfeiting operation, issued his own currency in 1923.[68] His power over this key border region, which was occupied by French and Belgian forces in 1923, also meant that he was associated with threats to German territory after the war.

A *Kladderadatsch* cartoon from September 1922 depicted Stinnes to this effect in the role of Oedipus, confronting a demonic sphinx across a chasm filled with human bones. The sphinx wears a Phrygian cap (commonly used to signify France in *Kladderadatsch*) and the caption reads: 'The Riddle of the Reconstruction: Who can solve the riddle of the crisis? Is it Oedipus? No, it's Stinnes!'[69] A *Simplicissimus* cartoon from the same year depicts Stinnes and Rathenau as *Die Weitblickenden* ('the farsighted ones') (Figure 4). Rathenau is perched on top of his stacked collected works, while Stinnes sits atop the smokestack of one of his factories and they argue: 'From here the view of

67 Quinn Slobodian, *Globalists: The End of Empire and the Birth of Neoliberalism* (Harvard University Press, 2018), 29.

68 Bernd Widdig writes that '[Stinnes's] larger-than-life stature, the many legends and fictional accounts circulating about him, lent him a dark and mysterious aura similar to that of Fritz Lang's figure Dr. Mabuse.' See Widdig, *Inflation*, 140.

69 *Kladderadatsch*, September 25, 1922.

Figure 4. *Top:* Arthur Johnson, *Kladderadatsch*, September 25, 1922. Caption: 'Das Rätsel des Wiederaufbaues. Die Sphinx: "Wer löst das Rätsel dunklen Sinnes? Ist's Odipus? Nein! Es ist Stinnes!"' – Translation: 'Who will solve the riddle of the crisis? Is it Oedipus? No, it's Stinnes!' Digitalisierungszentrum – Universitätsbibliothek Heidelberg. *Bottom:* Thomas Theodor Heine, 'Die Weitblickenden' – Translation: 'The Far-Sighted Ones' *Simplicissimus*, March 1, 1922.

the crisis is best! No from here!' while the German everyman, 'Deutscher Michel,' stands below with his pockets turned out.[70] This image is evocative in several ways. Firstly, it acknowledges the existence of the economic crisis, and by extension, the economy itself, as a terrain that can be understood as emergent and coming into view for a select few. Secondly, it recalls the root Latin variations of the term 'speculate' – *speculat-* ('observed from a vantage point'), and *specula* ('watchtower'). It was figures like Stinnes and Rathenau who were in the position to glimpse the outlines of the emerging and interconnected world economy. In a related sense, Stefan Andriopoulos argues more generally that Mabuse perhaps does not represent one specific figure, but that the dissolution of Mabuse's body at the end of the stock exchange scene, through the use of superimposition and the mechanisms of parallel editing, evokes the 'omnipresence of [the] "invisible aggregate person" of the modern corporation' itself.[71] He points out that it is only through the combination of these two cinematographic techniques that a representation of this aggregate figure can come into being. In this reading, the cinematic representation of Mabuse has a powerful knowledge-producing function. It gives the viewer, perhaps for the first time, a mental image of the invisible corporate 'citizen.'

It is clear from the outset in the film that Mabuse's power stems from his surveillance of the terrain of the financial world – a power that is clearly scopic throughout the film and is removed with Mabuse's own sight at its conclusion. I believe that the appeal of Mabuse to an audience of financial workers is due to the film's mobilization of this fantasy of power over this realm. In this light, consider also Thomas Elsaesser's reading of Mabuse, which draws from Thomas Pynchon's mention of the character in *Gravity's Rainbow* (1973). Elsaesser claims that Pynchon presents Mabuse as an industrialist 'anti-hero' whose struggle is 'a capitalist entrepreneur's war against a neo-feudal bureaucracy.'[72] A review in *Die Standarte* supports this reading, referring to Mabuse as 'a peculiarly demonic hero' (*eigenartig dämonisch Helden*).[73] Elsaesser continues:

> Mabuse becomes the 'character-mask' of which Adorno was to speak when he analysed captains of industry and finance in America, seeing the Rockefeller, Ford and Vanderbilt dynasties as the ultimately unacceptably

70 Widdig, *Inflation*, 139.

71 Stefan Andriopoulos, *Possessed: Hypnotic Crimes, Corporate Fiction, and the Invention of Cinema*, Cinema and Modernity (Chicago: University of Chicago Press, 2008), 125.

72 Elsaesser, *Weimar Cinema*, 162.

73 Review from *Die Standarte* (Berlin) quoted in *Film-Kurier*, May 18, 1922.

> human face of the anarchic forces of capital, especially in the sphere of public opinion. In Lang, the image of the stock-exchange speculator becomes emblem of the struggle between capitalism (monopoly capitalism, multinational capitalism) and civil society, democracy.[74]

A variety of readings of the figure of Mabuse are thus possible. He can be seen as a specific historical individual, as a conspiracy of many, or as the new aggregate form of organized capitalism. These interpretations are not mutually exclusive and are united by the common characteristic of power within the financial realm that transcends that of the everyday individual. In the *Simplicissimus* cartoon of the '*Weitblickenden*' Stinnes and Rathenau, these figures are clearly shown to have access to the spectral realm of finance and are paramount examples of the *homo economicus* of the new era. Not only are such figures more comfortable in the new conditions of modernity, but they specifically understand its codes and visual imagery since they have direct access to the worldview of the global market. The individual's loss of bearings (exemplified by the German everyman 'Michel' with empty pockets in the cartoon) and his inability to 'cognitively map' this new inhuman geography suggest the blindness of the modern subject to the accelerating forces of this new terrain of modernity.

In this sense the film can be read as an elaborate fantasy of empowerment for a populace beset by ongoing crisis. Given the degraded state of Weimar society, and the mistrust of the role of the state at the time, it is not clear that the audience would have understood Mabuse as a clear-cut villain. It is also questionable whether his adversary, and the representative of state power, *Staatsanwalt* ('state prosecutor') Wenk, can be understood as the hero of the film. Lang specifically calls Mabuse an '*Übermensch*'[75] while *Film-Kurier* refers to him as 'a genius.'[76] The popularity of the film clearly stems from a fascination with Mabuse's power over time and space and his mastery of finance. With this reading, I would also move beyond the interpretation of this and other films as merely 'pictures of their time' and attempt to determine how these texts were a part of the worldview of their time. Throughout the Weimar years, 'the business section of a newspaper was for most readers a "closed book"' and tabloids 'did not offer much economic coverage at all' until, by 1931, only a handful of German newspapers offered a 'high-quality coverage of economic affairs' and 'economic developments.'[77]

74 Elsaesser, *Weimar Cinema*, 162.
75 See Leiser, *Zum Beispiel: Fritz Lang*.
76 *Film-Kurier*, April 4, 1922.
77 Fulda, *Press and Politics*, 174.

At the same time, audiences were presented with explanatory narratives for the complexity of the world economy in films like *Dr. Mabuse der Spieler*, narratives which we will now examine more closely.

Dr. Mabuse and the Weimar Financial Imaginary

'Money was the Key to Every Lock'

In adapting *Dr. Mabuse der Spieler* to the screen, Lang and Harbou followed the original narrative but rewrote the plot significantly and, of particular interest to the present study, added the famous opening overture that depicts Mabuse and his gang of underlings orchestrating an elaborate stock market manipulation. It was a scene of market frenzy that was resolutely contemporary to the events surrounding the film's premiere. Tom Gunning claims that in the opening sequence of the film, Lang 'creates an image of the new "empty" and standardised space and time of modernity'[78] and locates Mabuse in the 'centre of the terrain of modernity and its network of events and messages against a background of the rationalised space and time of the contemporary environment.'[79] For Gunning, Mabuse's mastery of the technologies of time and space is key to his omnipotence. This mastery, however, 'cannot be visualized in a single shot or image, but rather becomes evident in the way different spaces and times interrelate in a film, producing a unique playing-field for the master criminal.'[80] Thus, Gunning directly identifies Mabuse with the experience of time and space in the modern world as influenced by the interaction of communications technologies in the form of 'the pocket-watch, the railway and the telephone with the cinematic device of parallel editing.'[81] Additionally, he points to the importance of Mabuse's mastery of currency and money as central to this spatiotemporal logic. Taking Anthony Giddens's lead, he argues that 'money is one of the major means of the "disembedding" of modernity,' and further that money is 'as Giddens puts it, "a means of time-space distantiation." Money provides for the enactment of transactions between agents widely separated in time and space.'[82] Gunning goes so far as to suggest that the 'disembedding of space

78 Tom Gunning, *The Films of Fritz Lang: Allegories of Vision and Modernity* (London: British Film Institute, 2000), 96.

79 Ibid.

80 Ibid.

81 Ibid.

82 Ibid., 103.

and time,' that is a key feature of our experience of modernity, is expressed in the 'whole institution of the stock exchange' in the film, but he does not push the argument further, instead interpreting Mabuse as an 'enunciator of modernity' within his larger thesis of the Langian 'destiny machine.'[83] In what follows, I will pursue this line of reasoning and suggest that *Dr. Mabuse* is not only about the experience of modernity in a general sense, but more specifically a narrative depiction of the new space of finance of its day.

Dr. Mabuse can be best understood in terms of the historical specificity of the activities it depicts rather than as simply a document of the 'disembedding' forces of modernity. By drawing attention to this specific context, I hope to avoid a more general trap that commentaries on fictions of finance can fall into. This would be the tendency to categorize financial activity according to a symbolic system of exchange in which there are varying levels of disassociation of the signifier from the signified. This generalization results in the dismissal of financial activity as merely an abstraction. Yet, as Leigh Claire La Berge points out, the tendency to accept financial activities as 'complex or abstract' and 'beyond our collective cognitive, linguistic, and epistemological reach' stands in the way of the ability of critical studies of finance to address financial activity across the disciplinary boundaries of the academy.[84] The material effects of finance capital are not abstract to the individual and financial activities are still embedded in their social and historical contexts. As La Berge argues, the assignment of 'the abstract' to finance agrees with negative critiques of financial activity as being estranged and external to what is considered concrete and real. Acceptance of the abstract nature of finance also easily aligns with anti-Semitic stereotypes of finance capital, and the important divergence in popular thought, across the political spectrum, between 'productive' and 'non-productive' capital. As discussed, *Dr. Mabuse* certainly traffics in the associations that would provoke such a reading, but there is also a historical specificity to the conglomerate of associations that he represents that would have been legible to audiences of the time. In short, while *Dr. Mabuse* certainly stages central crises of modernity, I want to tease out the specific associations that the film evokes in the context of the Weimar Republic, particularly with relation to class and society, speculation and gambling, overseas colonies, and the emerging image of the world economy.

83 Ibid.

84 Leigh Claire La Berge, "The Rules of Abstraction Methods and Discourses of Finance," *Radical History Review* 2014, no. 118 (December 21, 2014): 93–112.

It is in the opening sequence of the film that the nexus of meanings around money and society are most clearly articulated. The film opens on a hand of cards with eight photographs of Rudolf Klein Rogge in various disguises, thus immediately foregrounding the doubling of representation at play in the film. These are the disguises that Mabuse will don throughout the film: the anarchist agitator, the Dutch professor, the stockbroker, the young playboy, the wealthy elderly gentleman, the hypnotist, the elderly card player, and the drunk worker – an imperfect cross-section of identities across classes in Weimar society. Mabuse shuffles the cards and selects the image of the wealthy elderly gentleman as his first disguise. From his office, he proceeds to orchestrate the scheme to steal a commercial contract being carried by a courier on a train between the Netherlands and Switzerland that sets up his ultimate stock market manipulation.

The stock market depicted in the film is an elaborate set filled with a crowd of costumed extras on the central trading floor (Figure 5). It is introduced in a characteristically Langian, symmetrical wide shot that shows the trading hall dominated by a huge backlit clock. Truly a 'temple of time,' as Gunning names it, the hall is built in a stripped classical style, replete with a Doric colonnade around its perimeter. News of the attack on the courier reaches the floor, communicated in the film as an intertitle styled as a newspaper headline, and informs the market participants and the audience that this could spell disaster for Dutch coffee and cacao companies. Close-ups of the elegantly dressed brokers and traders on the floor show the news spreading by word of mouth while Mabuse looks on from an elevated perch, now disguised as the figure 'Sternberg.' The price of 'c. Holland' falls rapidly, as depicted by the frenzied clerk who repeatedly erases and rewrites the share price on the board. Mabuse waits until the price has dropped dramatically, then holds his hand up and exclaims 'I buy!' Shortly thereafter, word arrives on the exchange that the secret contract has been found, and the share prices rise once again. Mabuse sells his now inflated stock right before the bell that marks the close of the market and makes a fortune.

At the end of act one, after profiting greatly from a combination of thuggery and control of electronically transmitted information, Mabuse stands in the centre of the stock exchange disguised as a tuxedoed and elegant trader – master manipulator of the panicked crowd that surrounds him. Mabuse's masquerade in the overture gives him anonymous but privileged access to the inner sanctum of the stock exchange. At the same time, he controls the extended, and arguably more important, virtual space of the exchange. This point is driven home by the shots of the space behind the trading floor, under the clock, from which the news of the finding of the lost

Figure 5. The stock exchange scene in *Dr. Mabuse der Spieler* (Fritz Lang, 1922). Photo: Friedrich-Wilhelm Murnau Stiftung.

contract is delivered. This space, which is shown from an elevated vantage point inside a central office that looks back through two doorways to the trading floor, is the inner sanctum of the exchange. Featured prominently in this space, and framed by the doorway, is a large radio antenna, a technology that was only in its infancy as a popular medium at this time, that suggests a realm of communication and information beyond the human fray in the foreground.[85]

For all of its inclusion of cutting-edge technologies, however, the film does not include a key technology of the financial world – the stock ticker. Though the ticker had been invented in 1867,[86] and had been quickly adopted by English and American markets, the German exchanges at this time did not feature continuous price quotation, instead releasing prices twice a day to correspond with the morning and evening newspapers. This makes

85 Chapter 4 discusses Gerhard Lamprecht's film *Die Verrufenen* (1925), in which a stock trader character is shown listening to financial news on the radio in his own home. The difference of only a few years saw huge advances in the use of this technology.

86 Mary Poovey, "Writing about Finance in Victorian England: Disclosure and Secrecy in the Culture of Investment," in *Victorian Investments: New Perspectives on Finance and Culture*, ed. Nancy Henry and Cannon Schmitt (Bloomington: Indiana University Press, 2009), 50.

Mabuse's elaborate plot and his need to disguise himself amongst the other traders more understandable, as his physical presence on the floor would have been required to pull off this manoeuvre. Since no ticker is present, Lang chose instead to embody the continuous flow of price information in the form of the frenzied figure at the blackboard. As he races to keep up with the flow of numbers the clerk himself acts like a human ticker, a kind of automaton whose motions are fully at the whims of the market.

The image of the financial worker as automaton is not original to the film. In his 1920 work, *'Daum' marries her pedantic automaton 'George' in May 1920. John Heartfield is very glad of it*, George Grosz presents a critical portrayal of just such a figure. This painting (which includes elements of photo montage) had its debut at the First International Dada Fair on June 30, 1920 at a Berlin art gallery owned by Dr. Otto Burchard.[87] A thinly veiled portrait of himself as artist/automaton, the seated male figure in the painting is half human and half an assemblage of telephonic and telegraphic technologies. His body is a mass of machinery while a ticker tape emerges from his head, held by a pair of hands. A woman, her body exposed, turns away and reaches towards the edge of the frame, but looks back in his direction with a mixed expression of scorn and concern. A similarly disembodied hand as those that touch the ticker tape touches the woman's naked breast. The composition suggests sexual frustration and the seated automaton, with the fallen shoulders of a lifetime spent at a desk, is symbolically castrated, his eyes blank. The figures are set against the backdrop of a space that is urban but neither inside nor outside – neither private nor public – while an actual photo in profile of Grosz's wife Eva Peters ('Daum' being a thinly veiled reversal or her nickname 'Maud') appears in a window in the upper-left corner. Like the frenzied clerk in *Dr. Mabuse*, the male figure in the scene, who has become literally a mouthpiece for financial information, is a member of the *Angestellten* that Kracauer describes.[88] Writing in *Der Querschnitt* magazine in 1923, Margot Starke calls such a white-collar worker, an '*Untermensch*,' whose 'head is a calculator, his arms respectively a pencil and pen,' and who 'stands on two rulers' with a 'ledger for a body,' on which 'he writes most maliciously.'[89]

87 Wieland Herzfelde and Brigid Doherty, "Introduction to the First International Dada Fair," *October* 105 (July 2003): 93–104.

88 Matthew Biro also draws this conclusion in his analysis of Grosz's painting. See Matthew Biro, *The Dada Cyborg: Visions of the New Human in Weimar Berlin* (Minneapolis: University of Minnesota Press, 2009), 42.

89 First published as "Der Bankbeamte," *Der Querschnitt* 3 (1923), 138–39. Reprinted in Anton Kaes, Martin Jay, and Edward Dimendberg, eds., *The Weimar Republic Sourcebook* (Berkeley: University of California Press, 1995), 183.

Mabuse, the 'villain,' but also a clear representation of an *Übermensch* in the book and film, presents a fantasy of empowerment that is in stark contrast to the frenzied clerk, and would have resonated with the audience of the time. In this context, Mabuse is a heroic and virile figure, a master of the game that many in the audience themselves played. He effortlessly overcomes the rites of passage of the market and, in his various disguises, moves easily through the classes and types of Weimar society. The key to his success and access is money and his relationship to it.

There is another way that the film can be understood: as a document of the tension between older ideas of community and emergent realities of a society in which relationships were governed by exchange under capitalism. At the time of the film's release, with the rise of the new-money *Schieber* and *Raffke*, as well as the financial empowerment of women and their entrance into the workforce, Weimar society was undergoing a seismic shift. As one review explicitly noted, Mabuse represented the replacement of 'the old "subject," that prototype of yore' with 'the new "player" [Spieler], the type of today.'[90] In order to understand the film in this context, it is informative to turn to the work of Georg Simmel and, in particular, to his highly influential *The Philosophy of Money*. Though originally published as *Philosophie des Geldes* in 1900 and enlarged in a second edition in 1907, it should be considered a contemporaneous text of the early Weimar Republic.[91] It was republished after Simmel died in 1918, in the years leading up to the hyperinflation. The third edition appeared in 1920 and the fourth in 1922.[92] It was disseminated and widely read at that time, and Simmel's influence can of course be read directly in the work of Kracauer, who was his student and published an essay named after the sociologist in 1919. *The Philosophy of Money*'s central discourses of alienation, authenticity, and distance form the foundation of the intellectual tradition of the Frankfurt School and had a far-reaching influence on writers such as Stefan George, Rainer Maria Rilke, Robert Musil, and Walther Rathenau.[93]

In *The Philosophy of Money*, Simmel is primarily concerned with describing a theory of 'society' based on the function of money in human interactions. He writes that 'it should be recognized that most relationships between people can be interpreted as forms of exchange,' and further, that 'exchange

90 H. W., "Der Film der Zeit," *Lichtbild-Bühne*, April 29, 1922. Quoted in Jacques and Scholdt, *Mabuse*, 180.

91 See details of its complicated publication history in Georg Simmel, *The Philosophy of Money*, ed. David Frisby, 3rd ed. (London: Routledge, 2004), 526.

92 Frisby and Simmel, *Money*, xiii.

93 Ibid., xxvii.

is the purest and most developed kind of interaction, which shapes human life when it seeks to acquire substance and content.'[94] For Simmel, exchange permeates every level of human interaction forms the basis of his sociology. The concept of 'society' as distinct from 'community' as it emerged in the late nineteenth century in the work of Ferdinand Tönnies is key here.[95] Further work on this distinction also appeared at precisely the time that *Dr. Mabuse* was filmed in Max Weber's *Economy and Society* (1921) – a foundational text of the social sciences that attempted to systematically describe forms of economic and social relationships. The reorganization of society around relations of financial exchange also posed a challenge to the status quo of power relations based on title and rank that had begun to be cracked open after the First World War. At its core, this was the threat that Mabuse posed as a representative of the new class of *Raffke*. As David Graeber has put it more recently: 'Exchange, then, implies formal equality—or, at least, the potential for it. This is why kings have such trouble with it.'[96]

For Simmel, the act of exchange also admits individuals by default to the realm of a globally connected society. The category of society is thus 'supranational' and not reducible to a symbolic membership in a clan or group. In contrast with membership in the imagined community of nationhood, which relies on the positivism of constructed symbols and a metaphysics of presence, exchange puts people into a *de facto* relationship with one another that is of the most abstract character – that of the relationship of currency. For Simmel, the abstraction created by the 'money economy' opens up the realm of possibilities that allows for the constitution of society in the first place. And it is a cynical version of this theory of society that finds its articulation in Jacques's novel, which declares:

> ...there were no more private societies in 1921. Money was the key to every lock, a fur coat hid any profession, if you wore it, and a diamond pin outshone every disposition. One entered whichever society one wanted.[97]

The emergence of an awareness of the world market, or society as a supranational entity, threatened the *völkisch* idea of the nation and provoked the fears described in the reactionary reading of Mabuse. At the same time,

94 Ibid., 79.

95 Ferdinand Tönnies, *Community and Civil Society* (Cambridge: Cambridge University Press, 2001).

96 David Graeber, *Debt: The First 5,000 Years* (Brooklyn: Melville House, 2014), 109.

97 Jacques and Scholdt, *Mabuse*, 8. Author's translation.

alienation linked to the levelling of values as a corollary of the omnipresence of the money economy is what Kracauer criticized. In this sense, the world depicted by Jacques, and amplified in Lang and Harbou's adaptation – 'a geography crisscrossed and demarcated by the constant circulation of messages, messengers and message delivery systems'[98]– is not merely the more general 'terrain of modernity,' but is a reification of the money economy as a cinematic experience. This film and others like it performed a kind of 'cognitive mapping' for Weimar spectators and, in the face of the bewilderment of the collapse, provided a narrative geography with which to reconstruct an image of the world economy.[99]

Through his cynical detachment, Mabuse is presented as a master of the financial turmoil besetting the audience. The pleasure derived from witnessing this mastery explains why one review in *Film-Kurier* stated that, in this film 'the audience is pleased to recognize itself in its own environment.'[100] Given the film is a depiction of an arch-criminal, this statement is somewhat peculiar but can be better understood as describing the form of identification that I am suggesting here. Although he is ostensibly a villain, he is clearly a seductive figure and identification with him is not unlike that which occurs in the case of the villainous Gordon Gekko described in the introduction. Hardly any contemporaneous reviews of *Dr. Mabuse* are critical of the film's main character, instead presenting him, as one review put it, as 'something of an ideal figure of our day. No longer the clumsy heavy handed criminal kingpin of yore, it is no accident that he is a doctor with all the intellectual powers of his education available to him.'[101] The same review goes on to state

98 Gunning, *Lang*, 88.

99 The term 'cognitive mapping' is here borrowed (anachronistically) from Fredric Jameson. Though Jameson refers to the 'post-modern subject,' I argue that this inability to map the human-made informational sublime that replaces the role of natural, is experienced much sooner in the relation between finance and the space of the modern metropolis than Jameson suggests. He writes: 'So I come finally to my principal point here, that this latest mutation in space – post-modern hyperspace – has finally succeeded in transcending the capacities of the individual human body to locate itself, to organize its immediate surroundings perceptually, and cognitively to map its position in a mappable external world. It may now be suggested that this alarming disjunction point between the body and its built environment – which is to the initial bewilderment of the older modernism as the velocities of a spacecraft to those of the automobile – can itself stand as the symbol and analogon of that even sharper dilemma which is the incapacity of our minds, at least at present, to map the great global multinational and decentred communicational network in which we find ourselves caught as individual subjects.' Fredric Jameson, *Postmodernism, Or, The Cultural Logic of Late Capitalism*, Post-Contemporary Interventions (Durham: Duke University Press, 1991), 56.

100 *Film-Kurier* April 28, 1922.

101 Kurt Pinthus, "Dr. Mabuses Welt," *Das Tage-Buch*, May 6, 1922.

that 'adventurous types' like Mabuse are subject to the 'burning interest' of 'all people of our time,' some of whom may also be 'sneaking around' with similar schemes in their 'professions in the big cities.'[102]

Mabuse is an idealized *homo economicus* in that his schemes are driven by his conscious will and proceed with a clockwork rational precision. At the same time, his powers far exceed the rational, and he re-enchants the world of finance and speculation with his supernatural abilities. His cynical demeanour and emotional detachment are perfectly in keeping with the demands of the financial turmoil of the time. In a society reduced to constant financial precarity and speculation, '[e]very interaction has to be regarded as an exchange: every conversation, every affection (even if it is rejected), every game, every glance at another person.'[103] Appropriately, Lang titles the second half of the film *Inferno – ein Spiel vom Menschen unserer Zeit* ('Inferno – a game of the people of our time'), and Mabuse himself exclaims at several points in the film that 'everything is just a game!' The film is accordingly replete with cynical and instrumentalized relationships between Mabuse and other characters who are often seated across from him and the logic of monetary exchange permeates the film at all levels.

Simmel specifically attributed the rise of cynicism to the rise of finance capital at the time. He had a dim view of the financial worker, who he claimed was at the forefront of the turn to cynicism in modern life. For Simmel, it was the institution of the stock exchange that was at the heart of a change in attitude in society. As a space of modernity, the institution of the stock exchange provides a specific example for Simmel of the production of the cynical disposition:

> The nurseries of cynicism are therefore those places with huge turnovers, exemplified in stock exchange dealings, where money is available in huge quantities and changes owners easily. The more money becomes the sole centre of interest, the more one discovers that honour and conviction, talent and virtue, beauty and salvation of the soul, are exchanged against money and so the more a mocking and frivolous attitude will develop in relation to these higher values that are for sale for the same kind of value as groceries, and that also command a 'market price.' The concept of a market price for values which, according to their nature, reject any evaluation except in terms of their own categories and ideals is the perfect

102 *Ibid.*
103 Frisby and Simmel, *Money*, 79.

> objectification of what cynicism presents in the form of a subjective reflex.[104]

Beginning as it does with a scene on the stock exchange floor, *Dr. Mabuse* proceeds to portray for its audience the story of an individual who, through his calculating and cynical machinations, has conquered the adversity of their situation. This is cynical detachment as a survival strategy, a condition that is demanded of individuals caught up in the economic turmoil of the times. I believe that this and other examples that will be discussed here support the idea that the film stages the emergence of global finance for its audience and the resonance of Mabuse as a character stems from his mastery of the crises and seismic shocks of modernity's new financial flows. It is not merely the individual's induction into modernity as an abstract concept that is dramatized in *Dr. Mabuse*, but rather, the individual's induction into the world of speculation and financial exchange.

Spectres of the Past: Gambling, Colonies, and National Boundaries

While the figure of Dr. Mabuse was deeply embedded in the contemporary moment of the film's release, the constellation of associations and narratives that he embodied must also be read with reference to key historical resonances. I have pointed out the ways in which gambling should be considered separately from speculation in the film, but here I would like to return to the central trope of gambling in order to unpack key historical and geopolitical references within the gambling scenes that deserve closer scrutiny. As has been discussed in chapter 1, the historical ties between gambling and the establishment of the German state run deep. E. J. Carter has shown, the historical location of sites of gambling on the border of France connect the space of the casino to the idea of national territory in the German historical imaginary. In imperial Germany, gambling and financial activity were negatively associated with France. Gambling was seen as so counter to the image of German nationalism that, after unification in 1871, Prussian authorities banned casinos in this area, clarifying the change from a 'frontier' to a 'delineated border' and 'eliminating French influences.' This also had a direct bearing on the German attitude towards finance capital. Carter notes:

> the destruction of the Rhine casinos helped reinforce and perpetuate the distinction between industrial and financial, or productive and parasitic,

104 Ibid., 257.

> capitalism, contributing to a widely accepted birth narrative of the German nation-state: that it emerged from the collective repudiation of French-style financial immorality.[105]

During the Weimar Republic, the idea of gambling also recalled the recent national trauma of the Great War, and the very recent precedent for experiencing life and death as a process of gambling in the example of the German high command at the end of the war. According to Wolfgang Schivelbusch, 'Ludendorff had been called a "gambler" whose only strategy consisted of an all-or-nothing insistence on absolute victory.'[106] At the end of the Franco-Prussian War, France was said to have lost everything in a game of chance with Germany, in the First World War, it was Germany who had gambled and lost. Compounded by the ever-present pressure of foreign exchange (*Valuta*), the constant burden of reparation payments, and the loss of real territory after the war, the symbolically loaded stagings of gambling in *Dr. Mabuse* would have been evocative of this rich history for the viewing public of the time. Mabuse as the master gambler – whose name Jacques wanted to sound deliberately foreign and has the ring of the French *je m'abuse* ('I abuse myself') – can also be read as standing for the perception of France's corrupting influence. Mabuse's technological mastery, combined with his occult power, makes him a particularly fitting example of the combination of rational and irrational thought that governed the 'magical thinking' of the gambler (or speculator) at this time.

In the penultimate act of the first film (act five), this conflation of occult magical thinking, the laws of chance and contingency, the threat of border crossing, and the influence of France are all demonstrated. The act begins with Wenk awakening in a small boat adrift on a lake after being gassed and assaulted by Mabuse's henchman, Georg. Mabuse is then shown in his office picking through the contents of the state prosecutor's wallet. He tells Georg to return the belongings, since he is no vulture, but keeps a document proclaiming Wenk's power to arrest, and discovers another slip of paper that contains street addresses, along with words like 'Marmor,' 'Ananás,' and 'Venus.' These turn out to be the addresses and passwords for underground speakeasies. Following this discovery, Mabuse decides that Wenk and the playboy Edgar Hull must be eliminated. He hatches a plan involving Hull's

105 E. J. Carter, "Breaking the Bank: Gambling Casinos, Finance Capitalism, and German Unification," *Central European History* 39, no. 02 (2006): 207.

106 Wolfgang Schivelbusch, *The Culture of Defeat: On National Trauma, Mourning, and Recovery*, (New York: Metropolitan Books, 2003), 258.

romantic interest Cara Carozza, who has fallen under the sway of his will. Hull is to be lured to the Petit Casino – a new underground night spot at Haydn-Strasse 11 – and killed. Hull, however, discovers that Carozza may be duping him and notifies Wenk over the phone, who subsequently hatches a plan to spring a trap at the casino. Hull, Wenk, and Carozza all meet at the Petit Casino, which is an opulent club featuring a central circular enclosure that contains the gaming table. Players are seated in small alcoves resembling theatre boxes, gazing in on the croupier who emerges on a hidden elevator in the centre of the table. Here, the camera emphasizes the circular nature of the space by tracking around the croupier who welcomes the players to this 'highly modern environment' where they should nevertheless 'feel as if they are carried back to the golden age' where '*Erlaubt ist was gefällt...*' ('anything goes'). This reference to the pre-war 'Gilded Age' and '*Belle Époque*' of Paris is confirmed by the architectural style of the casino enclosure itself, which is decorated with the whiplash curves of Art Nouveau filigree.

An abrupt intertitle cuts away from the casino and announces 'the other world.' Here we see the Count and Countess Told waiting for a séance to begin after the arrival of a psychoanalyst (Dr. Mabuse) 'who is greatly interested in the occult sciences.' Mabuse arrives and appears drawn to the countess, who sits tracing her hand on the spirals printed on her dress, repeating the formal logic of the circle in the scene. Scenes of the casino and the séance are intercut and Mabuse is shown closing in on the countess, who he will eventually capture, while Wenk slips away from the gambling table to call in the police for a raid. In the confusion that follows, Mabuse's henchman Georg attacks and kills Hull in an alleyway near the casino and Carozza is apprehended by the police.

The Petit Casino scene evokes the symbolic association of casinos with France, and plays on the animosity towards France as an existential threat to the German nation at this time. Representation of this threat is accomplished formally in this section of the film through a series of images of border crossing and breach. Act five combines the space of the casino with that of the occult séance through the formal match of their circular configuration, but it also conflates the space of the city street and the threat of boundary crossing in a characteristically Langian gesture that combines images of a map with an architecturally elaborate transforming set. The map can be seen early in act five when Mabuse diagrams his plan for Hull's murder and describes the location of the Petit Casino to his henchmen. This map seems oddly anachronistic for the otherwise modern metropolis that *Dr. Mabuse* is set in, and shows a city that more resembles Lübeck, or another German city that had retained its mediaeval walls, than Berlin, which had by this time erased any trace of them. Mabuse traces a path from the casino, located just outside, through the walls of the city, to the intended place of the fatal attack on Hull. He taps his pencil on the site for emphasis and a circular iris superimposition reveals the crime scene itself. By locating the casino beyond the walls, Lang recalls its historical position as effectively outside the *polis* of German society, and its association with the frontiers of the nineteenth century. The collection of signifiers of French influence in the scenes that follow drive this association home. Further, the image of the circle occurs frequently in the film to denote levels of inclusion and exclusion. Once again, Mabuse is shown to command this space of traversal and invasion that would have resonated with the recent events of the war in the popular imaginary.

In addition to references to France as an extraterritorial space, both the novel and the film make several references to overseas colonies that would have been legible to audiences in the wake of Germany's recent loss of its own colonial holdings. In the novel, Mabuse frequently refers to his plan to found a colony in South Brazil called 'Eitopomar.'[107] He states:

> But in Eitopomar it will still be different! [...] There he had owned people, there nature had been his, there he had triumphed with his sails over the sea, his muscles and blood over the people, his will over nature. The palms of his plantation overran him with so many riches and piles of gold that he could be in contempt of them, because he was so free, free like a king or a god [...][108]

In the novel, the founding of Eitopomar is the central motivation for Mabuse's plans. Mabuse's colonial ambitions resemble those of Elisabeth Förster-Nietzsche and Bernhard Förster who established *Nueva Germania* during their colonial expedition to Paraguay in 1887. The unpublished sequel to Jacques's blockbuster novel was accordingly to have been titled *Mabuses Kolonie* ('Mabuse's Colony'). It is clear throughout the novel that return to this lost paradise serves as the motivation that drives his criminal enterprise:

> But the war had rooted him out of his paradise and driven him back to hateful, tiny Europe. He could not live in these lands. This was why he had founded a state within the organization of the state for himself, with laws

107 Gunter Scholdt points to the explicit links to German imperialism in Jacques's text, concerning *Eitopomar* specifically. He reminds us that *Eitopomar* is a composite of 'Eu – topos – mare' – 'a beautiful place by the sea' or 'beyond the sea/overseas.' See Jacques and Scholdt, *Mabuse*, 140.
108 Ibid., 30. Author's translation.

> that he alone wrote, with power over life and death. With [this state's] help he would hoard (*erraffen*) money in order to found his empire in the deep jungle of Brazil – the empire of Eitopomar.[109]

Jacques's second most popular novel after *Mabuse*, entitled *Piraths Insel* (1917), is even more overt as a 'metaphor of German colonial loss.'[110] It depicts the link between colonial power, primitive accumulation, and the modern economy and tells the story of its protagonist, Peter Pirath, who modernizes the economy of palm tree plantations on a Pacific island. Germany's loss of its colonies after the war was, of course, a significant material blow to its own economy and excluded it from membership amongst the select few European nations that could boast of their world-spanning reach.

In both the novel and film of *Dr. Mabuse*, there is an even more direct reference to German colonial holdings that links the image of colonies to gambling. In one scene, Wenk and Mabuse – disguised as an old professor – square off at the gambling table for the first time. Mabuse wears a pair of antique glasses described in the book as 'of Chinese origin' that he carries in a green sharkskin case.[111] During the course of the gambling session Mabuse utters the magical words 'Tsi-Nan-Fu' to Wenk, as part of a supernatural attack on his will. Historically, 'Tsi-Nan-Fu' referred to the 'Jinan prefecture' and Jinan, the capital of Shandong province in eastern China.[112] Shandong is significant in this context as it encapsulates the so-called 'Kiautschou Bay' concession – an area of land around Jiaozhou Bay on the southern coast of the Shandong peninsula that was leased to Germany by the Qing dynasty from 1898 until it was lost after the siege by the Japanese and the British of the German-held port of Tsingtao (now Qingdao) in 1914. Many German prisoners taken during this siege were not repatriated until as late as 1920.[113] As such, this was a reference to territory lost by Germany as a result of the outcome of the war. Jacques makes this link to territories in China unmistakable (though he refers to the mouth of the Yangtze at

109 Ibid., 30–31. Author's translation.

110 For more on *Piraths Insel* (1917), as well as the follow-up fragment that Jacques never completed, entitled *Mabuses Kolonie* (fragment, 1930) see Kristin Kopp, "Dr. Mabuse's Colonial Fantasies" (paper presented at the annual meeting for the Modern Languages Association, Vancouver, Jan. 11, 2015).

111 Jacques and Scholdt, *Mabuse*, 22.

112 Thanks to Erin Schlumpf for this translation.

113 Atsushi Otsuru, "Prisoners of War (Japan)," in 1914–1918 Online. International Encyclopedia of the First World War, eds. Ute Daniel, Peter Gatrell, Oliver Janz, Heather Jones, Jennifer Keene, Alan Kramer, and Bill Nasson, Freie Universität, Berlin, 2014. https://encyclopedia.1914-1918-online.net/article/prisoners_of_war_japan.

Shanghai, far south of Shandong province) in his version of the showdown between Mabuse and Wenk:

> Wenk fought off sleepiness. He sat up straight and looked at the green sharkskin case of the Chinese glasses. It seemed to him as if the glasses magnified the staring eyes of the old professor, blurring them, and a dim memory passed from them to his consciousness, of a day of travel. One morning on his travel to China, as if through a portal of his cabin [on a boat], he sees a thin shore, like a band, between the water and heavens. It is the mouth of the Yangtze. Indeed, the Yangtze.[114]

Images of sea travel and water invoke a land seen as if in a distant memory, and from a ship leaving its shores. In the film, this is the first time that Mabuse uses a command word as part of his hypnotic power. Evoking the name 'Tsi-Nan-Fu' at the casino connects the themes of gambling, the occult, extraterritorial space, and the image of liquid, once again, making clear the mercurial nature of Mabuse's power. The magic words will return in the second part of the film, uttered by Mabuse, disguised as the hypnotist, Sandor Weltmann.

As a result of the close timing of the release of the serialized novel and the film, the overt references to colonial and imperial imagery in Jacques's novel would have been legible to audiences of Lang's film. Here we can see that even without the explicit reference to Mabuse's colonial ambitions the historical traces of the lost colonies appear in the film. Similarly, the particular staging of the 'French' casino in the film functions both as a potent reminder of the importance of the Rhineland casinos to the German historical imaginary, as well as their liminal location as spaces of transgression and territorial threat. Beyond their relevance as markers of Germany's defeat, these spectres of the past also point to the awareness of Germany's reduced role in the world economic order after the First World War. As such, these additional resonances enrich our understanding of how key cultural memories connected to the historical role of gambling, finance capital, and the construction of Germany's place in the world economy were crystalized in the figure of Dr. Mabuse.

Under the Sign of Mabuse: Speculation, Numerology, and the Financial World Picture

Review after review of *Dr. Mabuse* noted that the film's success was largely due to the audience's identification with the film's central character and how

114 Jacques and Scholdt, *Mabuse*, 22. Author's translation.

well it depicted the contemporary environment. It seems fair to say that as an 'image of the times,' the film performed as much of a reflective function as it created a particular worldview. As a review in *Der Roland* magazine put it:

> Dr. Mabuse is – if I may say so – the first cosmic film, the first film with a worldview that projects an ethical and social world structure onto the screen. [...] [The film] removes the distance between cinema and reality. Of its pace and rhythm one can say: 'That's life.' With another film you have to adapt and adjust to its psyche. Here, every title, every picture says: 'That's you!'[115]

The everyday experience of speculation and financial crisis at the time of the film's release manifested as a superabundance of numbers in Weimar popular media. Whether in the form of stock quotations, the constantly fluctuating *Valuta* (currency exchange rate), or in the ever-increasing zeros on the constantly updated paper money, these numbers were part of the fabric of daily experience. Broadsheet pages of market price data were a feature of most major newspapers, appearing as a tangible projection of the market worldview – the production of prices for a world consisting of commodities (as discussed in the previous chapter). The juxtaposition of stock quotations with other news was a feature of the Weimar experience that was commented on by artists and writers at the time. In his 1929 novel, *Berlin Alexanderplatz*, Alfred Döblin punctuated his prose with random snippets of financial jargon and price quotations.[116] Similarly, John Heartfield's cover jacket design for Malik-Verlag's 1925 translation of Upton Sinclair's *The Moneychangers* (1908) featured an image of a busy trading pit overlaid on a field of newspaper stock quotations. The figures on the cover stand in the circular trading pit with their attention focused inwards on one another. The pit is like a small amphitheatre of concentrically arranged steps that suggest layers of access to this group, whose exclusivity is driven home by the outwardly turned

115 "Fritz Langs größter Erfolg," *Der Roland*, June 1, 1922. Author's translation.

116 There are several references to the media sphere of the market in Döblin's novel. On p. 17, he inserts the headlines: 'Market dull, later Bears very active, Hamburg depressed, London weaker.' On p. 107: 'Supply at the cattle market: 1399 steers, 2700 calves, 4654 sheep, 18,864 hogs. Market conditions: prime steers firm, otherwise quiet. Calves firm, sheep quiet, hogs opening firm, closing weak, overweights lagging.' On p. 150, in a sub-section entitled 'local news,' he writes: 'Quiet conditions prevailed in the stock market [...] Quotations on April 18 around 11 o'clock were: I.G. Dye Stuffs 260½ to 267, Siemens & Halske 297½ to 299, Dessauer Gas 202 to 203, Waldhof Cellulose 295. Bids for German Oil at 134½.' See Alfred Döblin, *Berlin Alexanderplatz: The Story of Franz Biberkopf*, trans. Eugène Jolas (London: Continuum, 2004).

backs of the traders. Perspectival space is erased outside this hermetic world by the sea of orderly columns of numbers that surround it.

Accordingly, *Dr. Mabuse* plays on the omnipresence of the code of the financial market. The film is punctuated throughout by sequences of seemingly meaningful numbers in a manner that produces the impression that Mabuse's plots are structured according to an overarching mathematical order. Mabuse's operations seem informed by a rational engagement with the numerical excess of the modern financial world. At the same time, his access to the occult and spiritual realm makes him a master of irrational and mystical forces. In what follows, these parallel aspects of Mabuse's power will be discussed in terms of how they served to reproduce the worldview of financial markets of this time.

In a key scene of the film, one of Mabuse's alter egos, the one-armed hypnotist Sandor Weltmann, performs for a packed house. In the novel, Weltmann is described as a Hungarian who had lost his arm in the Carpathian Mountains, referring most likely to the bloody First World War mountain battles between Russia and the Austro-Hungarian Empire.[117] With the creation of Weltmann, Jacques offers up a mirrored version of Mabuse as no longer the consummate insider, but rather the embodiment of the stranger or outsider on display to the general public. Weltmann embodies the occult, irrational aspect of Mabuse's power, as well as the clinical experimentation of psychoanalysis, his designation as a foreigner and stranger, and his visionary power over time and space. A sign on the marquee for Weltmann's act confirms this conflation of pseudo-science with magic. It promises 'experiments in mass suggestion, waking hypnosis, trance, natural magnetism, the secrets of the Indian fakirs, secrets of the inner life, and the subconscious of humans and animals.'

Inside the packed theatre, Weltmann prepares his first attraction for the crowd – an elaborate special effect set-piece that is original to the film. Serving little purpose to the plot, this scene is inserted as pure spectacle. Weltmann states his intention to demonstrate 'a typical case of mass suggestion similar to that underlying the tricks of the Indian fakirs!' Standing to stage left, he raises his hand and the proscenium seems to dissolve while a vision of a desert appears from which a band of figures marches slowly out onto the stage and into the auditorium. Though we only see it for a few brief

117 'Sie wissen, er ist bekannt, weil er nur eine Hand hat. Die andere liegt in den Karpaten – 1915!' Scholdt and Jacques, *Mabuse*, 116. Jacques refers to the battle between Austria-Hungary and Russia in the winter of 1915, also known as the 'Stalingrad of the first World War.' See Graydon A. Tunstall, *Blood on the Snow: The Carpathian Winter War of 1915*, Modern War Studies (Lawrence, Kan: University Press of Kansas, 2010).

moments, this appears to be a commercial caravan laden with wares. Several figures carry goods on their heads or shoulders and, along with three horses and a camel, there is also what appears to be a covered cart of some sort in the background. Though it is unclear exactly where these figures appear from, they are armed with long spears and their clothing resembles that of the North African Amazigh people – also known as the Berbers. Lang's inclusion of these figures is another reminder of extraterritorial trade as the Imazighen have historically been important traders across the Maghreb region and the Mediterranean. Since antiquity, they have also been considered outsiders – the term 'Berber' is derived from both the Greek *barbaros* (barbarian) – and they appear here as representatives of an ancient economic order.

The appearance of the Imazighen on-screen at this time could also be evocative of contemporary struggle against European colonialism. In 1921, Spanish colonial armies in the Rif mountains of Morocco had been defeated by Amazigh forces under the command of Abd el-Krim, a conflict that presaged other struggles against European colonization. Lang's inclusion of these figures underlines the associations at work in the appearance of this 'world-man' performer in front of the audience, both on screen and watching the film. Weltmann, visibly scarred from the war, conjures an image of overseas colonies and a colonized people who cross over into the space of the theatre. Then, with a wave of his hand, he effortlessly causes them to disappear. It seems clear that this is a representation of a fantasy of power over extraterritorial space – an association aided by the name Sandor, or Alexander, which as Tom Gunning suggests, evokes the memory of the world conquering emperor.[118]

Weltmann's performance in 'mass suggestion' brings forth this image of a caravan of nomadic people who move outside of the modern economy. Tom Gunning also points out that this 'performance is a high point of Mabuse's power' and 'his identification with the actual powers of the film he exists within,'[119] and certainly, a characteristically Langian meta-cinematic gesture is at work here. Weltmann's construction of a self-reflexive cinematic apparatus within the film is established by the device of a 'mass suggestion,' a collective vision and shared experience. In other words, his audience views the world as a product of their collective conscious minds – a succinct allegory of the cinema.[120] The image of the Amazigh is simultaneously recognizable, as well as enigmatic within the diegesis of the film. The

118 Gunning, *Lang*, 120.

119 Ibid., 112.

120 Raymond Bellour in fact saw this scene as demonstrative of apparatus theory. See Raymond Bellour, "On Fritz Lang," *SubStance* 3, no. 9 (April 1, 1974): 25–34.

question as to why Weltmann shows this particular group goes unanswered and has no parallel image in the rest of the film. The mystery of the image, its unknowable quality, dropped into the middle of the narrative with little explanation, causes a collision of worldviews and knowledge systems within the film. Here we glimpse an era in which time and space had not yet been conquered by modern technology. The nomadic Imazighen are transported into the commercialist excess of Mabuse's Weimar Republic and then vanish from the scene.

If we recognize this conjured caravan as a group of itinerant, nomadic *traders*, this illusion seems less out of place when compared to the rest of Weltmann's act. His subsequent tricks in this scene, which involve banknotes and the divination of numbers, complete the re-association of this mystical realm back to the concrete reality of the money economy. Immediately following this first illusion, Weltmann asks the audience to supply him with 'two two-digit numbers.' This is part of a larger trope that runs throughout the film involving combinations of numbers, often randomly assigned, that end up having significant import. For example, at the beginning of the film, one of Mabuse's henchmen robs a courier carrying a trade agreement on a train between Switzerland and Holland. In the rail car, we see the seat numbers 19 and 20, and another number beside the courier, 1126. The courier sits in seat 20 and, beside him, a superimposition reveals the commercial contract concealed in his briefcase. Mabuse's henchman Georg, who is seated opposite the courier, pretends to yawn and looks at his pocket watch – '8:19.' Cut to another of Mabuse's henchmen waiting by a car, who also looks at his watch – '8:20' – and starts his engine. Georg and the courier are shown again in the rail car, and Georg's watch now shows '8:22.' He assaults the courier, steals the briefcase, and throws it from the window of the moving train into the passenger seat of the passing car of Mabuse's henchman, who signals to a figure perched on a telephone wire. Back in his chambers Dr. Mabuse picks up the phone to receive the message 'Full hand!' (English in the original intertitle) signifying the end of the 'game.' The association with the card game blackjack[121] is explicit in this scene, with the action occurring across the threshold of the numbers near 21 that are essential to winning the game. A disguised Mabuse leaves his office after writing a series of numbers on a few banknotes that he places in the hat of a homeless war amputee (also one of his accomplices). One of the notes bears the serial number '1127,' and Mabuse proceeds to get into a car bearing the license

121 This game was most likely known in more numerical terms as *Einundzwanzig*, or *Siebzehn und Vier*, or possibly the French *Vingt-et-un*, at the time.

Figure 6. Stills from *Dr. Mabuse der Spieler* (Fritz Lang, 1922) that show the closely related sets of numbers that run through the film. Photo: Friedrich-Wilhelm Murnau Stiftung.

plate '2711.' Similarly, Edgar Hull is introduced in a note that Mabuse reads as a 'member of the 17 + 4 club.' This is the beginning of the intricate series of seemingly related numbers that appear throughout the film.

These close matches – usually off by one whole number – and numerical sequences occur frequently throughout the film. For example, after being hypnotized by Mabuse and forced to gamble away his money, the playboy and gambler Hull discovers a mix-up in the hotel records involving the room number of Mabuse's alter ego 'Mr. Balling' – presumed to be in room 111, but who is actually in 112 (Figure 6). A similar switch occurs in the auditorium where Weltmann performs when he asks for numbers to be called out. Mabuse's underling Spoerri is shown craning his neck to identify the seat that Wenk is occupying and incorrectly calls out 'number 12!' Wenk, actually seated in seat 11, agrees to volunteer in place of the absent audience member in seat 12.

Weltmann proceeds to perform an illusion that reveals that he has determined the contents of Wenk's pocket, revealing that he is carrying a browning revolver, a firearms permit, and 'two thousand-mark notes, printed in 1918, series D no. 65045 and series E, no. 5567.' After this, he hypnotizes Wenk – again using the words 'Tsi-Nan-Fu' – and compels him to leave the auditorium and drive off a cliff into a mine, in a car with the specific license number 3825. Cards shown on screen also add to this parade of seemingly connected numbers. Though there is no discernible meaning revealed in these patterns, their constant appearance gives the impression of a numerological or cabalistic code to be deciphered within the text.

What should we make of the elaborate spectacle of Weltmann's illusion that has been inserted into the film and is absent from the novel? How does this scene, which conflates a cinematic illusion of far-flung colonial Africa with concrete images of the money economy function in the context of the structuring logic of speculation, counterfeiting, and gambling? I suggest that Mabuse/Weltmann's production of an image of the world is another moment that the looming presence of the world economy is alluded to in the film. In a similar manner to the superimposition of Mabuse's face over the stock exchange, which announces his spectral power over this realm and his easy access to the abstract space of the market, Weltmann's illusions and tricks connect an image of the world back to the money economy and the numerical cypher that runs through the film.

This experience of the money economy as an ambient and seemingly connected numerical code was the subject of the first issue of *Der Dada* magazine from 1919, the cover of which displayed an evocative but nonsensical combination of numbers and symbols in various alphabets (Figure 7), and the contents of which combined appeals to Eastern religions with a call to its readers to 'deposit their money with the DADA bank.'[122] The magazine effectively mocked the ubiquity and urgency of the financial code that was increasingly present in the popular media and intruded into everyday experience but was decipherable only to an initiated few. As in this issue of *Der Dada*, *Dr. Mabuse* plays on the natural inclination to attempt to find patterns and correlations in numerical patterns, a process that is not necessarily rational, yet is central to the engagement with the numerical code of the financial market.

Weltmann's illusions conflate images of colonial power and fantasies of an uncanny 'omnipotence of thought' with a numerological world picture. This configuration is not unlike the combination of rational and irrational activity that informs the acts of speculation and gambling, in which logical behaviour and strategy exist alongside appeals to hunches, fears, and emotions. *Dr. Mabuse* played into, and reinforced, the popular perception of

122 Thanks to Kurt Beals for bringing this image to my attention. Kurt Beals, paper presented at the annual meeting for the Forschungsnetzwerk Berkeley, Tübingen, Wien, Harvard "Modeling the Future: Risk and Simulation," Internationales Forschungszentrum Kulturwissenschaften an der Kunstuniversität Linz, Vienna (May 31, 2014).

Figure 7. Raoul Hausmann and Johannes Baader, "Dadadegie," in *Der Dada*, issue 1, June 1919. DADA III:18:1. Kunsthaus Zürich Library.

gambling and speculation as one and the same, in contrast to the discourse that separated the two within the sphere of financial professionals. The film served a powerful expository function by providing a complex visual representation of the cultural codes associated with finance capital.

In his essays from the Weimar period, Siegfried Kracauer discusses the rise of Rudolf Steiner's anthroposophy in the spiritual vacuum and explanatory power that was previously assigned to religion. In Kracauer's judgment, the popularity of anthroposophy was due to its claim to 'have a scientifically verifiable method that allegedly will enable people to perceive supersensory realities as well as fathom human destiny.'[123] Anthroposophy thus provided a framework within which irrational spiritualism could co-exist with a claim to scientific verifiability. This is precisely the position that Mabuse, in all his disguises and personas occupies. His powers extend over both the rational terrain of technology and standardized time as well as the irrational notion of a predetermined fate in the religious understanding of the world. Faced with the shifting logic of currency speculation at the time of the film, individuals engaged with irrational and rational approaches as equally viable narratives – turning to both pseudo-scientific explanation as well as superstition and intuition.

State Power and the Defeat of Dr. Mabuse

Dr. Mabuse ends with a metaphor of vision, in the form of the blind counterfeiters who surround Mabuse when he is finally trapped in his own workshop and denied his power to fascinate with his gaze. This symbolic castration bookends the earlier image of omnipotent power linked to both his own vision and the world that he commands. Mabuse, once the demonic apotheosis of Freud's notion of humans as 'prosthetic Gods' through their use of 'auxiliary organs' of technology, has now lost his spectral and speculative mastery and is caught in the web of contingencies that he himself has created. His ultimate downfall sees him lose both his physical and non-corporeal mobility as well as his power over the money economy. He is caught in his own trap in his workshop with the blind men that he employs in his massive counterfeiting operation. Unable to control the blind counterfeiters with his hypnotic gaze, he succumbs to spectral visions of the victims he has left through the course of his criminal enterprise. He collapses in a pile of his own counterfeit currency, while the machinery of the workshop seems to come alive around him.

This final immobilization and neutralization of Mabuse's power is achieved through the blunt implement of state violence – in a shoot-out with his gang that sees the army called in. This is a reassertion of the law of the land over Mabuse's stateless and boundary-crossing activity and a reinforcement of the status quo. It stages the constant need to rein in the radically disruptive nature of financial forces within the modern nation state. In a letter, Jacques recounts the various criticisms that were levelled

123 Kracauer, *Ornament*, 132.

against him at the time of the novel's publication. He claims that the novel was 'attacked' for its apparent 'glorification of crime,' but protests that it was intended as a 'glorification of individual power' that 'must break the constrictions of the state.'[124] This is a very specific defence that will remind us of today's disciples of Ayn Rand and boosters of the libertarian fantasy of 'unregulated' or 'self-regulated' markets. As Quinn Slobodian has shown, the roots of this now prevalent fiction can be traced back to the writings of German and Austrian economists in the 1920s.[125] Slobodian argues that the neoliberal vision of a world open to freely flowing market forces arose in the wake of the First World War. As Ludwig von Mises wrote in 1927:

> For the liberal, the world does not end at the borders of state. In his eyes, whatever significance national boundaries have is only incidental and subordinate. His political thinking encompasses the whole of mankind.[126]

Mabuse then, can be read as the individual who has adapted to this new economic order – stateless, liquid, and flowing across all boundaries.

Siegfried Kracauer claims that the frequently occurring images of circles in *Dr. Mabuse* denote 'chaos.'[127] This is certainly a possible interpretation of the circle's appearance in the final scene, in the form of the uncanny expressionistic animation of objects in Mabuse's workshop. More often than as markers of chaos, however, circles appear throughout the film in a constant play of exclusion and inclusion, and as representative of a battle between stasis and circulation. Mabuse is in the end driven to madness through stasis and the condition of being trapped or confined. In Lang's next Mabuse film, *Das Testament des Dr. Mabuse* (1933), Mabuse' return in fully 'spectral' form would allow him to transcend this corporeal limitation once and for all. He becomes more powerful as an idea, as a thought in circulation, than he had ever been in human form alone. The dilution of his identity, begun at the beginning of the film through his random selection of disguises, thus finds its logical completion in the complete erasure of his identity. In the 1933 film, Mabuse is mute and immobile, but his powers of influence lie in the constant automatic writing of cyphers, plans, and endless combinations of numbers that this time have no pretensions to an underlying logic. Writing out endless pages of zeros, Mabuse evokes

124 Jacques, in a handwritten note from 1928, quoted in Jacques and Scholdt, *Mabuse*.
125 Slobodian, *Globalists*.
126 Ludwig von Mises, quoted in Slobodian, *Globalists*, 27.
127 Kracauer, *Caligari*, 83.

the endless addition of zeros to the rapidly inflating currency, but also the zero-sum game of the market, as if he were writing the narrative of 'fictitious capital' itself. Marx's alternate name for the formula M-M,' or 'finance capital' in Rudolf Hilferding's terms, was money that begets more money in an endless multiplication based solely on confidence in future value. In death, Mabuse is more powerful than ever, and like Marx's formulation of capital, he circulates, vampire-like. In a sense, Mabuse's entire enterprise collapses in on and erases itself as if mimicking the effect of speculation over time. As Urs Stäheli notes, in relation to the act of 'hedging' risk, 'the effect of true speculation is to eliminate itself.'[128]

This chapter has pointed to ways in which *Dr. Mabuse der Spieler* could have resonated with its audience in terms of the prevalence of financial themes and images of global extraterritorial space in the film. It seems clear that the 'double reflection' of meta-cinematic sequences in the film can be read in this light and, as Thomas Elsaesser argues of Weimar cinema in general, allowed spectators at the time to 'organize and experience their (psychic and social) reality in the cinema.'[129] However, this 'organization' is not merely a coming to terms with modernity in the general sense, but rather, with the specific scene of crisis that constitutes this key marker of modernity – an increasingly financialized everyday experience, and a growing awareness of the centrifugal forces of the world economy. The films discussed in this chapter, when read as part of the public discourse on the individual modern subject's relation to the world economy, become implicit in the creation of this particular worldview. The conflation of images of territorial loss with the economic amounts to what Wolfgang Schivelbusch has described as the 'replacement of the authoritarian *homo militaris* with the liberal *homo oeconomicus*,' that occurred during the Weimar Republic or, as chancellor Gustav Stresemann stated, 'the German economy would have to conquer what the German army had lost.'[130] As an anti-hero Mabuse represents a fantasy of mobility and power that is tied to the free flow of capital for the new demographic of financial workers identified by Siegfried Kracauer. Mabuse embodies the figure of the profiteer, the cosmopolitan Other, speculation as a daily reality, and the disruptive force of capital which, in the end, is too much of a threat and is neutralized by state power.

128 Stäheli, *Speculation*, 48.
129 Elsaesser, *Weimar Cinema*, 99.
130 Schivelbusch, *Defeat*, 281–82.

3. Women and Finance Capital in Weimar Cinema

Abstract: Chapter 3 takes up a central paradox of financial markets. While market participants were almost entirely male, financial activity is historically associated with the feminine. This chapter discusses the gendering of financial exchange and the depiction of women as both agents and objects of exchange in *Die Austernprinzessin* ('The Oyster Princess,' 1919), the little-known *Fräulein Raffke* ('Raffke's Daughter,' 1923), and *Die freudlose Gasse* ('The Joyless Street,' 1925). It offers the counterexample of an early and atypical film that featured a female speculator, *Die Börsenkönigin* (The Queen of the Stock Exchange, 1916), in order to discuss the depiction of financial independence in terms of its importance to first-wave feminism and the German women's movement. Also introduced is the trope of 'liquidity' – a central theme of this book.

Keywords: Woman as Speculator, Woman as Commodity, Gender and Finance, Liquidity, Asta Nielsen, First-Wave Feminism

The New Woman as Speculator

Introduction

In the established discourse on Weimar cinema, women are usually discussed in terms of their role as *objects* rather than active *agents* of financial exchange. However, a close examination of the depiction of women speculators reveals a more complex picture. Public and private space in Wilhelmine Germany (and continuing into the Weimar years) was highly gendered, and characterized by a doctrine of separate spheres, with men taking an active role in public space, and women largely confined to the domestic sphere of the family. Gender roles conformed to the notion of *Geschlechtscharakter* ('the character of the sexes'), which emerged in the eighteenth century and described 'the mental characteristics which were held to coincide with

---

Lyons, O., *Finance and the World Economy in Weimar Cinema*. Taylor & Francis Group, 2023.
DOI 10.5117/9789463727136_CH03

the physiological distinctions between the sexes.'[1] After the First World War, women increasingly participated in the workforce but this shift in women's role was gradual in practice. In popular media, however, it was manifested as a much more urgent phenomenon, creating the impression of violent rupture in traditional gender roles. Evidence of the perception of the threat of an emergent 'New Woman' can be found in all cultural domains in the Weimar period and appeared in a variety of forms in the cinema.[2] Accordingly, depictions of women and finance in the films of this time are highly varied and complex, reflecting both women's newfound financial agency while often also framing them as objects to be exchanged among men. Additionally, this tension surrounding agency and gender is reflective of the gendering of financial markets themselves.

In practice, the stock exchange was a highly 'male' space, with German women only gaining the right to access the Berlin trading floor in 1922, but seldom taking advantage of this new privilege.[3] Despite being the domain of men, however, the money economy and the activity of financial exchange is often represented culturally as an 'irrational' female force – a hysterical panicked mass phenomenon to be tamed by the rational male individual. This is a core contradiction of the mythology of financial markets and one that revolves around a clear gender binary. This gendered narrative is at the root of the over-identification with masculinity demonstrated by financial workers (still a common feature of discourse and popular representation of markets today) because of the cultural perception of financial labour as inherently 'feminized,' when compared to the 'productive' sectors of the economy.

Women speculators, when they do appear, challenge and threaten the gendered logic of financial markets and this chapter seeks to recuperate and interrogate the cultural resonances of these figure as they appear in several key films. In order to do so, we turn first to a lesser-known film, *Die*

1 Karin Hausen, "Family and Role-Division: The Polarization of Sexual Stereotypes in the Nineteenth Century – an Aspect of the Dissociation of Work and Family," in *The German Family: Essays on the Social History of the Family in Nineteenth- and Twentieth-Century Germany*, ed. Richard J. Evans and W. Robert Lee (London: Totowa, NJ: Croom Helm and Barnes & Noble, 1981), 51.

2 See Maria Tatar, *Lustmord: Sexual Murder in Weimar Germany* (Princeton, NJ: Princeton University Press, 1995); Patrice Petro, *Joyless Streets: Women and Melodramatic Representation in Weimar Germany* (Princeton, NJ: Princeton University Press, 1989); Richard W. McCormick, *Gender and Sexuality in Weimar Modernity: Film, Literature, and 'New Objectivity'* (New York: Palgrave, 2001).

3 Harold James, "Strukturwandel in Kriegs- und Krisenzeiten 1914–1945," in *Geschichte des Finanzplatzes Berlin*, ed. Hans Pohl (Frankfurt: Knapp, 2002), 165.

Börsenkönigin (1918), a film whose very title challenges presiding assumptions about the role of women in the Weimar financial markets. Then we will discuss the complex representations of women and financial exchange in in well-known films like G. W. Pabst's *Die freudlose Gasse* (1925), and Ernst Lubitsch's *Die Austernprinzessin* (1919), as well as Richard Eichberg's now virtually unknown *Fräulein Raffke* (1923).

Finance and Women's Emancipation in *Die Börsenkönigin*

The first two decades of the twentieth century were marked by a dramatic shift in the role of women in German society. Even before the First World War, women increasingly competed in the workplace for jobs traditionally only available to men. In February 1912, an exhibition was mounted at the Berlin Zoological Garden that brought this phenomenon into the popular consciousness.[4] Entitled *Die Frau in Haus und Beruf* ('Women in the Home and at Work'),[5] the exhibition was highly successful and widely reported on, even by *The New York Times*, which wrote that it showed 'every sphere of activity, domestic, industrial, and professional, which women have so far invaded.'[6] Organized by the women's rights activist Hedwig Heyl, the exhibition was an integral part of the growing awareness of the new professional roles women had begun to occupy, and the title was intended to 'honour equally the paid and unpaid contributions made by women to the nation.'[7] Attended mainly by women, the exhibition also had the practical effect of bringing women together in a mass of up to 10,000 at a time under its roof and in a manner that dwarfed the similarly new phenomenon of women gathering in large numbers at department stores.[8] *Die Frau in Haus und Beruf* was a watershed moment for the women's rights movement in Germany, and women who had been reluctant to march and demonstrate before 1912 increasingly left the domestic sphere and engaged in 'claim[ing] the streets as their own.'[9]

4 See Despina Stratigakos, *A Women's Berlin: Building the Modern City* (Minneapolis: University of Minnesota Press, 2008).

5 The exhibition was later cynically mirrored in *Die Frau in Familie, Haus und Beruf*, organized by Bruno Gebhard and Albert Wischek, under the supervision of *Reichspropagandaminister* Joseph Goebbels, on March 18, 1933.

6 "Woman's Work in Many Fields." *The New York Times*, February 25, 1912. Quoted in Stratigakos, *A Women's Berlin*, 97.

7 Ibid., 98.

8 Ibid., 105.

9 Ibid., 135.

Directed by Edmund Edel, the 1916 film *Die Börsenkönigin* was as much a creation of its star (Asta Nielsen) as it was of its director. Nielsen's power over her own image in the 1910s was unprecedented for a female star and eclipsed many of her male counterparts.[10] Nielsen had already negotiated a share in the profits of her films with *Afgrunden* ('The Abyss') in 1910, and had dramatized her own position of influence in the self-reflexive *Die Filmprimadonna* ('The Film Prima Donna') of 1914, which, as Heide Schlüpmann explains, considers 'the ways in which the star does not merely play a role, but rather influences the entire creation of a film.' Accordingly then, for this film, Nielsen controlled the mechanics of shooting, costuming and the darkroom process itself.[11] As such, the Danish Nielsen was a pivotal figure in the empowerment of women in cinema, primarily through her work in the German context. She has also been called cinema's first 'vamp'[12] and announced 'the coming of film as art in Germany.'[13] She was Europe's best-known actor in 1912,[14] later rivalling Chaplin in popularity and recognizability, especially amongst the European avant-garde.[15] Her career spanned some seventy films, including *Die freudlose Gasse*.

After the First World War, Nielsen's control of her roles and image began to be significantly curtailed by the rise of the male director/auteur, and she attempted to regain control by starting her own company, Art-Film GmbH.[16] Nielsen's influence was so great at the time that the question 'why is our film not considered art?,' asked in a 1919 *Film-Kurier* article, was given the answer: Nielsen would 'show film the way it had previously lost.'[17] Heide Schlüpmann points out that Nielsen's actions in this regard were at least, in part, a result of her objection to being frequently offered the role of sex worker (a staple role for women in Weimar cinema). When Nielsen did

10 See Heide Schlüpmann, "27 May 1911: Asta Nielsen Secures Unprecedented Creative Control" in *A New History of German Cinema*, ed. Jennifer M. Kapczynski and Michael D. Richardson (Rochester, NY: Boydell & Brewer, 2014), 44–50.

11 Schlüpmann, "Creative Control," 45.

12 Thomas Elsaesser and Michael Wedel, eds., *The BFI Companion to German Cinema* (London: BFI Pub, 1999), 182.

13 Thomas Elsaesser and Michael Wedel, eds., *A Second Life: German Cinema's First Decades* (Amsterdam: Amsterdam University Press, 1996), 7.

14 Jan-Christopher Horak, "Munich's First Fiction Feature: *Die Warheit*," in *A Second Life: German Cinema's First Decades*, ed. Thomas Elsaesser and Michael Wedel (Amsterdam University Press, 1996), 87.

15 See Geert Buelens, "The Manifold in One / and the One Manifold" – Asta Nielsen as an Icon for the European Avant-Garde," *Avant Garde Critical Studies* 28, no. 1 (May 1, 2013): 105–16.

16 Schlüpmann, "Creative Control," 48.

17 *Film-Kurier*, July 6, 1919. Author's translation.

take one of these roles, Schlüpmann argues that she was usually able to subvert the stereotype and 'convey her objection to the socially degrading presentation of women/actresses as objects,' a stance that meant she was misogynistically labelled as being 'difficult.'[18] Nielsen's resolve to maintain her own vision of and control over the portrayal of women in Weimar cinema is of particular interest in reading her earlier work. *Die Börsenkönigin* was financed by Nielsen herself and evidence points to her creative control over the film.[19] It is an example of what Schlüpmann identifies in Nielsen's work as a tendency to use film as a 'place of female self-determination, where gender relations might be redefined.'[20] Since there is currently little scholarship available on this film and it is not widely known, what follows is a detailed synopsis of the relevant sections that clarifies, and in some cases, corrects existing accounts of the film.

Die Börsenkönigin tells the story of a businesswoman and investor who owns a controlling interest in a copper mine that has fallen out of profitability. The film opens with an inspection by 'Börsen-Agent Goldstein' who subsequently recommends the selling of all shares in the mine, on the assumption that they are about to fall. The second scene of the film shows brokers and traders entering through a neoclassical façade onto a stock exchange floor, followed by an interior shot of the buying and selling of the 'Glückauf' mine shares (literally 'good luck' mine). The third scene introduces Nielsen's character Helene Metzler sitting at a gambling table with two elderly and elegantly dressed male card players. Helene is identified in some reviews as the owner of the mine, but it seems more accurate to say that the mine is a publicly traded company and that she is a majority share-holder. She learns of a 6 per cent fall in the value of Glückauf shares through the evening edition of a newspaper and retires to her opulent office to call the director of the mine on the telephone. After arranging to have the director report to her at home the next day, she returns to the card table to continue playing. He informs her that the mine's production is dropping, jeopardizing her entire fortune. After a heated discussion, Helene decides to visit the mine herself. Wearing pants was already a Nielsen trademark and, accordingly, after changing into a chic outfit that resembles a boiler suit, Helene descends into the mine where the director informs her that he

18 Schlüpmann, "Creative Control," 49.

19 Ibid., 47.

20 Heide Schlüpmann, "Asta Nielsen and Female Narration: The Early Films," in *A Second Life: German Cinema's First Decades*, ed. Thomas Elsaesser and Michael Wedel (Amsterdam: Amsterdam University Press, 1996), 118.

has made a discovery that could save its fate. At this point, Nielsen tells the director that if his discovery yields the intended profit, she will ask him to run the mine with her. She embraces him and a love interest is introduced that becomes central to the ensuing narrative.

In order to recoup her losses from the slump in the share price Helene directs the trader Goldstein to drive down the price of shares on the stock exchange so that she may buy as many of the discounted shares as possible. Unable to access the exchange floor herself, Helene acts through the intermediary of Goldstein. However, she also visits the exchange, eavesdropping on the action, and writing in her own notebook while she stands in the wings overlooking the floor (Figure 8). Particular emphasis is put on her authority over Goldstein in this scene, and she is shown reading instructions out of her notebook to him against the backdrop of the crowd of traders on the floor. Her visit is also marked by the traders who tip their hats to her as she is drawn away on a carriage outside but then chuckle, presumably at the sight of a woman at the exchange after she exits the frame. Director Lindholm's discovery in the mine yields a rich lode, but the story turns briefly to Helene's offer of a servant job to her younger 'penniless cousin Lina.' In her new position, Lina catches the eye of the newly promoted Lindholm and a love triangle between her and Helene develops during a party in honour of Lindholm's new discovery. Helene and Lindholm retire to seal their new business arrangement and Helene passionately embraces Lindholm, exclaiming that without his discovery she would have been ruined.

In one of the most striking compositions of the film, Helene is shown visiting the mine processing floor wearing her white frock dress and carrying a cane. Her figure is starkly contrasted by the female mine workers around her, who push large carts of ore around the factory grounds while dressed mostly in black, with shawls over their heads that are almost mediaeval in appearance. After nearly falling down the mine shaft in a swoon, Helene is steadied by the superintendent (Oberinspektor Müller) who 'is overcome by a surge of passion,' and she has to fight off his sexual advances.[21]

Her return home interrupts a flirtatious game of croquet between Lindholm and Lina, after which Lina opts to leave the services of Helene rather than suffer from seeing her and Lindholm together. As she is leaving, Helene witnesses Lindholm go to her waiting carriage and passionately kiss Lina. Helene returns distraught to her office and summons superintendent Müller to her – presumably the only person she can manipulate, if not fully

21 Intertitle: 'Der Oberinspektor Müller läßt sich in einer plötzlichen Aufwallen von seinen leidenschaftlichen Gefühlen hinreißen.'

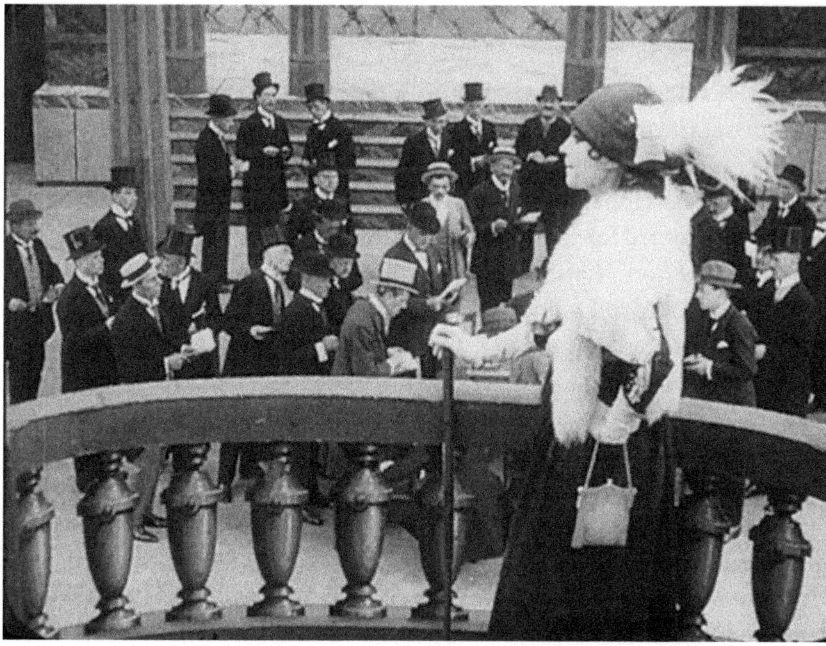

Figure 8. Helene (Asta Nielsen) standing in the wings overlooking the exchange floor in *Die Börsenkönigin* (Edmund Edel, 1916). Edition Filmmuseum press photo.

trust. She uses Müller's infatuation with her to persuade him to take over the supervision of the mines from Lindholm, imploring him by pressing herself against him. Here, rather than rely on her authority as a majority shareholder in the company, Helene relies instead on the power of her sexuality – a slippage that occurs several times in the film and will be discussed.

Müller takes the position and immediately (and inexplicably) orders that no further work be done in the mine that night, but Lindholm is shown returning to the mine to inspect the new tunnel – ominously descending alone in the mineshaft lift. Bad weather leads to a disaster in the mine while Lindholm is underground and Müller returns to tell Helene the news. Helene becomes hysterical with grief at the news of Lindholm's death and Müller once again makes unwanted advances towards Helene in her moment of weakness, but is again forcefully denied and this time thrown out. The final scenes intercut between the workers running through the mine grounds, towards and around the camera at the news of Lindholm's death, and Helene in her plush interior. In a striking sequence, Helene then runs first through the gardens of her stately home and then across the mine grounds and around the tailings ponds in an elaborate fur-lined dressing gown as the workers amass in front of the factory. She collapses in the arms of one of the miners who surround her, and exclaims 'what use are my riches when he, the dearest thing that I owned, is dead?'[22] The Queen of the Stock Exchange returns to her desk, dejected and forlorn. She declares that work at the mine will continue and that the workers 'should, under no circumstances, be the victims of the accident.'[23] This can be read in either of two ways: as sympathetic to the wages of the workers, or alternatively, as a callous disregard for the worker, stemming from her own unwillingness to halt production. Nielsen's performance, unless read entirely cynically, would seem intended to indicate the former reading, especially since she is amongst the workers, and favourably received by them, when she makes this announcement.

Die Börsenkönigin is an interesting case study in contradiction insofar as it gives Helene agency in the plot at the same time as it repeats many stereotypical associations of women and finance. In order to unpack the film's codes and assumptions, an overview of some of the key literature on cultural productions of women and finance is useful. Produced in 1916, *Die Börsenkönigin* predates the official admittance of women to the Berlin stock exchange floor in 1922, which coincided with the large increase in the number of white-collar workers discussed in the previous chapter. In the first few decades of the twentieth century, the number of German women employed in the financial and credit sector rose quickly, from around one per thousand (of working women) in 1900 to approximately one per every two hundred women in 1907. In 1907, 7% of German *Bankangestellten* ('bank employees') were women, a number that increased to 20% by the middle of the 1920s.[24]

The struggle for access to the exchange intensified after the turn of the twentieth century. It was led by women who, in many cases, were war widows taking over the businesses of their deceased husbands, and who strove to obtain equal access to credit and the mechanisms of the market. Because of the restrictions on women in business and entrenched sexism, prominent Berlin women began to organize a bank and credit organization that would cater to their specific needs. What was begun under the name of the Genossenschaftsbank selbständiger Frauen ('Independent Women's Credit Union') in 1910, was officially renamed the Frauenbank ('Women's

22 Intertitle: 'Was nützen mir nun meine Reichtümer, da er, das Liebste, was ich besaß, tot ist.'

23 Intertitle: 'Jetzt werde ich mit aller Kraft ans Werk gehen. Die Arbeiter sollen weiter ihre vollen Löhne erhalten. Sie dürfen keinesfalls die Opfer des Unglücks sein!'

24 Gilla Dölle, *Die (un)heimliche Macht des Geldes: Finanzierungsstrategien der Bürgerlichen Frauenbewegung in Deutschland zwischen 1865 und 1933* (Frankfurt am Main: Dipa, 1997), 194.

Bank') in 1913.[25] This was one of many women's organizations that were founded at this time by women to support their entrance into the work force. In 1914 alone, almost 70 associations for women clerks, such as the Berlin Commercial Alliance for Female Employees, were founded.[26]

The Frauenbank also published its own newspaper: *Frauenkapital – eine werdende Macht: Wochenschrift für Volkswirtschaft, Frauenbewegung und Kultur*,[27] ('Women's Capital: A Power in the Making – A Weekly Journal of Political Economy, The Women's Movement, and Culture') whose target audience was 'educated independent women who managed their own financial affairs,'[28] and which combined financial reporting with cultural and literary reviews, as well as travel reports. The Frauenbank thus regarded itself as an institution of the women's movement, as financial independence was seen as key to political and personal independence.[29] At this pivotal time for women's movements worldwide, financial independence was a stepping stone to later political independence and access to income. Control of and access to credit and financial markets was crucial to the mobilization of these movements in Germany, Sweden, Britain, Canada, and the United States.[30] The Frauenbank was, however, faced with adversity from its inception and dissolved in 1916, and its founding members were named in a lawsuit against the bank in 1918.[31] Among the challenges the bank faced over its short lifetime were the outbreak of the First World War shortly after its founding, and the failure to make 'intensive contacts' with the established male-dominated financial sector.[32] This last point echoes the description of the situation for women investors in Britain. Charles Dickens commented on the prevalence of women investors in the late nineteenth-century in Britain, but women were still barred from both the official halls of the exchange and the non-official,

25 Dölle, *Macht*, 197.

26 See Carole Elizabeth Adams, *Women Clerks in Wilhelmine Germany: Issues of Class and Gender* (Cambridge: Cambridge University Press, 1988).

27 Dölle, *Macht*, 203.

28 'Als Leserin hatte die Redaktion die gebildete, selbständige Frau vor Augen, die ihre finanziellen Geschäfte selbst regelte und deshalb mit den nötigen Zusammenhängen vertraut gemacht werden mußte.' Dölle, *Macht*, 204.

29 Urs Stäheli observes that in the American and English contexts early feminist writers and journalists pointed out the 'possibilities for women's emancipation in speculation.' Urs Stäheli, *Spectacular Speculation: Thrills, the Economy, and Popular Discourse* (Stanford University Press, 2013), 181.

30 See Pernilla Jonsson and Silke Neunsinger, *Gendered Money: Financial Organization in Women's Movements, 1880–1933* (New York: Berghahn Books, 2012), 216.

31 Dölle, *Macht*, 219.

32 Ibid., 220.

yet equally important places where men conducted business, such as pubs, coffee houses, restaurants in urban business districts, clubs, and fraternal lodges.[33] The situation was no different in the off-market spaces of Berlin, such as the legendary Café Bauer, which was renowned as a hub of financial news, as indicated by its subscriptions to over one hundred and twenty daily newspapers. Notably, in this important unofficial space of finance, women were only permitted with a male escort.[34]

Class and Gender in *Die Börsenkönigin*

The members and beneficiaries of the Frauenbank primarily belonged to the middle and upper classes of society, and their activities would have been less relevant to the working class or their exponents in organizations like the Spartakusbund. Class conflict is, however, alluded to several times in *Die Börsenkönigin*. First, Helene Metzler's attempts to help her young, penniless cousin, Lina, by employing her as a maid, is clearly not acceptable to the younger woman. Lina also chafes at her subservient position in the film's love triangle, and ultimately retains her dignity by refusing Helene as an employer rather than having to endure her union with Lindholm. Rather than harbour resentment, Helene is portrayed as very understanding and fair in this circumstance, and the film does not resolve Lina's departure with a simple break or conflict between the two women. Class is also clearly visually represented in the aforementioned scene in which Helene walks amongst the workers clad in white. This seems a clear indication of Helene's 'enlightened' position of power, as opposed to the dimly lit, faceless and voiceless working-class women.

Die Börsenkönigin was completed in 1916 but premiered on May 25, 1918, only a few months after the general strike that marked the birth of the republic. This delay was due to a legal battle with the distributor and Nielsen's return to Copenhagen to care for her ill daughter.[35] Its relevance to the German women's movement, and Nielsen's own position as a promoter of

33 George Robb, "Ladies of the Ticker: Women, Investment, and Fraud in England and America, 1850–1930," in *Victorian Investments: New Perspectives on Finance and Culture*, ed. Nancy Henry and Cannon Schmitt (Bloomington: Indiana University Press, 2009), 121–124.

34 Paul Lindau, "Unter den Linden," in *Great Streets of the World* (London: Osgoode, McIlvaine, 1892). Reproduced in: Iain Boyd Whyte and David Frisby, eds., *Metropolis Berlin: 1880–1940*, (Berkeley: University of California Press, 2012), 179.

35 Nielsen's own role as a mother intruded on her burgeoning film career, and she was away from the Berlin film world until 1918. See Asta Nielsen, "Mein Weg im Film – Teil 7: Die traurige Geschichte meiner Kriegsfilme," *Berliner Zeitung am Mittag*, October 6, 1928.

women's rights, becomes clearer given the contemporary context of both the Frauenbank as well as the undercurrent of class conflict that runs through several scenes of the film. But the film may have already seemed dated with regards to its politics at the time of its release. Though the film is pioneering in many ways, its full potential as a feminist text is undercut by a number of factors. For example, Nielsen's character cedes control to men at times – sometimes unnecessarily – and oscillates between a position of power and powerlessness throughout. That said, for the period, it remains trailblazing in its subject matter and depiction of a powerful female businesswoman.[36]

Helene is shown visiting the copper mine three times in the film, and each of these instances is shot on location in an industrial area. Early in the film she changes out of her stuffy upper-class dress and dons a sporty two-piece work suit, riding boots and a thick white toque, to accompany Lindholm to the mine. In this scene, which again demonstrates Nielsen's preference for *Hosenrollen* (roles in which she wore pants),[37] Helene very much embodies the figure of the new woman, unafraid to descend into the mine with Lindholm and intent on her task of surveying her investment. Her second visit to the mine stands in stark contrast to the first and produces an almost surreal juxtaposition of wealth and labour. Helene is shown visiting the mine without any particular purpose or plot motivation beyond 'inspecting her employees.' She walks amongst the toiling workers in a section of the mine that is solely populated by women in head scarves, while she, herself, wears high heels, a conspicuously frilled white dress, and carries a cane with a doily on the handle. The scene appears to be shot on location in a factory and pointedly shows the vast divide between Helene's position and that of the female mine employees.

Helene's third visit to the mine occurs after she learns of Lindholm's death in the mine collapse, and proceeds to run from the opulent gardens of her estate, through a landscape of industrial ruination, towards the waiting mob of workers who have gathered at the news of the disaster. Helene's crestfallen defeat at the close of the film can be read as demonstrative of the film's ostensible moral: that greed is ultimately destructive, although her methods are hardly excessive in this regard. Since the film was produced before, and then ultimately released after, the Bolshevik revolution of 1917,

36 Nielsen had already established herself for playing strong feminist roles, starring a few years before in *Die Suffragette* (Germany, Urban Gad, 1913), based on the biography of the English feminists Christabel and Emmeline Pankhurst who founded the Women's Social and Political Union in 1903.

37 Schlüpmann, "Asta Nielsen," 48.

its concession to the workers in the end may also have been a product of changing historical conditions. The moral of the film is ultimately, and conspicuously, only conveyed through an intertitle that could have been written in 1918 and is somewhat at odds with the tone of the rest of the film. The message that none of the workers should suffer in the face of this disaster might suggest that Helene is less hard-nosed in her business dealings than would have been the norm of the time, but the penultimate shots of the film also redeem Helene's position of power as she dictates her wishes to a room filled with men who hurry away to fulfil them. In this sense the film demonstrates an elementary class consciousness through Helene's concession to her employees. But at no point does the film suggest that the workers have any agency or rights of their own, and the relationship is closer to a fantasy of feudal benevolence. The film's muddled moral conclusion may very well have been the result of last-minute changes as without some concession to the workers the film would have been strikingly out of step with its time. As such, the film is demonstrative of a particular problem facing the women's liberation movement at the time. Whereas in 1916 it might have been received as a triumphant declaration of independence and power within the social sphere, in 1918 this jubilant message would have been tempered by the ongoing revolutionary struggle that called into question the very basis of these aspirations in its rejection of capitalism. Similar contradictions abound in the scene where Helene weeps in a self-conscious display of her own traditional femininity; here the film restores a normative ideal that confirms the limits placed on transgressive gender representations in the period.

Yet, the film also contributes to the changing of social norms for women. One remarkable aspect of *Die Börsenkönigin* is the nonchalant and natural way Helene conducts herself as a businesswoman. She performs her role as speculator, investor and ultimately boss of the men who obey her with very few concessions to the revolutionary nature of her position. The normalization of her role is demonstrated in the scene that introduces her in the film – sitting at a gambling table with two men, who treat her as an equal. The problem with her business venture, which she discovers when reading a newspaper, is as abstract and commonplace to her as the arbitrary rules of a card game, and it is presented in almost the same manner, as symbols on paper (presented to the audience in one insert of a stock quotation broadsheet) delivered to her in the comfort of a casino. In this respect, Helene's professional activity is naturalized and, with the exception of one scene in which the men at the stock exchange chuckle behind her back, the film makes a pointed effort to avoid having any of the male characters of note react to her as if her requests were anything out of the ordinary – a remarkable eschewing of the winking misogyny of many films of this period.

The film also makes nothing of the fact that Helene neither has a family, nor plans to have one, and thus, is not bound by the traditional role of motherhood. The absence of this concern, so prevalent in the public discourse on women's employment at the time, makes the film even more notable. In short, *Die Börsenkönigin* dramatizes a central conflict for women of the time in its presentation of a portrait of a strong independent woman who does not clearly fit within emergent notions of female emancipation. Instead, Helene engages with the centrality of money to the emancipation of German women in the early twentieth century.[38] Proletarian and middle-class women were caught between two possible paths: on the one hand, a liberal promise of independence through greater conformity with the capitalist economy and greater control of their finances, and, on the other, the gender-blind promise of class revolution from the left that pushed for real reforms and emancipation of women's bodies and reproductive systems, but that also often conflicted with the male proletariat's resistance to women's participation in the industrial workplace. The film stands as a testament to the optimistic expectation of the social advancement of women in the period, one that would fade toward the end of the republic. Throughout the life of the republic, women would gradually but conspicuously withdraw from the public sphere. Between 1918 and 1930, female membership in the National Assembly would drop from almost 10% to only 7%, and membership in labour organizations would also fall drastically.[39]

The Gendering of the Market in Financial Discourse

Even if few women took up the opportunity to physically attend the official exchanges, this is not to say that women did not speculate, especially during the inflation period. Instead, they conducted their business (at additional cost) through intermediaries in the banks, rather than taking up their newfound freedom of movement on the exchange floor. According to the

38 German women were put at a disadvantage by the Civil Code itself, at the end of the nineteenth century. The expectation of married women to prioritize their family duties over financial activity remained entrenched in the West German legal code until the 1970s. See Eve Rosenhaft, "Women Investors and Financial Knowledge in Eighteenth Century Germany," in *Women and Their Money 1700–1950: Essays on Women and Finance*, ed. Anne Laurence, Josephine Maltby, and Janette Rutterford (London: Routledge, 2009).

39 Katharina von Ankum, *Women in the Metropolis: Gender and Modernity in Weimar Culture* (Berkeley: University of California Press, 1997), 3–4.

contemporary press, the job title of *Börsianerin* ('female stock exchange speculator/broker') had not even been developed at the time of publication of one an article in the illustrated magazine *UHU* from 1927 entitled 'Die Börse: Der Ort, an dem ernste Männer hysterisch werden' ('The Stock Exchange: Where Serious Men Become Hysterical').[40] This article speculates that the lack of women on the floor was as much a question of the physicality of the exchange activity itself, comparing the 'bare-knuckle politics' and elbows of the floor traders to a boxing match.[41] Similarly, in 1924 German economist Willi Prion doubted 'if many women would take advantage of the [changes in the law]' and claimed 'the womanly disposition would barely cope with the nerve wracking, clamorous and barely civilized exchange trading.'[42] *Die Börsenkönigin* dramatizes this separation of space that affected Nielsen's character in one scene in which she visits the exchange floor, but stands in the *coulisse* (the wings, or gallery) in order to conduct her business through the intermediary of her broker Goldstein. At the same time, her presence is noted by the men who look up at her and seem to react to her subtle motions, while she remains intent on her own business.

The film is ultimately somewhat ambiguous in its depiction of the power relationships between men and women, juxtaposing Helene's professional power with her frequent use of her sexual power to convince men to carry out her will. Helene does not emerge clearly victorious in the end, but rather, is regretful of the actions she has taken to shore up her own fortune, and recognizes her inability to subordinate her romantic feelings to her business acumen. For example, in one scene Helene embraces Lindholm, taking a much more passive role and congratulating him on finding new material to mine (in her own mine). She exclaims: 'Without your discovery I would be ruined. Now you will share in the profits with me.'[43] This concession to a man who is effectively her employee, is framed in the film as an act of passion on Helene's part and complicates a reading of the film as a triumphant portrayal of a successful businesswoman. Helene can of course do whatever she wants with her money but this gesture seems different than an example of a lavish

40 Olearius, "Die Börse: Der Ort, an dem Ernst Männer hysterisch werden," *UHU*, January 1927, 106. Author's translation.

41 Ibid.

42 Friedrich-Wilhelm Henning, "Börsenkrisen und Börsengesetzgebung von 1914 bis 1945 in Deutschland," in *Deutsche Börsengeschichte*, ed. Hans Pohl (Frankfurt: Knapp Fritz GmbH, 1992), 229. Author's translation.

43 Intertitle: 'Ohne Ihre Entdeckung wäre ich ruiniert. Nun werden Sie den Ertrag mit mir teilen.'

gift to her lover given that the film has spent so much time building up her business acumen and independence.

During her second visit to the mine, which immediately follows this scene, Helene is also unable to descend into the mine as she had before, and swoons at the edge of the shaft – a (possibly intentional?) gesture that clearly feminizes her and which later leads her to seek the solace of Lindholm back on her estate. This particular mixture of economic power and powerlessness continues to be played out in Helene's garden, where, though she is on her own property, she relies on Lindholm for physical and mental support. The film also spends an inordinate amount of time depicting the power relationship between Helene and her cousin, and rival for Lindholm's affections, Lina, thus displacing Helene's real economic power and entrepreneurship into the realm of petty melodramatic conflict between the female characters. In so doing, Helene's authority as an employer is undercut, not by a man, but by another woman through a personal conflict. This is a subtle development but one that allows another way of reading *Die Börsenkönigin* in a less progressive light, and anticipates the clichés of depictions of women and finance in Weimar cinema that the film otherwise avoids. The conflict with the younger woman, to whom she had offered herself as a guardian, also underscores the incompatibility of Helene's sexuality with the traditional construction of motherhood.

In two cases (with Lindholm and Müller), Helene uses her sexuality to implore men to carry out her will. But neither instance in the film seems to warrant this extra dimension since, in both cases the men are her employees and do not need to be convinced in standing to gain from her plans. The manner in which these interactions take place is also important, as, in both cases, the added sexual dimension is spontaneous and Helene's otherwise rational plans are aligned along the vectors of desire and seduction. In broader terms, Helene consistently reifies her own physical relation to individuals with whom an idealized 'rational actor' would only have an instrumental relationship. This is significant because it casts Helene, as representative of the female speculator, back into the realm of the irrational and into the gendered binary that characterizes market participation and also forward toward the emerging cliché surrounding women and financial exchange in later examples from Weimar Cinema.

The film's equivocal portrait of female independence mirrors the ambiguity of many of the women's rights movements of its time. While mobilization for women's emancipation resulted in the revolutionary reforms of the Weimar constitution, the real frequency of women in the work place continued at the slow pre-war rate, and the conditions of their employment and wages did not improve for the most part.[44] Women did not in practice suddenly gain the independence and freedom promised to them in the constitution, and representations of independent women shifted from such multifaceted portrayals as Nielsen's, towards the now familiar figure of the New Woman as threatening 'vamp.' Thus, the New Woman simultaneously *appeared* more frequently and became more *visible*, but was reintegrated into a patriarchal logic of representation that constituted her freedom as a challenge to hegemonic male power.

The film holds back from presenting a conclusive portrait of a powerful woman. In fact, the ambiguity around gender and power in the film is more demonstrative of internal tensions within financial labour itself, and the film is thus revealing of a deeper structure of gender relations. An article in *Simplicissimus* from 1921 characterized the commotion on the stock exchange as 'hysterical' while referring to the Börse as a *Herrentempel* (temple of men), stating:

> Yesterday I was on the stock exchange floor for the first time. It was like a temple of men. I once (accidentally) spent a half year in an asylum for incurable maniacs. This place made the stock exchange seem almost cosy by comparison. That evening I read in the newspaper: 'On the markets today there was great calm and restraint...'[45]

Like the aforementioned article in *UHU*, this article repeats the connection to hysteria, adding a key contemporary discussion of gender to the equation. The article describes the activity of the exchange in detail, with special attention paid to the monolithic nature of the gender represented. It concludes with a cartoon depiction of a woman selling fruit, subtitled 'The Only Woman in the Stock Exchange (even though women are officially permitted): The Banana Woman in the Foyer.' The article specifically describes the activity of the exchange members as being 'nothing like the calculating businessman in his office assessing all possibilities and weighing the pros and cons of a potential business, but rather, the exchange acts as rushed and frenzied as a hysterical woman.'[46] It notes that: 'the three thousand serious, business-minded gentlemen who operate on the Burgstrasse consider it a great day if by some coincidence an "overheated mood" grips them and a buying frenzy (*Kauflust*), or its opposite, races through the soul like a contagious

44 See Ankum, *Women in the Metropolis*.
45 *Simplicissimus*, May 4, 1921, 75. Author's translation.
46 Olearius,"Die Börse," 106. Author's translation.

fever, about as sane or competent as an excited diva who in one moment is cheering to the heavens, and in the next is deathly depressed.'[47]

Though an exclusively male space, the market is a site of feminized behaviour – an observation that rhymes with the idea of financial labour as 'unmanly.' But, as has historically been the case, and has remained so throughout much of the twentieth century, exchange floors are typically associated with a *surplus* of masculine overcompensation and aggression, and economic and financial language is rife with metaphors of violent struggle, virility, and male-dominant sexuality. How is this surfeit of masculinity to be reconciled with the common perception of speculation as associated with a lust and frenzy that is coded in feminine terms? Urs Stäheli argues for the common conception of the subject of financial markets and the idealized speculator as the masculine *homo economicus* working against the 'feminine' vagaries of the market. He claims that 'speculation was represented as feminine, while speculators were presented as men – or, to be more precise, the "feminized market" necessarily turned the speculator into a man' through their performance of a rational 'science' of speculation. Thus, masculinity was *performed* as an active resistance to the overwhelming 'femininity' of the frenzied crowd.[48]

As compared with the ideal *homo economicus*, 'a figure who lacked any particular quality' and who was described in investment guides as 'disembodied,'[49] Helene is portrayed as all too embodied, lacking the mastery of abstraction required by successful speculators. Helene's redemptive turn at the end of the film complicates her motivations, and though she aligns sex with commerce through her actions, she does not maintain a calculating control over her own sexuality. Her femininity and conflicting motivations are thus analogous to well-established depictions of financial markets as 'scenes of uncontrollable desire and unpredictable change.'[50] However, Helene's genuine involvement and concern with her lover in the

47 Ibid.

48 The crowd at the stock exchange, though a multitude of men, has been historically constructed by various commentators as feminine. It is a collection of conflicting motivations, wants, and desires and as in Poe's *Man of the Crowd* 'has given way to manic behaviour.' One side effect of this gendering of crowd behaviour was the suggestion by brokers such as William Worthington Fowler that women may in fact be more suited to working in finance than men because 'speculation derives its food from excitement, and women often feed on excitement.' Fowler goes on to report that 'there are no more eager and venturesome gamblers at Baden Baden, in Germany, than women, and there are no more eager and venturesome speculators in stocks, than women.' See Stäheli, *Speculation*, 175–76.

49 Ibid., 172.

50 Ibid., 175.

film adds a depth to her character that goes far beyond the one-dimensional motivation of seduction.

In *Die Börsenkönigin*, Asta Nielsen presents her audience with a complex and multi-dimensional portrait. Helene's tragic story both presents an emancipatory path for a strong female character and yet still partakes of the equivocal stance towards women's emancipation that anticipates the retrenchment of women's rights in ensuing decades. What we are left with in terms of a representation of finance and speculation, is a multi-faceted engagement with emancipation and capital, and one that perhaps honestly sums up the complexity of the personal and professional relations in the instrumental sphere of capitalist exchange.

Women as a Medium of Exchange

Financial Agency in *Die Austernprinzessin* and *Fräulein Raffke*

Though Asta Nielsen's role in *Die Börsenkönigin* was atypical in terms of its depiction of female agency, the film still foreshadows the complex interplay of sexuality and financial exchange of Weimar cinema. Consider, for example, Ernst Lubitsch's *Die Austernprinzessin* (1919). In this comedy, the female lead and daughter of the American *Raffke* and oyster magnate, 'Mister Quaker,' is played by the well-known film comedienne, Ossi Oswalda. She is introduced in the film throwing a tantrum upon discovering that the 'Shoe Cream King's daughter' has married a count. This motivates the plot of the film, as her father consoles her by claiming that he too will 'buy her a prince.' Though prompted by his daughter, Mister Quaker also has an ulterior motive in arranging her marriage – to buy his way into established society.[51] Thus, the film's plot is advanced based on the purely transactional function of the daughter's marriage and the film would appear to initially be an example of an emerging tendency in Weimar cinema – to depict women as a medium of exchange.

In the film, commerce, marriage, and financial exchange are played out through Oswalda's body as display object. In one scene, notable for

51 As Ofer Ashkenazi has pointed out, though not explicitly coded as Jewish, Lubitch's tendency to portray 'the protagonist's desperate endeavours to integrate into a society that is reluctant to accept them' means that the 'Jewishness' of the character of Quaker can be 'inferred.' See Ofer Ashkenazi, "Rethinking the Role of Film in German History: The Jewish Comedies of the Weimar Republic," *Rethinking History* 14, no. 4 (December 2010): 573.

its length, and which Bela Balázs described as 'downright obscene,' she undresses and is bathed by her servants.[52] While this scene seems specifically constructed for scopic pleasure, Janet McCabe and Sabine Hake point out that the matrix of looking and desire is complicated in the film. In fact, the plot is driven by the desire of the Oyster Princess herself and her multiple suitors, rather than being completely shaped by her father's will. McCabe reads desire in the film as aligned with the female gaze,[53] and there is a sense that the film is driven by the Oyster Princess's own agency, with the (impoverished) Prince Nucki's fate fully in the hands of this daughter of new money. As Sabine Hake has argued, *Die Austernprinzessin* is an important example of the emergence of 'girl culture' that made the figure (and myth) of the 'New Woman' so visible in the cinema of the 1920s.[54] Hake suggests that this film is also significant as an early example of the transformation of women's bodies as spectacles and, by extension, the representation of women as 'products' or 'commodities' on screen – a transformation that is visualized through 'a spectacle that imitates early forms of the conveyor belt' where the Princess is pampered and primped for her husband-to-be and eventually 'enters the drawing room – very much like a luxury item on display.'[55] This transformation would seem to anticipate an emerging cliché of Weimar cinema – the depiction of women as *objects* rather than *agents* of exchange – but the film complicates any such simple reading of agency since, as Hake points out, in *Die Austernprinzessin* 'it is the woman (i.e., the product) who does the "buying."'[56] The film's ambivalence concerning the financial agency of women is worth noting and, indeed, it 'moves back and forth between subversion and affirmation'[57] of both traditional versus modern gender roles, as well as the historical lack of agency amongst women in their financial affairs and their emergent financial power. As such, like *Die Börsenkönigin*, though less obviously, it straddles the line between the

52 Quoted in Janet McCabe, "Regulating Hidden Pleasures," in *Light Motives: German Popular Film in Perspective*, ed. Randall Halle and Margaret McCarthy (Detroit: Wayne State University Press, 2003), 24.

53 Ibid., 34.

54 Sabine Hake, *Passions and Deceptions: The Early Films of Ernst Lubitsch* (Princeton: Princeton University Press, 1992), 82.

55 Ibid., 87.

56 Ibid., 91. For an in-depth analysis of the complex commentary on the ways in which matchmaking in this film plays across boundaries of class and religion, see Valerie Weinstein, "(Un) Fashioning Identities: Ernst Lubitsch's Early Comedies of Mistaken Identity," in *Visual Culture in Twentieth-Century Germany: Text as Spectacle*, ed. Gail Finney (Bloomington: Indiana University Press, 2006), 120–133.

57 Ibid., 94.

idea of women as agents of exchange and the cliché representation of women as objects to be exchanged in much of Weimar cinema.

Die Austernprinzessin anticipates a very similar film that was released a few years later: Richard Eichberg's *Fräulein Raffke* (1923). A drama with comedic elements, the film is very similar in its plot but is clumsier and less known, lacking the humour of the 'Lubitsch touch.' As in *Die Austernprinzessin*, the plot of *Fräulein Raffke* is driven by the marrying off of the female lead by her rich father. Even more so than in Lubitsch's film, the figure of the *Raffke* is contrasted with established society, and in one scene in a respectable night club, the drunken Emil Raffke is accosted by other, seemingly more high-born, patrons who yell '*Raus mit dem Schieber!*' ('Get that swindler out of here!'). Emil Raffke is so desperate to improve his standing by attaining a noble son-in-law that he remains blind to the swindle being pulled under his own nose by Baron Egon von Geldern (Hans Albers), who, penniless himself, wishes to marry Raffke's daughter for her wealth. Raffke's daughter, Lilli, however, marries for love against her father's wishes and is cast out of the family. The newly-weds quickly fall on hard times and, at this point, the transactional relationship between Baron von Geldern and Lilli Raffke takes on an added dimension. Unable to woo her into marriage, the baron determines a way to gain access to her wealth by approaching her with a seemingly friendly offer of credit that her husband can pay back after they get back on their feet. The catch is that Emil Raffke must sign as the guarantor. Unable to get her father's signature, Lilli Raffke then commits a swindle of her own by forging it.

At this point in the film, Lilli crosses a moral and legal line, and her transgression is doubly upsetting to the symbolic order of the film as it occurs across the binary of subject and object in relation to the act of financial exchange. By taking matters into her own hands, Lilli betrays her father's trust but also betrays her position as object to be exchanged within the film. The expected subordination of women as symbolic objects of exchange within a patriarchal system is of course not original to Weimar cinema, and has been widely commented on.[58] Lilli's act of rebellion is so threatening to this order that it is depicted with an explicit destabilization of the visual frame, as if to indicate that a radical transgression is taking place. In the scene that follows the forging, Lilli wanders through the streets and, in a

58 See Claude Lévi-Strauss, *The Elementary Structures of Kinship*, rev. ed. (Boston: Beacon Press, 1969), and the critical response of Gayle Rubin, "The Traffic in Women: Notes on the 'Political Economy' of Sex," in *Feminist Anthropology: A Reader*, ed. Ellen Lewin (Malden, MA: Blackwell, 2006).

trick-shot superimposition, is beset on all sides by policemen – a frenzied hallucination of guilt. Then, a ghostly apparition of a line of judges stands before her while one points his finger at her and the word *Wechselfälscherin* ('contract forger') appears on the screen. In a notable break from the otherwise conventional cinematography of the film, this scene is captured in a highly expressionist manner. Dissolves and superimpositions are used and an image of an alleyway is double exposed and rotated, giving the impression that the public space of the street itself has become unmoored from its static foundations. The scene underlines the double transgression taking place. Not only is Lilli taking an active role in her own fate in the exchange process, literally emerging into the public space of the city as she does, but she is also betraying the symbolic order of money through the act of counterfeiting.

The only other use of superimposition in *Fräulein Raffke* occurs in a direct visual representation of the space of finance capital at the beginning of the film. In the opening scene, Emil Raffke is depicted seated in his office directing his employees and wildly gesturing while speaking on the phone. This is followed by a complex, multiple-exposure shot that introduces the interconnected world of his business endeavours. In this shot, the seated businessman is depicted with a telephone on both ears and, on each side of the frame, superimposed spaces represent respective domains of his far-flung business. From this visual composition we learn that he is a livestock magnate, as images of pigs and cattle in a stockyard are juxtaposed with a train passing over his head. This brief stylistic gesture aligns the formal mechanics of the cinema with those of the market apparatus and lends the otherwise comical character of Emil Raffke a degree of scopic mastery that sums up the extent of his riches to the viewer. The film makes less use of superimposition than *Dr. Mabuse der Spieler*, but this is another example of how this visual convention was used to show the extended space of the market. It is instantly recognizable as such and legible as indicative of the multi-temporal and spatial disjointedness of market activity. Such formal compositions, and the development of this convention, were essential to the moving image's representational power with respect to invisible financial forces. A similar formal composition also appears in Wilhelm Thiele's *Die Dame mit der Maske* ('The Woman with the Mask,' 1929), to which Hans Richter's 1928 experimental film *Inflationsbild* was appended. It is in these two examples of superimposition in the film that the 'unseen' space of financial exchange is made visible – first as an example of mastery in the case of the father, and later as an example of transgression in the case of the daughter.

Fräulein Raffke was released in the same year as Karl Grune's canonical film *Die Strasse* ('The Street,' 1923) and also contains scenes in which the space of the city street is dissolved through trick effects. *Die Strasse* has been widely credited with inventing many of the conventions of the 'street film,' establishing the figure of the (female) sex worker as transgressing the threshold between the public and private spheres. In the film, a simplistic binary is established between the interior domestic space and the threatening public street. The male protagonist is lured into the street by the attractive force of electric light and the allure of the transgressive woman, but soon finds himself faced with mortal danger, and subsequently retreats to the domestic sphere where his wife and safety await. Grune's film differs from *Fräulein Raffke* in its cautionary view of urban modernity, which associates the allure of the sex worker in the street with the breakdown of domesticated normative life, and thus allegorizes the alienating environment of the modern city. *Die Strasse* has often functioned synecdochally for the entirety of Weimar cinema's representation of the emergence of women into the public sphere, and the 'threat' of female sexuality to male identity. Yet this well-worn narrative of the Weimar era should be questioned in terms of its potential reification of the rules of gender division, 'kinship systems,' and the fraught Oedipal narrative of Weimar cinema espoused by Siegfried Kracauer that was later taken up by Peter Gay in his history of the Weimar period.[59] *Fräulein Raffke* is much more subtle in its associations, and I suggest that its reliance on expressionist devices to portray this effect may also be couched within the larger framework of what I want to establish under the heading of *moments of liquidity*, a concept that combines economic discourse with these visual effects of superimposition and dissolution. These destabilized images stage a new subjectivity in disequilibrium in the field of new financial flows and crises. In short, I am reading this effect, which is usually bundled under the expressionist aesthetic, as historically moored in a social-economic field. This filmic effect relies on the context of financial transaction within *Fräulein Raffke*, and other films, and refers to the formal 'liquefaction' of the image as simultaneous with plot developments that hinge upon the transitional state of insecurity brought on by significant financial transactions, or, in this case, the forging of just such an exchange.

In financial terms, the property of 'liquidity' refers to the degree of ease by which a commodity, asset, or security can be bought or sold. It thus contains within it the connotation of speed, that is, how rapidly an item can be sold, or brought to market, or the degree of possibility that ownership or the identity

59 See Peter Gay, *Weimar Culture: The Outsider as Insider* (New York: W.W. Norton, 2001).

of an item might shift. Significantly, real estate is the example most often employed as a counterpoint to the idea of liquidity, as it is usually defined as an 'illiquid' asset that requires the 'friction' of a lengthy process to buy and sell and, not coincidentally, is imbued with a high degree of use value in the Marxian sense. Thus, the concept of liquidity also has a spatial dimension, as well as strong implications for the geography of the modern city. The central tensions of modern development, be they wholesale capitalist land transference, as in the case of Haussmann's Paris, or the creep of urban gentrification that ignites so much debate in the twenty-first century, revolve around the varying degree to which individuals can consider their place of habitation to be permanent – in the Heideggerian sense of 'dwelling' – or how domestic space can be considered 'liquid,' transferable, and ultimately destructible, in order to make way for further profit-generating permutations within the terrain of the city. This process also directly disrupts the arrangement of domestic space, and thus, categories of gendered activity tied to the public and private realms. In the case of *Die Austernprinzessin*, *Fräulein Raffke* and, as we shall also see in *Die freudlose Gasse* (1925), key plot crisis points are driven by the pressure of finance capital, as it impedes on established categories of gender and public and private space. Far from being abstracted in these films, however, the effect of this pressure is embodied in the figure of women who stand at the threshold between agency and objectification – often in liminal roles that establish women as extensions of a medium of exchange.

The Role of Finance and Speculation in *Die freudlose Gasse*

With a subtle touch that transcends the often-aphoristic plot points of the aforementioned films, G. W. Pabst's *Die freudlose Gasse* brings the abstract, international forces of finance capital into the streets of interwar Vienna, thus personalizing financial crisis in a manner not seen before in German-language cinema. The film foregrounds the sexual and financial economy of a cross-section of the population of Vienna, played out in the public and private spaces of the city through the exchange of money, meat, and human flesh. Almost all of the female characters of *Die freudlose Gasse* are faced with the dilemma of turning in desperation to prostitution in order to survive and women's sexuality is seen as dangerous and excessive in the film, resulting in the murder of both Lia Leid and the loathsome butcher Josef Geiringer at the hands of women. This fraught depiction of female sexuality is in keeping with representations of women's uncontrolled desires, in ways that were linked to social disorder and male anxiety in the shifting gender roles of the time. In many Weimar films, excessive female sexuality is thus either tamed through a recuperation into a traditional familial role or punished through violent murder (as in the case of Lulu in *Die Büchse der Pandora* ('Pandora's Box,' 1929).[60]

Die freudlose Gasse, like *Die Strasse*, is also part of the cynical tradition of the *Aufklärungsfilme* of Richard Oswald and others, such as *Die Prostitution* ('Prostitution,' 1919), which were ostensibly intended to 'warn young women about pimps and prostitution but in reality were vehicles for depicting sexual violence and bondage.'[61] What is less well understood about *Die freudlose Gasse*, however, is how central financial themes are to the plot and how the film conflates financial and sexual exchanges in the figure of the prostitute. Here, the film will be discussed in terms of the importance of financial speculation to its plot as well as its creation of an allegory of the economy that depicts women as a medium of exchange.

Set in Vienna of 1921, but shot in Berlin, *Die freudlose Gasse* is widely considered a masterwork of Weimar cinema. This is all the more remarkable given that until only recently, available versions of the film were cobbled together from limited and heavily censored material. Although it is still definitive, the version restored by the Munich Filmmuseum, and released as a DVD in 2009, will be referenced here since it is a vast improvement on previous versions in terms of its completeness.[62] In this edition, the

60 See Tatar, *Lustmord*.

61 Peter Jelavich, quoted in Jill Suzanne Smith, "Richard Oswald and the Social Hygiene Film: Promoting Public Health or Promiscuity?," in *The Many Faces of Weimar Cinema: Rediscovering Germany's Filmic Legacy*, ed. Christian Rogowski (Rochester, NY: Camden House, 2010), 14.

62 This is still by no means a definitive version as it is estimated that 700 metres of film are still missing from Pabst's original cut. According to Stefan Drössler: 'The surviving script of the film is so extensive that Pabst kept deviating from it, eliminating, combining, or rearranging many scenes. Thus, it is as unreliable as the film's foreign versions, which all fall short of the film's documented original release length.' The first reconstruction of the film was completed in 1989, a second in 1998, and this third version was completed in 2009 for the Filmmuseum Munchen DVD edition. See Stefan Drössler, "The Restoration," in *31st Pordenone Silent Film Festival Catalogue*, ed. Catherine A. Surowiec (Gemona: La Cineteca del Friuli, 2012), 120. "Edition Filmmuseum Shop – Die Freudlose Gasse Edition Filmmuseum 48," http://www.edition-filmmuseum.com/product_info.php/language/en/info/p81_die-freudlose-gasse.html. For further discussion of the history of the censorship of certain scenes of the film, and of versions of the film that have appeared over the years, see Sarah Hall, "Gender, Space, and Economics in G. W. Pabst's *The Joyless Street* (1925)," in *Weimar Cinema: An Essential Guide to Classic Films of the Era*, ed. Noah William Isenberg, (New York: Columbia University Press, 2009), 150; Patrice Petro, "Film Censorship and the Female Spectator: The Joyless Street (1925)," *The Films of G.W. Pabst: An Extraterritorial Cinema*, ed. Eric Rentschler (New Brunswick: Rutgers University Press, 1990). I was fortunate enough to see the most definitive of the various restorations in the form of an archival 35mm print at *Le Giornate del Cinema Muto* film festival, Pordenone, 2012.

centrality to the plot of the financial magnate Don Alfonso Canez as well as the speculator Egon Stirner, is much clearer. Pabst's film differs from the source material of Hugo Bettaur's novel, particularly in Pabst's addition of the speculator Canez and other financial themes.[63]

In versions of *Die freudlose Gasse* previous to the 2009 restoration, Grete Rumfort's actions, and those of the other main female characters, were presented primarily as reactions to two of the male villains in the film – the butcher Josef Geiringer and her boss Trebitsch, who fires her for resisting his sexual advances in his office. The role of Canez was significantly downplayed and the scene that introduces him in a nightclub was highly truncated in earlier versions. In this recent restoration, the role of the foreign speculator Canez becomes more apparent, and he is revealed to be a much more important character. In versions previous to the 2009 restoration, the club scene where Canez is introduced opens with the introduction of Stirner as a character. In the 2009 restoration, Canez is introduced after the iconic scenes of the line-up outside the butcher shop with the intertitle: 'Meanwhile in another section of the city, in the Hotel Carlton. Don Alfonso Canez from Valparaiso checks in with 10,000 dollars in his pocket and the intention of making half a million in three weeks.' The lengthy nightclub sequence that follows shows Canez meeting Mr. Rosenow, general director of the Central European Bank. This sequence also introduces several other key characters of the film, such as Lia Leid and Regina Rosenow, while showing their connection to Egon Stirner and Canez.

During their meeting, Rosenow proposes to Canez that since 'Vienna is cold and needs coal,' they should buy shares in the Petrowitz mine, but not before they launch rumours of a strike that will lower the stock price. After buying the stocks low, their plan is to then reveal that there is no strike and 'sell and earn half a million in gold.' The film is set in 1921, at a time when Vienna was experiencing hyperinflation and drastic shortages in coal that directly affected its population, adding a level of historical realism to this scene.[64] This financial deception is also an original addition by Pabst and distils the complexities of the business interactions in the novel into this one transaction. His creation of Canez serves the purpose of simplifying the financial swindle and presenting it as the machination of a clear-cut villain.

63 For a comprehensive and current overview of the relationship between the various editions of the film and the original novel see Alexandra Seibel, "Vienna, Girls, and Jewish Authorship: Topographies of a Cinematic City, 1920–40" (PhD diss., New York University, 2008).
64 See Rudolf Kloss, "The Coal Supply of Austria after the Revolution of 1918," *Annals of the American Academy of Political and Social Science* 98 (November 1, 1921): 16–19.

By choosing coal, a shortage of which would have dire consequences in a Vienna winter, Pabst raises the stakes of the financial deception. To Canez and Rosenow, coal has no use value, and is nothing more than a commodity on the exchange, the price of which can be easily manipulated regardless of the consequences. Pabst drives this distinction home just prior to the scene of the meeting in the Hotel Carlton. In the hotel lobby, on his way to meet the bank director Rosenow, Canez is approached by two men, one of whom holds architectural plans and the other a rendering of what appears to be a large house or hotel. These men are clearly looking for an investor but Canez, living up to the stereotypical depiction of the parasitic speculator, or *Raffke*, is much more interested in the get-rich-quick swindle with Rosenow than in the construction of a building with a specific use value or the purchasing of an illiquid asset.

After the market manipulation is agreed upon, Egon Stirner, private secretary to Rosenow, arrives at the hotel and learns of the plan. In the next scenes, which were restored for the 2009 version, Stirner, a middle-class social climber and white-collar worker, is revealed to be romantically involved with Rosenow's daughter, Regina. While dancing, they disappear to another room to talk. Regina Rosenow suspects that Stirner is interested in her solely because of her wealth and tells him that the only way to convince her otherwise would be for him to 'become as rich as she is' and that she 'doesn't care what he has to do to achieve it.'[65] Stirner confesses his love for her but shortly after is shown in the same room embracing Lia, the wife of Dr. Leid, who asks him to go in disguise to a dangerous part of town to make love 'where there are real whores and apaches.'[66]

It seems clear from the 2009 restoration that Stirner's actions are also more central to the plot of the film than has been previously noted. For example, Stirner is involved with at least three women in the film – most significantly, with Marie Lechner (played by Asta Nielsen) who also lives in the same building as Grete Rumfort. Lechner's proletarian background, and deeper level of poverty, is introduced early in the film through domestic scenes that depict her father as a drunk and their house in a shambles. In comparison, Rumfort is the daughter of a civil servant fallen on hard times because of the hyperinflation, and her family is depicted as adhering to a code of honour that (presumably) befits their

65 Intertitle: 'Ja, Sie müssen ebenso reich werden wie ich – oder ich ebenso arm wie Sie. Dann könnte ich Ihnen glauben!' and 'Wie Sie das Geld verdienen, das ist mir völlig gleichgültig.'

66 Intertitle: 'Nein, nicht hier, Egon ... Ich möchte lieber in einem finsteren, gefährlichen Haus, wo es richtige Dirnen und Apachen gibt...'

social rank. This could be interpreted as the key difference that drives Lechner to prostitution, while Rumfort only comes close. However, a much more direct motivation for Lechner's actions is revealed in the side plot of Egon Stirner and his involvement with Canez's plans. In a restored scene that takes place after the market-cornering scheme is introduced, Lechner is shown entering Stirner's apartment and confessing her love for him, saying that she will do anything to make him happy. He replies that '[t]hese days money is all one needs to be happy!' and reveals that if he had $100, he could earn $1,000 in a few days.[67] She replies: 'If that makes you happy, I'll get the $100!' In this restored version, Stirner, and by extension Canez, are much more central to the plot, and Lechner's involvement with Canez becomes clearer, as she attempts to sell him her body to bring the promised money to Stirner. This is one of the clearest equations that the film makes between women's bodies and financial currency, as Lechner's body becomes the very currency through which Stirner speculates on the stock exchange.

Lechner's offering of her body for Stirner's benefit is abruptly revealed to have been a mistake that leads to her own downfall. After she witnesses Stirner with Lia Leid in an adjoining room of the Melchiorgasse brothel, she herself murders Leid in a fit of rage – a crime which both Stirner and Canez are then accused of perpetrating. Stirner is apprehended in the interstice and Regina Rosenow immediately jumps to the conclusion that her directive to become rich by any means necessary has been taken too far (by Stirner).[68] Lechner eventually confesses and Stirner is released; Canez having been already set free due to 'diplomatic immunity.' At this point, it is revealed that Lechner's prostitution to Canez was redundant, as it turns out that Stirner also asked Lia Leid to let him sell her jewellery in order to buy into the Canez/Rosenow scam. This both nullifies the purpose for Lechner to resort to prostitution in the first place and reveals Stirner's duplicity – he effectively hedges his risk through his manipulation of both women in order to speculate with their money.

In both the restoration and previous versions of the film, the Canez/Rosenow swindle causes Grete Rumfort's father to lose his life's savings – thus driving Grete to despair and almost to prostitution in her search

67 Intertitle: 'Also siehst du, zum Beispiel: Wenn ich morgen 100 Dollar hätte, so könnte ich an der Börse damit bestimmt 500 verdienen – und übermorgen 1.000...'

68 She is one of the first to suspect Stirner, stating: 'Sie haben Lia Leid ermordet und beraubt, um einen Börsencoup zu machen und reich zu werden.' (trans. 'You've murdered and robbed Lia Leid to pull off your stock exchange scheme and become rich.') *Die freudlose Gasse*, intertitle.

for food and money. Her father, *Hofrat* Rumfort,[69] is a civil servant who receives word that his position is being dissolved and that he will receive a severance payment in the form of a lump sum of cash. An amateur investor himself, he decides to gamble his severance pay-out on the stock market. Through his rapt attention to the newspaper early in the film, the elder Rumfort learns of the (false) rumours of a strike at the Petrowitz mine, and he brings his money to his broker on the rational assumption that the shares will fall. After bringing home luxurious foodstuffs to his starving family, he tells Grete the reason for his presumed impending windfall in terms that are more sophisticated than most plot points based on stock market speculation at this time. He exclaims that 'the newspaper has reported that the Petrowitz shares have fallen sharply again' and that 'that means we're rich!' because he 'speculated *à la baisse*!'[70] Pabst could easily have used a more straightforward plot device here and simply tied Rumfort's financial losses to the later fall in stock prices, an arguably more understandable development. Previous censored versions of the film do in fact simplify this financial transaction to make it appear that he assumed that he was about to profit from the increase in the stock price, rather than from its fall. But instead, the use of this French technical investing term in the intertitle indicates not only that Rumfort himself is a sophisticated enough investor to understand what 'short selling' is – a much riskier manoeuvre than buying shares – but that the audience is presumed to be as well. This speaks to a level of financial literacy that is accurate to 1921, the year the film was set, when Vienna was also in the grip of a speculative fever.[71] It also speaks to the financial literacy of the Weimar Republic audience of 1925. The financial sophistication of the plot is further underlined when Rumfort's broker calls him and tells him that he must 'cover'[72] the losses, as the term 'cover' refers to the fact that the losses from a miscalculated short sale can exceed the total amount invested, and theoretically have no limit. Not only is Rumfort jobless and penniless, but he now owes the broker more than his initial investment. From the 2009 restoration, it becomes apparent that the plot of *Die freudlose Gasse* is directly driven by the financial actions of its characters, and Canez in

69 The designation *Hofrat* signifies his former career as a respectable bureaucrat.

70 *Die freudlose Gasse*, intertitle: 'Die Zeitung vermeldet daß die Petrowitz-Aktien wieder bedeutend gefallen sind … Das heißt, daß wir reiche Leute sind! Ich habe à la baisse spekuliert!'

71 Sylvia Nasar, *Grand Pursuit: The Story of Economic Genius* (New York: Simon and Schuster, 2011), 267.

72 Intertitle: 'Die Petrowitz-Aktien sind um mehr als 100 Prozent gestiegen. Du wirst decken müssen. Ich selbst bin so gut wie ruiniert…'

particular. While most of the characters are already in a state of poverty at the beginning of the film, it is the speculation of Canez and Rosenow that is the engine of the plot and catalyst for crisis in the film, and it is this speculation that creates narrative tension and drives characters over the edge.

Property and Prostitution in *Die freudlose Gasse*

The 2009 restoration of the film paints a much bleaker picture than previous cuts and is much clearer as a damning critique of speculation and finance capital. It suggests that both Grete Rumfort and Marie Lechner's fates are dictated by speculation and that the only factor that redeems Rumfort is her class position. The concrete reason Grete does not need to immediately resort to prostitution is that, right after she and her father both lose their jobs, she proposes they rent out one of their rooms to Davy, an American Red Cross officer. Thus, the economic management of the home comes into play, as well as the Rumforts's ability to leverage their own property. The importance of their property is visualized in a scene in which Davy's companion breaks a pane of glass in the window of their flat. After this literal gesture of insecurity and breach of the home, Grete leaves to call a glazier. But at this very moment the financial security of the house is once again placed in jeopardy when Grete's father terminates Davy's tenancy after learning that Davy has (rightly) accused one of his family members of stealing canned food. In a significant expressionist flourish, a ghostly apparition approaches Grete from the direction of the broken window, and she registers a horrified look. A defocused figure is superimposed over the wall and window of the apartment, and approaches the camera until he is so close that a massive superimposition of his outstretched, demanding hand fills the frame (Figure 9). It turns out to be the glazier, not physically threatening Grete, but politely requesting payment for the repair of the window. Nevertheless, the film here visualizes how the spectral realm of finance threatens the very security of the home. This shot is another example of a moment of liquidity, for both Grete and the spectator, in the way it binds the liquefaction of the film frame and its staging of unstable subjectivity with the disruptive power of financial transaction and exchange. Even the relative stability afforded by property ownership is dependent on the foreign buying power of Davy's American dollars.

As Sarah Hall has argued of *Die freudlose Gasse*, both 'geography and real estate figure in the formation of identity and morality of the society being

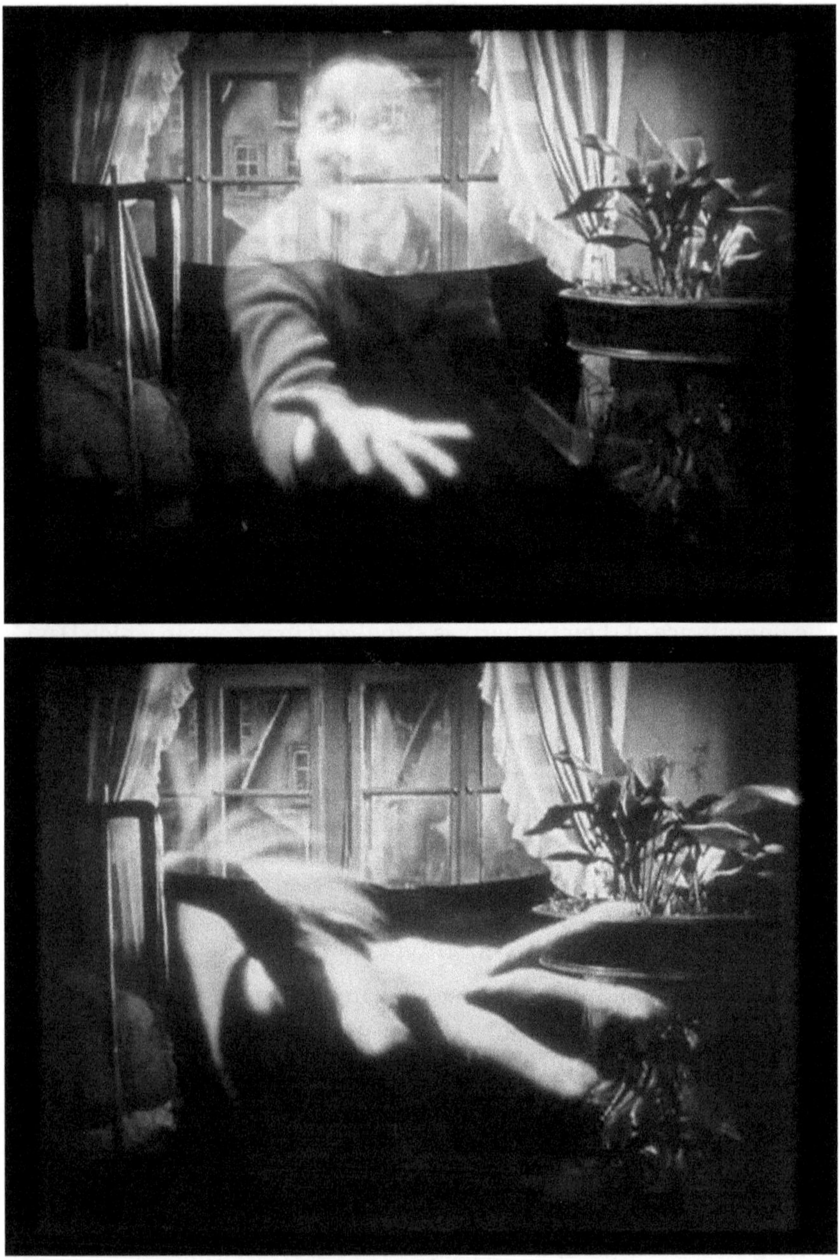

Figure 9. A spectral figure encroaches on the domestic space in *Die freudlose Gasse* (G. W. Pabst, 1925). Copyright: Filmmuseum München.

depicted.'[73] Hall sees the film's depiction of space as key to understanding how gender and the economy are intertwined in the film:

> Like the other Weimar street films, [*Die freudlose Gasse*] served as a space of projection and negotiation for a range of truly modern fantasies and nightmares about life beyond the four walls of a home. What distinguishes it from them is how it prompts us to think about the relationship between space, vision, power, and the economy, especially in as far as all four involve gender.[74]

Unlike other so called 'street films,' such as Karl Grune's *Die Strasse* (1923) and Bruno Rahn's *Dirnentragödie* ('Tragedy of the Street,' 1927), *Die freudlose Gasse* does not limit danger to what lies physically beyond the domestic sphere, but rather allows it to permeate the film in unseen and non-corporeal ways, and to disrupt both the public spaces and the private dwellings of the city.[75] The centrality of the stock swindle as a plot motivator structures *Die freudlose Gasse* according to a financialized spatial logic. For the female inhabitants of the Melchiorgasse, the physical boundary between the domestic and public spheres is effectively effaced, since they have no reasonable expectation of privacy. Places of work, businesses such as the butcher shop, and even the street itself, are compromised by men's expectations that sexual acts, linked specifically to financial exchange, could occur at any place and time. The constantly looming presence of prostitution, as a business transaction, threatens to erase any vestiges of privacy for women. Additionally, while male characters are responsible for driving the narrative crisis in the film, women usually occupy a reactive role, and are ultimately tasked with re-establishing the order of the family unit. This distribution of functions can be seen in the overt examples of Marie Lechner's abusive father, as well as the control that Geiringer the butcher wields, but it is also at the core of the financial subplots. Canez and Rosenow are responsible at the most abstract level for the stock swindle, while Stirner and the elderly Rumfort create the concrete need for money through their

73 Hall, "Inflation and Devaluation,"143.

74 Ibid., 153.

75 Bruce Murray characterizes these 'street films,' or *Aufklärungsfilme* as 'affirming patriarchal concepts of the family and sexuality,' but also points out that 'conservative religious and political organizations had argued that they tempted more than they deterred.' Bruce Arthur Murray, *Film and the German Left in the Weimar Republic: From Caligari to Kuhle Wampe* (Austin: University of Texas Press, 1990), 81–82.

attempts at speculation. In each case, it falls to women to cover the costs of their endeavours as well as protect their domestic property.

Die freudlose Gasse inherits its critique of the conflation of sexuality and economic exchange from Hugo Bettauer's original novel (*Die freudlose Gasse*, published in 1924). Bettauer used the novel to explore ideas that he had developed in his magazine *Er und Sie*: *Wochenschrift für Lebenskultur und Erotik* ('He and She: Weekly Magazine for Lifestyle and Eroticism'), which advocated for liberal sexual reform. The film's revelation of the 'relationships between economics and marriage and sex reform' were key to its appeal amongst women, as well as to why it was received as so controversial by critics and censors.[76] As Sabine Hake has argued, the film can be read in terms of its portrayal of women's agency and in the context of other melodramas that offered 'a point of identification for female audiences searching for figures on which to project their own desire for freedom from patriarchal domination.'[77] Similarly, Patrice Petro claims that melodramas simultaneously displayed not only a 'projection of male anxieties and fears,' but also women's own 'dissatisfactions with traditionally defined gender roles and their desire for a transformation of those roles.'[78] Petro's groundbreaking reading of the film informs the analysis undertaken here but, as Jan-Christopher Horak points out, it was based on the highly censored and truncated version that was available at the time.[79]

In the 2009 restoration of the film, it becomes clear that the order of events promotes an alternative understanding of the role of female agency in the film, especially given the radically different conclusion of the restored edit.[80] Contrary to previous edits of the film – which concluded as a classically complete narrative in the romantic pairing of Davy and Grete – this more definitive version ends with a scene in which the building containing the brothel is attacked by an angry mob, and burns as a result. Just prior to this, Else, who has returned from murdering the butcher Geiringer, and her lover

76 Hall, "Inflation and Devaluation," 152.

77 Sabine Hake, "Who Gets the Last Laugh?," in *Weimar Cinema: An Essential Guide to Classic Films of the Era*, ed. Noah Isenberg (New York: Columbia University Press, 2009), 124.

78 Petro, *Joyless*, 34–36.

79 See Jan-Christopher Horak, "Film History and Film Preservation: Reconstructing the Text of The Joyless Street (1925)," *Screening the Past*, no. 5 (1998).

80 Petro identifies the version of the film she worked with in the following passage: 'Following the theatrical resolution of Grete's story, there is a cut to an angry crowd of women who gather outside the brothel. At first, the appearance of this crowd seems somewhat confusing; not only does the women's anger at Frau Greifer seem narratively unmotivated, but they are also cast as anonymous, symbolic extras.' Petro, *Joyless*, 212. In the current restoration, it is clear that the angry mob is reacting to the murder of Geiringer and is pursuing the culprit, Else, to the brothel.

are trapped in their attic apartment but manage to lower their baby to the waiting crowd before dying in the blaze. This new version of the film thus downplays the romantic resolution focused on Grete that Petro describes, making it something of a false ending.

Die freudlose Gasse is widely understood to be a damning condemnation of the effects of economic hardship on the morality of a society. As Bernd Widdig has argued, the film depicts the circumstances under which women became 'commodified' through prostitution during the inflation period.[81] This was of course a common theme in Weimar cinema, in such films such as *Dirnentragödie* (1927), and Joe May's *Asphalt* (1929), amongst others. Perhaps the most frank and cynical mobilization of this theme was in Gustav Ucicky's *Café Elektric: Die Liebesbörse* ('Café Electric: The Love Exchange,' 1927), released in the same year that prostitution was decriminalized in Germany. The film stars Marlene Dietrich as a rich daughter of a construction magnate who falls for a cynical con-artist and pickpocket. It revolves around the titular night spot, in which incredibly frank sexual interactions are reducible to a form of monetary exchange.

Depicting the ills of prostitution was a convenient method of representing the breakdown of socio-economic forces by projecting them onto the bodies of women as 'commodities.' However, I would like to focus on the specific relationship between the figure of the prostitute and the gendering of financial markets in Weimar cinema. As Susan Buck-Morss notes, drawing on Walter Benjamin's reading of Baudelaire on prostitution, the prostitute is a 'dialectical image, she is the "seller and commodity in one."'[82] Further, Buck-Morss points out that Marx suggested that 'if the whore is a commodity and seller in one, so of course, are all wage-labourers under capitalism.'[83] This abstracted idea of prostitution is central to many critiques of exploitation under capitalism. As David Graeber has argued, drawing on the work of Gerda Lerner, the history of prostitution has paralleled the development of market economies and leveraged debt since antiquity. As an example, Graeber points out that even though the laws of ancient Mesopotamia defined marriage as an act of 'taking possession' of a woman – for an amount explicitly defined as the 'price of a virgin' – it forbade a husband from selling his wife or a member of his family. At the same time, it was common practice

81 For further discussion of this conflation, particularly as it pertains to the effects of inflation, see the chapter 'Gender and Inflation' in Bernd Widdig, *Culture and Inflation in Weimar Germany* (University of California Press, 2001).

82 Quoted in Seibel, "Vienna," 201–2.

83 Susan Buck-Morss, "The Flaneur, the Sandwichman and the Whore: The Politics of Loitering," *New German Critique*, no. 39 (October 1, 1986): 121.

for a man seeking a loan to use family members 'as surety, and if he was unable to pay, they could be taken away as debt pawns in exactly the same way that he could lose his slaves, sheep and goats.'[84] Thus, the introduction of the idea of debt served as the catalyst for overcoming the selling of family as property or into bondage and prostitution. With this example in mind, *Die freudlose Gasse* is deeply archaic in terms of its portrayal of the nexus of debt, financial exchange, and prostitution – it is Grete's father's debt that makes her turn to prostitution as a last resort. As Gerda Lerner has argued, the development of commercial prostitution in antiquity as a profession, and its separation from sacred ritual, was essential to the establishment of categories of 'respectability' for women.[85] Accordingly, the film relies heavily on this archaic separation of a 'respectable' woman (Grete Rumfort) from her 'non-respectable' counterpart (Marie Lechner) along these very lines.

The film's conflation of financial exchange with the figure of the woman can also be read according to biblical depictions of the city as a place of commerce and decadence, and by extension the market itself, as feminine. Fritz Lang's *Metropolis* (1927) made this comparison explicit in its use of a passage from the Book of Revelation during the famous scene that features Brigitte Helm as ersatz Maria dancing in the 'Yoshiwara' nightclub. In that scene, her frantic dancing is intercut with a rapid montage of leering men and their disembodied eyes. A page of text from the Bible appears on screen, describing Maria as '*Die grosse Babylon*' – the 'mother of prostitutes' and personification of the great capital city and birthplace of civilization. In *Metropolis*, as in the Bible, the ills of financial exchange and civilization are projected onto the body of the 'dishonourable' woman. This comparison was also made by D. W. Griffith in his use of biblical imagery and a depiction of Babylon as a critique of capitalism in *Intolerance* (1916). Griffith went so far as to re-enact Edwin Long's 1875 painting *The Babylonian Marriage Market* for scenes in which 'prostitution provided a metaphor in which the mysteries of sexuality and those of the marketplace converged – the commodity form become flesh and blood.'[86] The biblical figure of the city as the grotesque whore sitting on both 'seven hills' and 'the water' (an image that describes a commercial port) has long served as a useful foil for 'patriarchal hatred of the city.'[87] In a similar sense, prostitution and the brothel in *Die freudlose*

84 David Graeber, *Debt: The First 5,000 Years* (Brooklyn; London: Melville House, 2014), 180.

85 Gerda Lerner, "The Origin of Prostitution in Ancient Mesopotamia," *Signs: Journal of Women in Culture and Society* 11, no. 2 (January 1986): 236–54.

86 Miriam Hansen, *Babel and Babylon: Spectatorship in American Silent Film* (Cambridge: Harvard University Press, 1994), 229.

87 Graeber, *Debt*, 183.

Gasse serve as a surrogate for the nexus of finance capital and the spaces of exchange and commerce in the modern city. Out of this, an allegory of the economy emerges in the film that is highly elucidating of the popular perception of finance capital at this time.

The Allegory of Economy in *Die freudlose Gasse*

As Sara Hall has argued, specific characters in *Die freudlose Gasse* stand in for aspects of the inflation-era economy.[88] A contemporary review by Heinz Michaelis in *Film-Kurier* confirms that individual characters in the film could be understood at the time to embody key ideas.[89] The butcher Geiringer controls the real foodstuffs that retain use value outside of the shifting symbolic value of money, and is thus representative of the goods-rich farmers in the economy following the First World War. Michaelis equates Geiringer with the desperate period itself that, like 'Moloch,' devours 'everything that is too weak to resist it.'[90] Canez represents the influx of foreign speculators, rich in dollars and ready to take advantage of the volatile economic situation. Grete's father, *Hofrat* Rumfort, stands at the other end of the economic reshuffling that followed the war. Like many civil servants, his previously respectable pension would have been ravaged by the inflation and though he retains the trappings of the upper middle class, he is close to impoverishment.

Grete Rumfort is the only woman who thrives (in a limited sense of the term) by the end of the film, but she too succumbs to the forces of financial speculation and nearly turns to prostitution, after her father speculates and loses all of his savings. The mechanism that almost draws her into the employ of Frau Greifer's brothel is the fur coat that she buys from her after learning of her father's presumed gain on the stock market. The coat comes to play a key role in the reestablishment of her security in the film when her husband-to-be rescues her from an uncertain fate in the brothel. Grete, having finally succumbed to Greifer's pressure to work for her in the brothel, is found by Officer Davy wearing only a revealing undergarment. Whereas the transition of the other female characters into prostitution is more or less certain, the bourgeois Grete is an exception – and this is made clear in this

88 Hall, "Inflation and Devaluation," 142.

89 'Das Individuum wird zum Typ, der Typ zur Manifestation der Idee.' ('The individual becomes a stereotype, the stereotype a manifestation of an idea.') Heinz Michaelis, "Die freudlose Gasse: Uraufführung in Mozartsaal," *Film-Kurier*, May 19, 1925.

90 Ibid.

highly problematic scene. After she is nearly sexually assaulted by the head waiter of the brothel, Davy finds Grete in the brothel (which, hypocritically, he is patronizing) and flies into a rage at the revelation that she is apparently a prostitute. Notably, he exclaims that he has already given her money for the rent, and violently throws more money at her. It is only after the same waiter pleads with Davy to give Grete another chance, by revealing that '*sie ist unschuldig!*' ('she is innocent,' a turn of phrase that also implies 'she is a virgin') that Davy has a change of heart. In this pivotal scene, Grete's father also joins in the rescue of his daughter. In a sense, Grete is here allowed her speculative gesture of purchasing the glamorous luxury item of the coat, as it pays off in her procurement of a suitable suitor. Davy embraces Grete while draping her near-naked body in the fur coat. As they leave, the assault on the brothel by the residents of the Melchiorgasse begins, and a hastily discarded cigarette causes the fire that will burn it to the ground.

Officer Davy is another Pabst invention and is not present in the Bettauer novel. His presence, as a representative of the Red Cross, is a transparent allegory for the influence of Anglo-American financial and political power following the First World War, and in particular of the Dawes Plan that had only recently been implemented before the film was made. He insists on overpaying for his room in the Rumforts's flat, transacts his business in dollars, and feeds Grete's family with canned goods – the quintessential example of American commodities. Davy is overtly aligned with the patriarchal rescue of Grete, but at a formal level he also functions to smooth over the rupture between the public and private realms in the film. The brothel, on the other hand, functions as the space in which the inherent tensions between the private and public realms are completely revealed. Further, the brothel is the space in the film in which the members of the upper and lower classes, juxtaposed in the many parallel montages of the film, ultimately collide.[91] When Davy, in the midst of his rage at discovering Grete, opens the wrong door, he is confronted with a scene that breaks down any remaining barriers between the established private and public roles of women in the film – that of mother and prostitute – when he discovers Else and her partner nursing a baby. As Alexandra Seibel notes, in this scene, 'the traditional model of femininity which neatly separates the role of woman as either mother or whore, either confined to the realm of the domestic or to the domain of the street, is fundamentally eroded.'[92]

91 Seibel, "Vienna," 194.

92 Ibid., 224–25.

It is significant that Grete's happy ending and coupling with Davy – which was edited as the final scene in earlier censored versions – takes place with the couple framed by the very window that had been previously featured in the expressionist trick shot that signified the threat of financial ruin. It is difficult to determine how to read this overly saccharine ending to Grete's story, as so much of the rest of the film is infused with a knowing cynicism and a constant undercutting of the expectation that any character might act on a motivation other than self-interest. Keeping to an allegorical reading, I would suggest that the only saving grace for the residents of the Melchiorgasse is the influence of foreign money, and an element of chance. It might also be suggested, given the hyperbolic chivalry of Davy's character in comparison to the others, that his role as saviour and protector be taken with a grain of salt. It is certainly feasible that the film shows how Grete is now 'subordinated under the patriarchal order of her husband and provider,'[93] or that she has undergone the ultimate form of commodification, succumbing to the financial advantage of the American and becoming a possession of her husband. Financial exchange is definitely at the heart of this new relationship, and the earlier suggestion that Grete '*ist unschuldig*' carries a third meaning in German of being 'free of debt,' or 'not indebted.' She is thus represented as suitably 'untainted,' in the sexual and financial sense, for marriage and, in the archaic financial logic of the film, Davy has paid the 'bride-price' to release her from debt but also to possess her. In this sense, the disruptive and dissolving force of finance capital that is at times the engine of women's agency, is ultimately solidified along the lines of familiar gender roles. But, as Sara Hall has pointed out, the film's ambiguous depiction of patriarchy challenged the status quo of its time and the frank revelation of the transactional nature of Davy and Grete's relationship can also be read as revealing the of the role of finance and debt in the long history of the subjugation of women. As David Graeber argues, the interchangeability of money, debt, and honour is a central feature of modern society that was instituted by the spread of financial markets and has driven the subjugation of women. That the film makes this gendered logic of capital markets particularly clear is perhaps another reason why it was so heavily censored after its release.

There is one character in the film whose story highlights this in interesting ways through her role as an exception to this logic. Lia Leid, who meets her end at the hands of Marie Lechner, challenges a simple binary construction of active and passive gender roles with relation to both financial exchange

93 Ibid., 225.

and prostitution. While relegated to a minor role in the film, she featured prominently in the novel, in which Lechner's murder of Leid is motivated not only by her discovery of Leid with her lover, but also 'out of (racist) hatred for a woman she already knew from her school days.'[94] Bettauer presents Leid as an 'unsympathetic man-eating, explicitly Jewish female character that would calculably cater to anti-Semitic resentment' as a prototypical Jewish 'femme fatale.'[95] Some background on the complicated nature of Bettauer's relationship to Judaism is helpful here. Bettauer, Jewish by birth, converted to Protestantism over the course of his life. In the novel, he appears to have, like many 'assimilated' Jews in Germany and Austria, projected 'his own antipathy against Eastern Jews onto the body of the modern Jewess'[96] – though it is impossible to know if this was sincere or cynical. Bettauer's popularity as a writer was at least partially reliant on his ability to tap the prevailing anti-Semitism of his time, but his relationship to Austrian Jewry was highly complicated. His best-known work, *Die Stadt ohne Juden* ('The City Without Jews,' 1922), which was adapted to the screen by Gustav Ucicky in 1924, clearly shows the complexity of his various portrayals of Jews. In that film, the virulently anti-Semitic mayor of Vienna (modelled on Karl Lueger, mayor of Vienna, 1897–1910) banishes all Jews from the city, because he deems their influence to be corrupting. However, the city soon grinds to a halt, as many of its most prominent businessmen, politicians, bankers, and other members of established society are forced to cease their daily activities. The film is thus a piercing and chilling indictment of anti-Jewish sentiment. Bettauer himself was shot by a young National Socialist vigilante, and lay on his deathbed during the filming of Pabst's film.[97] His murderer's motive had as much to do with Bettauer's Jewish identity as with his sexual progressiveness and championing of sexual emancipation in his erotic weekly magazine, *Er und Sie*.[98]

Lia Leid maintains a key characteristic in the film that also appears in the novel, in that she is the only woman who inverts the gender roles of prostitution. When she and Stirner plan their erotic role-play on the Melchiorgasse, it becomes clear that she, in fact, 'pays' Stirner to accompany her by giving him her jewels in order to fund his stock market manoeuvre. This transaction is even foreshadowed in their first scene together, in which Stirner, seated

94 Ibid., 240.

95 Ibid., 242.

96 Ibid., 243.

97 Ibid., 183.

98 His murderer's wife had apparently consulted Bettauer in 'intimate marital matters.' Seibel, "Vienna," 183.

below Leid, pulls her into an embrace, but only after grabbing and pointedly looking at her pearl necklace. While the anti-Semitic undertone of Bettauer's novel is largely absent from the film, it is significant that Canez's partner in the stock market scheme is the Jewish banker Rosenow. Pabst also visually indicates the Jewish identity of Lia Leid through the casting of Tamara Tolstoi whose 'wild hair and the black makeup around her eyes reinforce her appearance as the exotic, "Eastern" looking woman.'[99] By reversing the sexual power dynamic between her and Stirner encounter, Leid upsets the established codes of bourgeois courtship, a fact that is further driven home by her desire to 'role play' a dangerous liaison with him. By also reversing the direction of the financial transaction, and by providing the capital for Stirner's stock market venture, Leid's actions combine the erotic and financial acts of exchange in a manner that upsets established gender codes of the time.

Leid is an example of the Weimar trope of the vamp and *Luxusweib* ('luxury woman'), or the 'mistress whose sexual permissiveness is mirrored in her excessive forms of consumption,' and who can be interpreted as a 'capitalist, secular version of the pre-capitalist witch.'[100] Further, Leid doubly embodies the threat of both the dissolution of familiar bourgeois marital relations and the inversion of economic and social expectations of masculinity – as a racialized femme fatale figure. Sexual power relationships and exchanges are key to how *Die freudlose Gasse* represents the mechanisms of finance and Leid's eventual murder fits the narrative of the punishment of excessive female (also now Jewish) sexuality in Weimar cinema. As such, she is a transgressive figure, and upsets the traditional gender order. She is also a key figure of rupture within the economic allegory of the film as a female character who coolly engages in speculative activity, combining her sexuality and financial might to control the actions of Stirner. It is ironic that Leid meets her fate at the hands of Lechner, played by Asta Nielsen, for Leid's role as the only true example of the woman as speculator in the film was a type invented and promoted by Nielsen, and portrayed by her in *Die Börsenkönigin* almost a decade earlier.

As mentioned, the brothel is the space in which all levels of Viennese society collide, and in which the inherent injustices of this society come to the fore. As such, its destruction in the end is cheered on by the residents, in

99 Seibel, "Vienna," 248. See also Lisa Silverman, "Der Film ohne Juden: G. W. Pabst's *Die freudlose Gasse* (1925)," in *Rethinking Jewishness in Weimar Cinema*, eds. Barbara Hales and Valerie Weinstein (New York: Berghahn Books, 2020).
100 Widdig, *Inflation*, 211.

a similar fashion to the orgasmic release of the sublimated rage of the masses that takes place in Fritz Lang's *Metropolis*.[101] In *Metropolis*, the destructive force of technological change and modernity is also represented in the form of a demonic woman. The character of ersatz-Maria is a product of arch-capitalist innovation in Lang's futuristic vision – a mechanical worker/robot that threatens to destroy both the workers as well as the corporate elite who created her. In *Die freudlose Gasse*, the brothel is a place of decadence and can also be understood as a reification of abstract market forces in the film. Thus, it is appropriate that, at the conclusion of the film, the rage of the residents of the Melchiorgasse is directed at it rather than at a specific figure such as Canez.

The film provides a space in which to think through an erotics of finance and money itself. The *Kauflust* (desire to buy) described in the aforementioned *UHU* article of 1927 can here be literally be taken as erotic desire itself, and is displayed in the example of Stirner and Leid. Here, the common definition of greed as the love of money subsumes the function of erotic love itself. The brothel becomes a surrogate for the *Börse* and is ultimately burned in impotent effigy, in lieu of real revolutionary confrontation with the institutions of repression which keep the Melchiorgasse down. But the brothel also functions as a heterotopia of the real arrangements of the economy, and in this sense more clearly reveals its structuring logic. The characters of the film, already a cross-section of society, all visit the brothel at some point and in some capacity. The Marxian revelatory aspect of the film's portrayal of Viennese society allows a new form of visualization, that of class-consciousness as a cross-sectional image of society. Heinz Michaelis noted in his contemporary review that 'none of the destinies of these individuals could be separated,' and that the film was an immense success in showing the 'universal in its details,' and revealing the 'macrocosm from within the microcosm.'[102] The film provides a visual structuring logic that facilitates *seeing* this interconnectedness, which had not yet been accomplished so effectively. This tendency will be returned to in chapter 5, in terms of the rise of macroeconomic concepts of the global economy.

101 See Andreas Huyssen, "The Vamp and the Machine," in *After the Great Divide: Modernism, Mass Culture, Postmodernism*, Theories of Representation and Difference (Bloomington: Indiana University Press, 1986), 65–81.

102 Heinz Michaelis, *Film-Kurier*, May 19, 1925.

4. Finance, Liquidity, and the Crisis of Masculinity in Weimar Cinema

Abstract: Chapter 4 addresses depictions of finance and masculinity in Weimar cinema, addressing the many 'moments of liquidity' to be found in key films. Continuing from the previous chapter, it discusses the conflation of women and water in *Berlin: Die Sinfonie der Großstadt* ('Berlin: Symphony of a Great City,' 1927) in order to further develop the conflation of finance, liquidity, and a crisis of gender in *Der letzte Mann* ('The Last Laugh,' 1924) and *L'Argent* ('Money,' 1929). This chapter then turns to Gerhard Lamprecht's film *Hanseaten* (1925) – an important yet unknown film, which has escaped inclusion in the Weimar film canon altogether, and provides a key image of reactionary stabilization to this study.

Keywords: Masculinity, Liquidity, Gender and Finance, Reactionary Modernism, Klaus Theweleit, New Objectivity

The Threat of Dissolution

Introduction

Cultural representations of finance and speculation in the Weimar Republic cannot be separated from questions surrounding the representation of gender. This chapter builds on the preceding chapter by turning to the question of the fraught construction of masculinity under capitalism and the related 'ideal' of a stable industrial capitalism based around the patriarchal family and a fixed notion of national identity. In order to do this, I will begin by fully articulating what I have called 'moments of liquidity' – drawing on Zygmunt Bauman's idea of 'liquid modernity.'[1] I will discuss this aesthetic gesture in

1 See Zygmunt Bauman, *Liquid Modernity* (Malden, MA: Polity Press, 2000).

Lyons, O., *Finance and the World Economy in Weimar Cinema*. Taylor & Francis Group, 2023.
DOI 10.5117/9789463727136_CH04

its clearest articulations, which can be found in F. W. Murnau's *Der letzte Mann* (1924) and Marcel L'Herbier's *L'Argent* (1929). I will also discuss how representations of liquid and water, in films such as Walter Ruttmann's *Berlin die Sinfonie der Großstadt* (1927) and *Die Büchse der Pandora* (1929), invoke the idea of overseas space of international trade and flows of capital. I will then examine the trope of liquidity in its relation to established discourses on the construction of masculinity during the 'period of stability' of the Weimar Republic (1924–29), and in terms of the particular construction of masculinity that emerged in the *Neue Sachlichkeit* ('new objectivity') movement.[2] Finally, I will turn to Gerhard Lamprecht's little-known feature film *Hanseaten* (1925) as an example of a reactionary text that mobilizes a fantasy of patriarchal control as a bulwark against the threat of subjective dissolution that is portrayed in images of liquidity and accelerated capital flow. *Hanseaten* puts forward an image of a national and autarkic economy that rejects the emerging importance of the global market. While this film tries to stabilize categories of masculinity, nation, and productive capital, it ultimately collapses under the weight of its own inherent contradictions but, nonetheless, is highly illustrative of central tensions inherent to the construction of masculinity and the Weimar economic subject.

Liquid and water appear as metaphors for trade and economy, as well as the destructive force of capital on the individual, in a wide range of representations in the 1920s. This metaphorical conflation of flow and dissolution with liquidity works across categories of subjectivity, gender, and national identity. In particular, the crisis of gender in the face of a 'liquid modernity' has a specific contour that can be traced within the fictional productions of the Weimar Republic. The severity of the economic crises of the period resulted in the production of a large number of films that portray the destructive and destabilizing effect of economic forces on individual subjectivity and the performance of masculinity. Within these films, moments occur in which a particular set of aesthetic choices made in the construction of the image are combined in order to render visible the financial undercurrents of the plot. The effect under discussion does not coalesce as a specific formal device, such as parallel montage or the dissolve, but rather occurs as a combination of techniques that liquefy or dissolve the space of the image and of individual characters, usually combined

2 For a discussion of the construction of the threat to masculinity posed by the accelerated crises of modernity, see Klaus Theweleit on the armoured male body in Klaus Theweleit, *Male Fantasies*, vol. 2, *Male Bodies: Psychoanalyzing the White Terror* trans. Stephen Conway, Erica Carter and Chris Turner (Minneapolis: University of Minnesota Press, 1989).

with the added anchoring signifier of a plot development that indicates the intruding force of the money economy as a threat to the individual. Here I will discuss the appearance of this trope in several key films of the Weimar Republic. In so doing, I will unpack the concept of 'liquidity' in its relationship to modernity, finance, and gender and discuss its specific historical resonance at this time.

Mercurial Modernity: Women and Water in *Berlin: Die Sinfonie der Großstadt*

The association of women with modernity is a central trope of Weimar culture. As Patrice Petro writes: 'Berlin also served as the decisive metaphor for modernity. Modernity, in turn, was almost always represented as a woman.'[3] This is clearly illustrated in the climactic narrative set piece at the centre of *Berlin: Die Sinfonie der Großstadt* (1927), which 'builds its investigation of the city's spatial and visual fragmentation around the spectacle of woman' and thus equates the suicide of its unnamed female character with the crisis of modernity itself.[4] Petro supports her argument for the centrality of the modernity-as-woman thesis with reference to the work of Klaus Theweleit's *Männerphantasien* ('Male Fantasies,' 1977):

> [The] remarkable juxtapositioning of women and cities [...] is probably rooted in the historical fact that the entire ancient world built its great cities on rivers and coastlines, because water transport was superior then. The freer forms of commerce among the cities released a certain proportion of women from the most stringent patriarchal relationships and monitoring. As early as the Gospel of St. John, we find Babylon described as 'the whore sitting beside the waters.'[5]

While Petro acknowledges the importance of the history of trade and economy to this association of modernity with women, she moves away from the centrality the centrality of the economy in this image. As discussed in the previous chapter, the association of women, prostitution, and commerce is key to understanding how representations of markets are gendered. In this sense, Ruttmann's use of this imagery deserves closer scrutiny.

3 Patrice Petro, *Joyless Streets: Women and Melodramatic Representation in Weimar Germany* (Princeton, NJ: Princeton University Press, 1989), 41.

4 Ibid., 43.

5 Klaus Theweleit, quoted in Petro, *Joyless*, 39.

Firstly, it is significant to note that the suicide of the woman is directly preceded by the only intertitles of the film, which separate this event from the flow of imagery and imbue it with significance. This set piece begins with scenes depicting the distribution of the *Berliner Zeitung* in the streets followed by a man opening a newspaper. The perspective switches to his view and a broadsheet is shown with a sequence of expanding words superimposed over it that read: '*Krise – Mord – Börse – Heirat – Geld*' ('Crisis – Murder – Stock Market – Marriage – Money'). *Geld* is repeated several times with increasing frequency, followed by a point of view shot from a rollercoaster that is reminiscent in its motion to the rise and fall of a financial chart. The sequence ends with the suicide that marks the midpoint of the film. Significantly, the woman kills herself by jumping into the Landwehr canal – one of the central arteries of commerce of Berlin. In *Sinfonie*, the woman stands as a metaphor for the crisis at the heart of modernity, but the conflation of money and commerce with mortality, her 'dissolution' into the river, and the merging of her body with the liquid body of capital exchange is significant. This sequence can be considered another example of a moment of liquidity that fuses cinematic techniques of dissolution and the liquid itself with thematic elements that make specific reference to the forces of finance and speculation and the mercurial nature of capital.

As discussed in chapter 1, metaphoric associations between women and trade were part of the established imagery and self-representation of financial markets. For example, in Emil Hundrieser's statue of *Weltverkehr* ('world trade') of 1880, which adorned the main hall of Anhalter Bahnhof in Berlin, an angelic female figure with bared breast representing world trade is flanked by two naked youths, one of whom holds a locomotive engine in his arms. This statue also symbolizes the separation of the masculine and feminine spheres in economic metaphors. The youths gaze upward at the angelic figure, holding in their hands the tools of the modern economy. The winged female figure symbolizes movement and flight, and is at the same time sexualized in her semi-nudity, as well as the added resonance of the term *Verkehr* ('trade') itself which, as Todd Samuel Presner points out, can be translated as 'intercourse.'[6] In this respect the phallocentric logic of this arrangement becomes apparent, as the male figures hold the tools of modern trade, and are poised to venture out into the new terrain of the global

6 *Verkehr* can be translated as 'intercourse,' derived from *Geschlechtsverkehr* ('sexual intercourse'). See Todd Samuel Presner, *Mobile Modernity: Germans, Jews, Trains* (New York: Columbia University Press, 2007), 311.

Figure 10. *Kladderadatsch*, September 1923. Caption: 'Die Valuta-Rire: Halb zog sie ihn, halb sank er hin' – Translation: 'The Valuta-Laugh: he was partly pulled and partly sank in.'

market, while the winged female form symbolizes the *medium* of exchange and transportation itself. Other depictions are less subtle in their association of women with currency and water. A cover of the satirical magazine *Kladderadatsch* from 1923 shows a naked female nymph, representing *Valuta* ('foreign currency') with a dollar sign in her hair, emerging from a river to tempt the German everyman 'Deutscher Michel' (Figure 10).

While currency was often represented in female form, mythological representations of the active trader took on the male form of the winged god Merkur ('Mercury' or 'Hermes'). The presence of Merkur, '*der Gott des Handels*' ('the god of trade'), was already a feature of the architectural adornment of the official exchanges, and was taken up in the popular press. He appeared frequently in magazines, and served to combine the association of trade with power over distance with his older association as the messenger of the gods. He is also a boundary-crossing figure who moved freely between the worlds of the mortal and the divine. As a masculine symbol of trade, he suggests the figure of *homo economicus* who is able to navigate the fraught borderlands of venture capital while maintaining a rational disposition in the face of risk and uncertainty. A painting by Adolf Hirémy Hirschl from 1898 evokes the mythical role of Hermes as the mediator between the lands of the living and dead, able to cross over into the dangerous underworld while being immune to its dangers (Figure 11). Significantly, his gaze is fixed on his intended course and he ignores the crowd who pull at him from all sides, and particularly, the woman who is featured in the foreground, begging him to take her back to the world of the living.

In another already mentioned image, the 1921 *Simplicissimus* caricature *Der Welthandel* ('world trade'), Merkur lies wounded on a dock with his left leg amputated (Figure 1). A French and an English officer stand above him and the caption reads: 'Why can't this guy walk anymore? We've only cut off the German leg.' As a characteristically trite image from the satirical magazine *Simplicissimus*, it demonstrates an awareness of Germany's importance in the new global economy, and its 'hobbling' at the hands of the allies after the First World War. This image signifies castration and loss of wholeness that resonates on several levels. The defeated male figure lies on a dock against a backdrop of the seething ocean, while blood streams freely from his wound. This violent image of bodily harm contrasts the figure of Merkur against the ground of the seething water as an image of a threatening, engulfing presence, emphasized by storm clouds in the upper right corner. This depiction of Merkur as the German male body wounded at the hands of its enemies can clearly be read as equating an attack on the economy with an attack on the integrity of the nation itself. Furthermore, the ocean and the blood are rendered in the same magenta/red tone, as if to imply that by compromising his bodily wholeness, the figure of Merkur would give way to the formless power of the open water. In the cartoon example of Merkur, the literal streaming away of his corporeal

Figure 11. *Merkur*, as depicted in: Adolf Hirémy Hirschl, *Souls on the Banks of the Acheron*, 1898. Oil on canvas. From the collection of the Österreichische Galerie Belvedere.

form is associated with the dynamics of international war reparations and geopolitical economic negotiation. It is clear in the culture and imagery surrounding financial markets of this time that there is a delimitation across gendered lines: women are associated with dissolution, water, and capital flows while men are positioned as stabilizing figures who must navigate a course against this threatening backdrop.

Destabilizing Flows and Male Identity

In his deep analysis of the construction of fascist masculinity in the Weimar Republic, Klaus Theweleit discusses the long history of the symbolism of liquid in medicine and psychology. He draws attention to the feeling of 'streaming' and 'flowing away' discussed by Wilhelm Reich in relation to the expansive feeling of sexual desire and orgasm. Theweleit points out that Sigmund Freud, in his own comments on religion in *Civilization and its Discontents*, refers to the 'oceanic' feeling 'of something limitless, unbounded' but, in the end, Freud 'refuses to concede that the ego lacks definite boundaries.'[7] After some consideration, Freud rejects the concept of the 'oceanic feeling.' For Freud, the construction of the mature ego and

7 Sigmund Freud, quoted in ibid., 251–52.

self depends on the rejection of the 'vestigial, infantile feelings of lack of differentiation from the external world' implied in the feeling of 'streaming-away.'[8] But, it is precisely this feeling of unbounded energy and desires that so often appears in representations of finance and speculation, in a mixture of erotic, religious, and transgressive imagery, and 'threshold' experiences – those moments of breaking through a barrier or passing to a new state of being. As discussed in chapter 2, in *Dr. Mabuse*, the act of speculation is linked to a state of frenzy and a succumbing to the dematerialization of the modern market and communications apparatus as a form of intoxication. Mastery is not only a question of rational control, but of being comfortable with occupying this state of flow and of reading and harnessing the hysteria of the crowd, while at the same time succumbing to its movements. Fictional representations of individuals caught up in this flow of money and capital usually render its dangers specifically in terms of a threat to corporeal and subjective wholeness. While Theweleit's argument stems from the specific case of the armoured masculinity of fascism, it extends to the general construction of the 'hard' masculine exterior. A similar assertion of masculinity occurs in the face of the flows of capital and desire that drive financial markets. This is often manifested in an overcompensatory masculinity set against the feminized work of the marketplace, and as a vestige of an older form of 'hard' or 'solid' masculinity connected with physical labour. Zygmunt Bauman sets up a dichotomy between the earlier condition of 'solid,' 'heavy' or 'condensed' industrial modernity, and the 'light,' 'liquid,' 'diffuse' modernity of the late twentieth-century, post-industrial condition. His argument is explicitly economic at its core and is grounded in the context of German socioeconomic literature when he claims that:

> 'melting the solids' meant first and foremost shedding the 'irrelevant' obligations standing in the way of rational calculation of effects; as Max Weber put it, liberating business enterprise from the shackles of the family-household duties and from the dense tissue of ethical obligations; or, as Thomas Carlyle would have it, leaving solely the 'cash nexus' of the many bonds underlying human mutuality and mutual responsibilities.[9]

Bauman and Max Weber's position are already informed by an acknowledgement of gender roles and political implications and, at the very least, suggest the disruptive effect of these conditions on such 'solid' notions as

8 Theweleit, *Male Fantasies*, vol. 1, 251.

9 Bauman, *Liquid Modernity*, 4.

the familial unit. It is important to acknowledge as well that this condition of impermanence is neither universal, nor is it experienced as desirable in the everyday sense. It is also implicitly bound to questions of class and social mobility. For Bauman, it represents a reversal of the long-held idea that the establishment class would desire and promote conditions of permanence and stasis. Instead, under the new order of 'light' and 'liquid' modernity, status and power are defined in terms of mobility and velocity – the act of change itself. In financial terms, it is the power afforded by maintaining a state of 'liquidity,' or of avoiding the problem of having money bound up in an immovable commitment or investment.

To illustrate how mastering this position can be represented as desirable when, for most, it is experienced as undesirable precarity, I would like to turn for a moment to a more contemporary example. The seduction inherent in mastering a position of 'liquidity' is perfectly articulated by the character Gordon Gekko in Oliver Stone's *Wall Street* (1987) when, in the position of the surrogate father figure, he admonishes his protégé Bud Fox:

> Wake up will ya pal? If you're not inside, you're outside, ok? And I'm not talking a $400,000 a year working Wall Street stiff flying first class and being comfortable, I'm talking about *liquid*. Rich enough to have your own jet. Rich enough not to waste time. Fifty, a hundred-million dollars buddy. A player, or nothing.

As a morality play, Stone's film was an utter failure. It has instead lived on in financial circles precisely because of the seductiveness of the character of Gekko and dialogue like this and the famous 'greed is good' speech. In interviews, Michael Douglas complained that after playing the role he was constantly approached by traders who told him 'you're the reason I got into the business' – even though he was the ostensible villain of the film.[10] But Gekko articulates something key here. Fictional figures like Mabuse or Gekko who have ability to withstand the flows of capital – and indeed to thrive – are powerfully seductive as models of an idealized modern form of masculinity. Gekko and Mabuse recognize that the appeal of this power is intimately connected to fantastic mobility (to 'have your own jet') and power over the clock (to 'not waste time'). Bauman writes that 'it is the high and mighty of the day who resent and shun the durable and cherish the transient, while it is those at the bottom of the heap who – against

10 Josh Freidman, "Michael Douglas, Smiling Now," *Los Angeles Times*, September 20, 2001, https://www.latimes.com/archives/la-xpm-2001-sep-20-ca-47641-story.html.

all odds – desperately struggle to force their flimsy and paltry, transient possessions to last longer and render durable service.'[11] Figures able to negotiate this new terrain will thrive in the reconfigured social relationships of modernity, but also with the constant threat of the loss of all measures of permanence. This is doubly problematic to notions of masculinity because it calls into question the structures that ensure its clear definition: the patriarchal family unit, the association of physical labour with production, and the separation of masculine forms of labour in the public sphere from feminine labour in the domestic.

The reaction to the disruption of seemingly stable signifiers of masculinity in the Weimar Republic was extreme. As Theweleit suggests, drawing on Deleuze and Guattari:

> The contradiction runs as follows: the process of primary accumulation in industry opens up the borders of a hitherto unknown human productive potential, setting in motion streams of money, commodities, and workers, and propelling itself forward on the streams of sweat and blood of workers and non-European peoples. Running parallel to that is a process of *limitation,* directed against the evolution of human pleasures. Deleuze and Guattari call the first process *deterritorialization*—the opening up of new possibilities for desiring-production across the 'body with organs'—and the second process *reterritorialization,* which is the mobilization of dominant forces to prevent the new productive possibilities from becoming new human freedoms.[12]

Thus, the disruptive and deterritorializing potential of capitalism collides with a reactionary backlash, as was the case in the Weimar Republic. It bears mentioning here too that the idea of deterritorialization is conceptually indebted to the notion of *schöpferische Zerstörung* ('creative destruction') that was later popularized by Joseph Schumpeter but first articulated by Werner Sombart to describe the revolution of 'late capitalism' initiated by the First World War.[13] Thus, this particular articulation of capitalism's deterritorializing power arose as a side-effect of the mass liquidation of (male) bodies during this industrialized war. The National Socialist obsession with the threat of 'international Jewish finance capital' was one such reaction to the threat of dissolution of masculine identity itself, and to the erasure of

11 Bauman, *Liquid Modernity*, 14.

12 Theweleit, *Male Fantasies*, vol. 1, 264.

13 Werner Sombart, *Krieg und Kapitalismus* (Munich: Duncker & Humblot, 1913).

the oedipal construction of the male subject.[14] The response is well known, in the championing of an overcompensatory productive masculinity that put a violent end to the notion of a masculinity that had been adapted to the changed conditions of the modern economy. Overcompensatory masculinity is not only a feature of reactions against finance capital, but historically, and to this day, is part of the performance of masculinity of financial sector workers.

Capitalism and *Der letzte Mann*

Another canonical Weimar film that clearly works with the trope of liquidity is F.W. Murnau's *Der letzte Mann* (1924). In the crisis moment of this film, the main character (played by Emil Jannings) breaks down after losing his position as a hotel porter – a job that gives him financial security as well as a sense of standing within the community. Faced with the potential embarrassment of revealing this job loss at his daughter's wedding celebration, he opts instead to sneak into the hotel at night and steal his former uniform. After the wedding festivities, the film's most notable and formally innovative visual effects are employed to represent the porter's inebriated dream-state fantasy of power. His dream is brought on by the silent on-screen representation of the music of a trumpet played by one of two drunken men outside his apartment, thus calling his attention to the exterior world outside the wedding, where his problems still exist. The trumpet is then shown pointed at the camera, as if hailing the audience in a direct address, and the image then seems to liquefy and melt into an abstract wash of light and specular highlights. The effect is likely accomplished on or in front of the lens itself, most likely by adding fluid or jelly to it – a technique often used to soften the image (Figure 12). The porter is shown sleeping, and a huge expressionist approximation of the revolving doors at the entrance of the hotel is superimposed across his face, again playing on the explicit theme of thresholds and interior and exterior space in the film.

The porter is then shown emerging from these doors, standing proud and confident in front of a group of six bald men who are struggling to pick up a suitcase left at the hotel door. He shoos the men away and effortlessly raises a heavy suitcase above his head with one hand – a significant prop that had appeared earlier in the film and, because of his difficulty in lifting it, was the cause of his dismissal. The six men, who bear a more than passing resemblance to the titular character of Murnau's own *Nosferatu:*

14 See Sander L. Gilman, *The Jew's Body* (New York: Routledge, 1991).

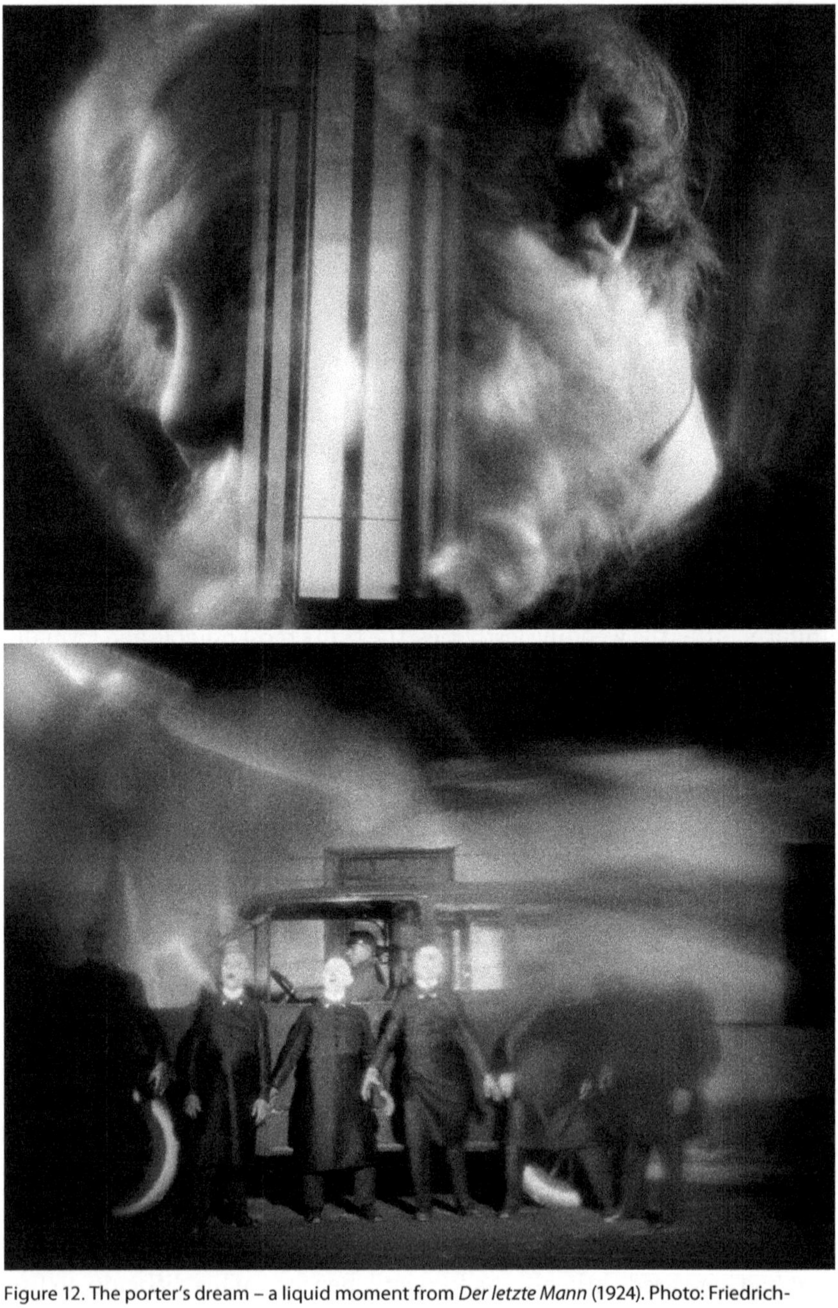

Figure 12. The porter's dream – a liquid moment from *Der letzte Mann* (1924). Photo: Friedrich-Wilhelm Murnau Stiftung.

Eine Symphonie des Grauens ('Nosferatu: A Symphony of Horror,' 1922) in their costuming, lack of hair, and uncanny poses, gaze with mouths agape at the porter's feat of strength. As the porter walks out of the frame, a thick transparent liquid flows over the lens, distorting and dissolving the men, and scattering the light. The scene cuts to a similarly 'liquified' image of the porter, now passing back through the revolving doors which open onto the *Hinterhof* ('inner courtyard') of the tenement in which he lives. The courtyard is filled with the entire cast of the film who applaud his superhuman strength. As Janet Ward writes, 'the tenement is the "interior façade" of the doorman's life to which the hotel provides the exterior; hence it is only logical that the two become sublated in his moment of intoxicated stupor.'[15] The porter thus redeems his symbolic role as gatekeeper, in this case guarding the semi-public realm of the *Hinterhof* from a group of strangely vampiric men. In this oneiric space, the technique of liquefaction functions to remind the viewer of the looming presence of the outside economy, and the porter's loss of his ability to keep order in his own home.[16] Even in this fantasy of empowerment, the threat of dissolution encroaches on the edges of the frame. His precarious position is revealed, and the presence of a group of vampiric men waiting to fill his position drives this home.

I would like to suggest that it is this combination of formal effects and thematic details in this moment of liquidity that ties the threat of financial ruin in the film to the general concept of financial dissolution. In addition, I would like to discuss the self-referential nod to *Nosferatu* – an under-discussed element of *Der letzte Mann* – in this context. *Nosferatu* has been read as representative of the influx of immigrants from the East, or the plague and death that followed the First World War,[17] but the figure of the vampire also evokes the disruption of capital within the fabric of the city, and has been used by Marx to describe capital itself as 'dead-labour, that vampire-like, only lives by sucking living labour.'[18] This connection with capital accumulation should remind us of the original motivation behind the vampire's movement from his home to the modern city. In both Murnau's film and Bram Stoker's original novel, *Dracula* (1897), Count Orlok/Dracula's original intent in hiring Jonathan Harker (Thomas Hutter

15 Janet Ward, *Weimar Surfaces: Urban Visual Culture in 1920s Germany* (Berkeley: University of California Press, 2001), 189.

16 The term 'economy' comes to us via Latin from the Greek: *oikonomia*, meaning 'household management.'

17 See Anton Kaes, *Shell Shock Cinema: Weimar Culture and the Wounds of War* (Princeton: Princeton University Press, 2009), 109–10.

18 Karl Marx, *Capital: A Critique of Political Economy*, vol. 1 (London: Penguin Books, 1981), 257.

in Murnau's version) is to certify a real-estate transaction involving the purchase of properties in London. In *Nosferatu*, the vampire arrives on the shores of 'Wisborg' as a rich man intent on buying land through the deranged real-estate agent Knock. In this sense, Nosferatu plans to invade the space of the city by using his financial power, and represents the threat of foreign capital. Steve Pile has argued that the vampire 'embodies pure economic ideas, such as: the importance of long-term investment strategies; ensuring the security of the money supply; thinking about property far into the future; and the immortality of money-in-circulation in the capitalist economy as opposed to the mortality of money itself.'[19] We are also constantly reminded in the vampire myth of the creature's close association with real estate, and the boundary between private and public space, through the well-known restrictions placed on a vampire's movement. In most narratives featuring the figure of the vampire, he (usually male) must be invited in before being able to enter a domestic interior (usually by a woman). In *Der letzte Mann*, the image of a multitude of vampiric men waiting at the door of the hotel thus functions in conjunction with the porter's role as gatekeeper, as an image of the encroaching threat of capital on the space of the tenement building itself. In this sense, and in combination with the visual effect of liquefaction of the image itself, Murnau's inclusion of this figure creates one such moment of liquidity that resonates beyond the text itself.

In keeping with the importance of action around liminal spaces, *Der letzte Mann* sets up an obvious spatial dichotomy between the upper-class world of the Atlantic Hotel and the working-class tenement building. Significantly, much of the action takes place not within the rooms of these buildings but on the thresholds and within the corridors, doorways and stairwells. Jannings, in the role of 'doorman,' stands at the barrier between these two worlds and tenuously clings to the modicum of acceptance into the upper-class world that his uniform alone seems to provide. His uniform also allows him to act as a symbolic emissary of this upper-class world to his neighbours when he returns home. It enables him to maintain the illusion of superiority that is at the fragile core of both their esteem for him, and his self-image. The porter's physical task, standing in the liminal space between the class strata of modern society, reminds spectators of the precarious nature of such categories of distinction. Similar to many members of the *Angestellten*, he stands within reach of the wealth of the upper classes, but

19 Steve Pile, *Real Cities: Modernity, Space, and the Phantasmagorias of City Life* (London: Sage, 2005), 111.

is easily disposed of and ultimately excluded.[20] Nevertheless, he relishes in his symbolic power over his neighbours, a power that is derived solely from the token uniform, the Wilhelmine style and military cut of which are emphasized by his constant salutes. This illusory appearance of nobility that separates him from his class conditions has become essential to his identity. His disrobing in the film – when he is demoted to position of bathroom attendant – thus provokes a crisis of masculinity. This castrating act reminds the viewer that the Wilhelmine conception of a militarized masculinity is constructed and performed through displays that occur in the public sphere. The film is spatially constructed across a clear gender binary: between the performance of masculinity in the public sphere – all of his co-workers are male – and the private sphere, which is primarily the space of women – his daughter's wedding and the mocking comments and sidelong glances of his neighbours (almost all of whom are women) after his downfall. However, as we shall see, this public/private binary breaks down in a key scene at the end of the film, which also has important implications for how the film portrays masculinity.

The final scenes of *Der letzte Mann* have often been criticized for the conceit of the Hollywood-style 'tacked-on' happy ending. After showing the porter's complete defeat, the film introduces an unlikely plot twist. An insert of a newspaper article announces that the porter is the sole inheritor of the fortune of an American millionaire who happened to die in the men's room while the porter was on duty. The apparent irony of this plot twist was duly noted by reviewers of the time and it has been alleged that the studio, Universum Film AG (UFA), stipulated that the ending be included, because the film would otherwise not be commercially viable.[21] Whether the ending was forced on Murnau or not, the chance reversal of the porter's fate functions to further underline the fragility of the construction of masculinity and financial independence in the film. In these final scenes, the film mocks the association of virility with economic power by making the doorman's rescue a matter of pure chance. Further, and in a similar manner to the role played by Davy – the Red Cross officer in *Die freudlose Gasse* – the American origin of this financial windfall plays again on the historical circumstances of the rescue of Germany's economy under the

20 See the essays "Those Who Wait," and "Revolt of the Middle Classes," in Siegfried Kracauer, *The Mass Ornament: Weimar Essays*, ed. Thomas Y. Levin (Cambridge, MA: Harvard University Press, 1995).

21 For a discussion of how this ending came about see Klaus Kreimeier, *The Ufa Story: A History of Germany's Greatest Film Company, 1918–1945* (Berkeley: University of California Press, 1999), 144–5. See also *Murnau's 4 Devils: Traces of a Lost Film* (Janet Bergstrom, 2003).

Dawes Plan of 1924, which marked the beginning of the 'period of stability.' This extraterritorial financial force enters the film as an absurd joke, but a joke that undercuts the idea of reward for hard work or the idea of the 'self-made' man. As such, it performs a central cynical function in the plot – that it is not necessarily the industrious who are rewarded, but rather, the lucky.

It is important to note, however, that this twist also reveals money's emancipatory power in the Weimar imagination – its function as a catalyst for the overturning of entrenched orders of subjectivity such as gender and class. It is this financial windfall that ultimately frees the porter from the crushing dictate of the film: i.e., that he conform to the gender and class roles ascribed to him. As an example of this transgression, consider the scene in which the porter, now rich and dining in the hotel restaurant, descends to the basement bathroom where he was previously employed, and interacts with the new bathroom attendant. In this long and drawn-out melodramatic interaction, the porter reaches out and embraces the man, kissing him tenderly on the cheeks while his soap-covered hand caresses his hair. All semblance of the hard exterior of the uniform has melted away as the porter covers the man's head with suds, another boundary crossing reminder of liquid. It is significant that this scene also takes place in the private interior of the men's washroom, a significant departure from other interactions between men in the film that introduces a new intimacy not seen yet between any men in the film.

Since the porter had no hand in his own financial windfall – the money does not stem from the realm of 'productive' capital – it can clearly be seen as undercutting any performance of masculinity. Given this potential undermining of the association of financial stability and masculinity virility, Sabine Hake asks: 'does the main character in *The Last Laugh* announce the long awaited demise of patriarchal authority or its replacement by more elusive structures of domination and control?'[22] Hake points out that the film is part of the 'emancipatory process' in Weimar culture that goes beyond 'essentialist gender binaries,' and blurs 'traditional categories of identity.'[23] Further, she claims that Jannings's 'overdetermined' performance 'connects the crisis of masculinity to more fundamental questions about gender relations and family life.'[24]

22 Sabine Hake, "Who Gets the Last Laugh?," in *Weimar Cinema: An Essential Guide to Classic Films of the Era*, ed. Noah Isenberg (New York: Columbia University Press, 2009), 124.
23 Ibid.
24 Ibid.

In materialist terms, this 'emancipatory' potential of Weimar culture was driven by shifts in the tectonic plates of capitalism that subsequently resonated outwards as aftershocks through the categories of gender and culture. In *Der letzte Mann*, however, capitalism's non-negotiable demand that the new destroy the old is also revealed, but the chance circumstance of a financial windfall also saves the old man from the fate of obsolescence. In the case of ruin or salvation for the porter, capital demands that individuals adapt to its ebbs and flows, and remain 'liquid' in the face of dissolution. Using this framework, the original German title of the film – which translates to 'The Last Man' rather than the English title, 'The Last Laugh' – takes on a new resonance that is specific to the particular erosion of Wilhelmine masculinity in the face of new flows of capital in the Weimar Republic. In this sense, the film can be read as illustrating the death of an older concept of masculinity while developing a formal visual vocabulary that heralds in the new 'liquid masculinity' demanded by finance capital.

Power, Vision, and Liquid Masculinity in *L'Argent*

Marcel L'Herbier's *L'Argent* (1928) also clearly mobilizes the trope of liquidity in Weimar cinema and demonstrates the link between finance capital and a crisis of masculinity. *L'Argent* presents two competing versions of the modern male subject both striving for mastery of the terrain of the global economy. Although a French production, it was distributed widely as *Geld! Geld!! Geld!!!* ('Money! Money!! Money!!!') in Germany by UFA in 1929, and featured two of Germany's major stars of the time – Brigitte Helm and Alfred Abel. *L'Argent* transposes the action of Émile Zola's 1891 novel into the 1920s through the use of contemporary devices such as the radio, the telephone, the airplane, and electric light. The original novel is an urtext of fictional representations of finance, and influenced later literary depictions of the financial world such as Frank Noriss's novels *The Octopus* (1901) and *The Pit* (1903).[25] Though much of the novel is not portrayed in this adaptation, the film version is incredibly rich and employs many of the major tropes and themes used to create an image of the world economy that are discussed throughout the present study. As Margrit Frölich has shown, the production of the film is also a significant example of international film financing as it

25 See Renata R. Mautner Wasserman, "Financial Fictions: Émile Zola's *L'argent*, Frank Norris' *The Pit*, and Alfredo de Taunay's *O Encilhamento*," *Comparative Literature Studies* 38, no. 3 (2001): 193–214.

featured a script written by L'Herbier and sold to UFA under the condition that the famous French filmmaker would be its director.[26]

The plot of the film revolves around the rivalry between two titans of finance: Nicolas Saccard and Alphonse Gundermann. Brinkmanship on the stock exchange between these two men forms the background for Saccard's attempt to rescue his failing Banque Universelle with the launch of an oil prospecting venture in colonial 'British Guiana' (now Guyana) headed by the daring aviator Jacques Hamelin. However, while Jacques is away, Saccard manipulates news of the expedition to gain advantage on the exchange, and also attempts to steal away Jacques's wife, Line. The film is important both as a representation of financial markets and as an actual photographic document of the stock market of in the late 1920s. Scenes shot on location at the Bourse de Paris (Paris stock exchange) over a bank holiday contained hundreds of extras, and featured the space and technology of the exchange in detail. Extensive footage revealed the inner workings of the Bourse and its state-of-the-art communication systems, both electric and pneumatic. In his attempts at verisimilitude, and since the film was made on the verge of the coming of sound, scenes of the Bourse were accompanied by sound effects at some screenings. As one reviewer noted, the addition of sounds was also a result of the difficulty inherent in visually representing the modern market:

> To represent the sophisticated mechanisms of the modern stock market, one must get lost in difficult un-cinematic details that the audience would find boring. [...] L'Herbier convincingly brings the superficial tempo of a big bank to the fore, and the skilful montage of typewriters, quotation boards, telephones, and a thousand other office technologies lend the film a believable atmosphere. The stock exchange scenes are also fascinating. The excitement of the people on the exchange is clearly demonstrated. The accompanying sound effects should have been softened, but still helped the impact of the stock exchange scenes.[27]

The film opens with an exterior shot of the Corinthian colonnade that separates the interior floor of the Paris Bourse from the street. A vast crowd

26 For a comprehensive overview of the international venture that funded the film, see Margrit Frölich, "Playing the European Market: Marcel L'Herbier's *L'Argent* (1928), Ufa, and German-French Film Relations," in *Continuity and Crisis in German Cinema, 1928–1936*, ed. Barbara Hales, Mihaela Petrescu, and Valerie Weinstein (Rochester: Camden House, 2016), 273–90.

27 Georg Herzberg, "Geld! Geld!! Geld!!!," *Film-Kurier*, March 16, 1929.

is assembled on the steps, forming the *petite bourse* of unofficial traders. The opening montage then takes us into the hall of the exchange and shows the floor from a god's eye perspective. The narrative then begins in the closed chambers of the *société anonyme* 'Caledonian Eagle.' This closed society is revealed to be an association of shareholders who are arguing over whether to support the ventures of the film's main protagonist, the 'audacious speculator' Nicolas Saccard.

Saccard's identity in Zola's novel as a Catholic monarchist is absent from the film, as are the connections between his business ventures and the Catholic church's goal of reconquering Jerusalem to make it the seat of the papacy.[28] The criticism of the connection between organized religion and capital in the novel is entirely absent in the film, replaced with a more general and moralizing critique of the effects of greed. In Georg Herzberg's German review, however, the film was dismissed as a failure as a morality play since its depiction of greed was deemed ambiguous and because Saccard's manipulation of information in the film was understood as *de rigueur* for market activity at the time:

> Both successes and failures are shown in the film, but they are hard to believe. One cannot simply hold the world stock markets in suspense with a few bluffs or antics [...] For the viewer, it is completely unclear why Saccard is convicted. If people are dumb enough to buy his newly issued certificates, then let them pay for them.[29]

Herzberg's review reflects the cynical mood of the time concerning financial activity. Saccard is convicted in the film of manipulating the news of Jacques Hamelin's flight, spreading an untrue rumour of his death, and then using the false information to buy up more shares before releasing the news of the successful flight. That this was not seen as problematic by the reviewer speaks both to the fact that such manipulations of the press were fairly common at the time and accepted as part of the everyday business of the marketplace.

Saccard's main investment scheme in the film is updated from the era of the railroad to the new age of petroleum. His Banque Universelle falls into disrepute amongst French investors due to the actions of his rival, the 'old and powerful' banker, Alphonse Gundermann (played by Alfred Abel). In the novel, Gundermann is a 'Frankfort Jew' who is 'ready to buy and sell

28 Wasserman, "Financial Fictions," 196.
29 Georg Herzberg, "Geld! Geld!! Geld!!!," *Film-Kurier*, March 16, 1929.

France in the interest of German-based Jewish money-interests.'[30] This association is absent from the film, as is the novel's portrayal of Saccard as virulently anti-Semitic, though it may have been read into the film by audiences familiar with the original. Similarly, the novel's suggestion of a financially backed crusade to bring Christianity to the Holy Land, led by the development of railways and public works, is replaced in the film with the more abstract idea of searching for oil in British Guiana. This change is also significant in that it fittingly updates the financial backdrop of the narrative, locating it firmly within a world of fungible commodities like liquid crude oil and replacing the outdated association of finance with the age of industry.

L'Argent features the French actor Pierre Alcover as Saccard and the German actor Alfred Abel as Gundermann. At the time, Abel was at the height of his fame following his role as Joh Fredersen in *Metropolis* (1927), and was one of Germany's most recognizable stars. German reviewers accordingly picked up on the opposition between France and Germany and commented on the film's depiction of finance capital in nationalist terms. One German reviewer praised the film but claimed that it would be more popular to a French audience, given its 'topicality with regard to France's current banking scandal.'[31] This most likely refers to the explosive arrest of Marthe Hanau in December 1928, a month before this review was written. Hanau, a confidence woman and founder of a financial newspaper, was highly connected within French elite circles and defrauded investors out of some 150 million francs.[32] Herzberg compared the German favourably to his French counterpart, calling Gundermann a 'noble opponent' who 'does everything with a knowing smile.' Further blurring the boundary between actor and role, Herzberg goes on to state that 'Alfred Abel is in every way the opposite of the *Raffke* type' that Saccard embodies, shifting the use of this term from referring to the German war profiteer to referring to the figure of the unscrupulous French speculator.[33]

Early on, the film provides one of its most compelling images of the world economy. When Gundermann's agent, Salomon Massias (Alexandre Mihalesco) returns from the 'Caledonian,' he is granted an audience in Gundermann's vast chambers, but before entering, is made to wait in a concealed antechamber. The walls of this small cylindrical room are completely

30 Wasserman, "Fictions," 208.

31 *Film-Kurier*, January 9, 1929.

32 See Janet Flanner, "The Swindling President – II," *The New Yorker*, August 26, 1939.

33 Georg Herzberg, "Geld! Geld!! Geld!!!," *Film-Kurier*, March 16, 1929.

Figure 13. The representation of flows of capital in Gundermann's antechamber in *L'Argent* (Marcel L'Herbier, 1929). Photo: Flicker Alley.

covered by a mural showing global trade routes – a view of world trade from a vantage point reminiscent of pre-Copernican maps of the heavens that placed humanity at the centre of the universe (Figure 13). Followed by a circular pan of his quarters, these images impress upon the viewer the vast power and reach of Gundermann who, we are informed, 'controls much of the world's oil' – that liquid lifeblood of the modern economy. Gundermann as 'master of the universe' is at the centre of this web while the thick glasses of the courier remind us of the scopic nature of this power. The stage is set for the central rivalry of the film to play out between the two bankers. After becoming a pariah in financial circles, Saccard devises a spectacular scheme and the majority of the film is largely constructed through the intercutting between Jacques Hamelin's (Henry Victor) voyage to British Guiana and Saccard's scheming back in Paris.

The film is a masterpiece of the 'unchained camera' of the late silent cinema, making use of all manner of cinematographic technologies to propel the audience into, around, and through the spaces it depicts. For example, after agreeing to finance Hamelin's flight, on the condition that the aviator work to discover new oil fields, Saccard is depicted in his office waiting for news of the transatlantic voyage. As in the antechamber scene, this is one of several points in the film that map the space of the global market onto the architecture of the film. Leading up to this sequence, Line Hamelin (Mary Glorie) is shown waiting attentively, listening for news of her husband on the radio. L'Herbier cuts between her and scenes of frenzied trading on the Bourse. Images of the hall of the exchange are transposed with images of Hamelin's plane, then a pan down from the night sky brings us to an office overlooking the Place de l'Opéra where Saccard and Line Hamelin are attending a celebration of the daring voyage. The camera pans over the waiting crowd in the square and the anxious investors on the exchange. Line is drawn to Saccard's office by the flickering of lights in the window, and crosses the room to look out on the square. Saccard, from the beginning, has been obsessed with Line Hamelin. In one shot pairing, Saccard is shown entering the office while Line waits at the window, silhouetted by the strong light streaming into the room. Here, the trope of the exchange of women in lieu of money is introduced into the film, as it becomes gradually clear that Saccard intends to control Line through his control over her husband's finances. He proceeds to harass and then attack her but is fiercely rejected.

This scene is the symbolic core of the film and forms a powerful representation of the informational world-picture of the market. It visualizes the gathering of financial news, by comparing it with the mechanism of the camera itself. News of the flight is highlighted by the intercutting of newspaper headlines, which at times seem to capture the attention of Saccard and Line, as if present with them in the scene. For example, light streams through the window, beaming through the space like streams of electronic news itself. A small model of Hamelin's plane is caught in the spotlights and projects a shadow onto the wall, further conflating the spaces of the film. Saccard's office effectively becomes a camera obscura within which the events of Hamelin's flight are projected and captured. The intercutting between this space, the exterior of the square, and the shots of headlines flowing in from far away, combine into a vision of fantastic scopic reach. Saccard's power is here shown to be linked to the specular mobility of the sphere of information – a combination of visual information and televisual power that anticipates a much later stage of the technical apparatus of the world markets. His power stands in direct contrast with Hamelin's more muscular command of the physical space of the world as an aviator. As such, *L'Argent* is similar to *Dr. Mabuse* in the way it recognizes the importance of metaphors of vision to the representation of the modern market. Even more than *Dr. Mabuse*, however, *L'Argent* depicts the flow of information in terms of the characteristics of the transmission of light, or the diffusion of energy through space, a reference to the newly invented technology of the radio that features prominently in the film. The image of a web of point-to-point nodes in a telegraphic network is replaced by the radiant model of wireless transmission.

L'Herbier's film captures the essence of what can be called a financial imaginary, or financial worldview. This image of the economy, that has today taken a much clearer form, given the wide range of screen-based technologies that are central to financial activity, was nascent at the time of *L'Argent* and was first made visible on screen in scenes such as this. The film renders the terrain of the world economy visible and promotes a fantasy of omnipotent visibility that reinforces the 'efficient market hypothesis' – the idea that prices represent all available information, that information is available to all market participants in a transparent manner, and that this information is instantaneously available through the technologies of the market. This conception is at the core of claims, such as Joseph Schumpeter's, that markets reflect an accurate picture of the world, and is ingrained in the idea of the validity of markets to set prices for commodities. As discussed in chapter 1, this 'strong' form of the efficient market hypothesis is blind to the real frictions inherent in the gathering and disseminating of financial information and ignores the possibility of time-based arbitrage and privileged access to information – i.e., acting on information gleaned before other actors in the marketplace. The efficient market hypothesis is, however, a central fiction of the day-to-day operation of the market, without which there would be no possibility of agreement on the price of a security as it appears on an index. As such, it gained importance in the twentieth century as information technologies made the promise of price availability an increasingly tangible goal of stock markets. As has been discussed here, this was one of the first and most successful efforts to create a form of simultaneity across space and time in the project of modernity. In *L'Argent*, it is given visual form through the cross-cutting in this scene, creating an illusion of instantaneity where Jacques Hamelin's actions are immediately perceivable to these distant observers.

In the scene overlooking the Place de l'Opéra, the nebulous optical fidelity at the edges of the frame of wide-aperture shots rhymes with the theme of financial liquidity in the film. This is a constant formal characteristic of Jules Kruger's exquisite cinematography,[34] and it is no accident that many shots are defocused and soft. As Ronald Blumer points out, this was a feature of L'Herbier's style that was also present in his film *Eldorado* (1921).[35] L'Herbier and other French impressionist filmmakers of his time indulged in such effects as part of their interest in capturing the elusive quality of *photogénie*. The effect is sometimes used in a generic manner, to soften the features of female characters like Line Hamelin, whereas, up until the end of the film, Jacques Hamelin is presented in muscular compositions and sharp focus. The differentiation between 'masculine' and 'feminine' lighting techniques was commonplace and used in generic ways, lending Line and the Baronness Sandorf (Brigitte Helm) a shimmering presence.[36] However, L'Herbier uses it more in shots of Line that depict her in distress, which, in the film, is always the result of Saccard's deception or her realization of his plot concerning her husband. The technique is not, however, only reserved for women and, as will be shown here, it appears in significant ways in relation to the theme of masculinity and financial liquidity. For example, the introductory shot of Gundermann in his chambers uses the technique to obscure his features and to dissolve the outline of his figure into the surrounding room. Additionally, his office is always depicted in wide shots in which the boundaries of the room are lost in the blurring effect of the lens.

34 Kruger was already renowned for his work on *Napoleon* (Abel Gance, 1927).

35 In *Eldorado*, a blurred effect was achieved not only through the defocusing of the lens, but also through the application of filters or materials to the lens to blur individual characters. The effect was used to signify that a single dancer, in a line of other in-focus dancers all on the same focal plane, was 'lost in faraway thoughts.' Ronald H. Blumer, "The Camera as Snowball: France 1918–1927," *Cinema Journal* 9, no. 2 (April 1, 1970): 34–5.

36 See Richard Dyer, "The Light of the World," in *White* (London: Routledge, 1997).

The technique is frequently employed in *L'Argent* and is also used to show the dissolution of architectural spaces, creating a feeling of instability in many scenes. The film stresses the boundaries of the image of space contained within it to show the constant presence of the intensities of the world beyond the frame. Painter and filmmaker Fernand Léger, who designed some of the sets for L'Herbier's *L'Inhumaine* (1924), was interested in utilizing film sets and the image itself to achieve the sublime goal of modern architecture – what Siegfried Gideon referred to as the creation of the visual effect of 'parallax' – essentially, the suggestion of movement in static architecture through the use of new materials that opened up structures, allowing them to be experienced in terms of its shifting planes and revelation of viewpoints.[37] Art historian Elie Faure dubbed the appearance of this impulse on film *cineplastics*, and claimed that 'architecture in movement [...] should be in constant accord, in dynamically pursued equilibrium, with the setting and the landscapes within which it rises and falls.'[38]

This effect is most apparent towards the end of the film in a scene in which Saccard throws a party to celebrate his (at this point) successful financial venture. Here, Line Hamelin, fed up with Saccard's violent sexual advances and growing control over her life, resolves out of desperation to shoot him. She is stopped at the last moment by Baroness Sandorf, who slyly realizes that Saccard's death would not bode well for her own speculative manoeuvres. This elaborately lensed and dreamlike scene takes place in a large nightclub set. The high-ceilinged space is supported by imposing columns, and the central floor is taken up by a reflecting pool over which two bejewelled women dance on a catwalk for the entertainment of the crowd. A band plays in front of a massive bank of church organ pipes that lend an air of the sacred to the proceedings. The archaic character of the architecture is amplified by the presence of a large frieze at the other end of the hall which depicts a man leading a bull. A woman reclines on the bull's back, half standing while small waves of water lap at her feet. Possibly meant to evoke the myth of the rape of Europa, the image foreshadows Saccard's assault of Line Hamelin later in the scene and is a signifier of the overcompensatory performance of masculinity so common in finance capital. Shots of the club

37 See the introduction of the idea of experience of 'space time' as an aesthetically desirable goal in modernist architecture: Sigfried Giedion, *Space, Time and Architecture: The Growth of a New Tradition* (Cambridge, MA: Harvard University Press, 1967), originally published in 1941. See also the equation of 'space time' with the effect of parallax in Peter Collins, *Changing Ideals in Modern Architecture, 1750–1950*, 2nd ed. (Montreal: McGill-Queens University Press, 1998).

38 See Anthony Vidler, "The Explosion of Space: Architecture and the Filmic Imaginary," *Assemblage*, no. 21 (1993): 46.

Figure 14. *Top*: Hamelin loses his ability to focus his sight. *Bottom*: a point-of-view shot of his hand, which appears to dissolve with the breakdown of optical focus. *L'Argent* (Marcel L'Herbier, 1929). Photo: Flicker Alley.

space become increasingly abstract as the intensity of the events increases, and Saccard's backstage attack on Line makes up her mind to murder him. Women are increasingly associated with images of liquid in the scene, as the tension builds to the near murder of Saccard. As the liquidity of the image itself threatens both the solidity of the space through dissolves and camera movements, it also threatens Saccard, who seems to have gone too far in his scheming, and the vertiginous representation of this space threatens to collapse. Here, women are again representative of dangerous, uncontrollable forces in the financial scheme of the film. Stylistically, this is rendered through the loss of optical clarity of the frame itself.

Metaphors of vision and blindness are central to both *Dr. Mabuse der Spieler* and *L'Argent*'s depictions of the terrain of finance and modernity. For example, Hamelin's flight in *L'Argent* ends with his successful return, but significantly, the strain of the voyage leaves the aviator blind. The optical effect of dissolution or liquefaction is used most strongly in the scene depicting Hamelin's loss of sight (Figure 14). This symbolic castration robs him of not only his sight, but also his career and mobility, thus removing him from his position of mastery over time and space. Thus, his loss foregrounds Saccard's own mastery in a gesture that seems to already assign the then new mobility afforded by flight to a secondary position in comparison to the spectral power over distance of communications technologies and the velocity of money itself. Saccard's competition with Hamelin is played out as a battle of worldviews. Hamelin, tall and athletic, bears a scar across his face that is reminiscent of a *Schmiss* – a fencing scar thought to be a mark of honour among nobility. He is a man of action whose financial successes spring directly from his use of his body in motion and its association with the power of the machine. He is also portrayed as popular with the masses and initially resists the world of financiers who want to use his popularity to promote their own schemes to develop a pipeline across Europe and into North Africa. In contrast, Saccard is the epitome of the *Raffke* and financial marauder, who harnesses the web of communications technologies, including the radio which is featured heavily in this film, and acts through the power of information. While Hamelin's mobility is tied to his body and the airplane that is the extension of his physical power, Saccard is immobile yet omnipresent. While Hamelin flies, Saccard is in a sense 'already there' through the mechanism of the telegraph and the radio. The power that this gives Saccard is made clear when he orchestrates false reports of Hamelin's crash and failure. The 'news' of this event nearly drives Line to suicide but Saccard's revelation that the news is false relieves her, and he consoles her in another deceitful attempt to woo her.

The contrast between the two men is made even starker in the parallel montage that shows Hamelin at work in the oil fields while Saccard buys gifts for the aviator's wife back in Paris. Accordingly, and in contrast to Saccard's mastery of electronic communication, Hamelin and his wife are limited to sending messages through the slow medium of physical letters. In one sequence, Hamelin, on the job site, looks up from a letter from his wife and a reverse angle shows workers assembling an oil derrick. The focus blurs, anticipating his loss of vision, and eventually fades to black. The film cuts to a scene depicting Saccard in Paris staring at a stock ticker, a collision of imagery that makes plain the two levels of vision at work in the film. Hamelin, the engineer and explorer, represents an enlightenment model of the conquest of space, tied to the line-of-site optical surveillance of territory. Saccard (and Gundermann), on the other hand, represent a mode of vision reliant on the informational web of communications technologies that maps the world through the lens of the market. This is driven home when Hamelin, unable in his weakness to read a predatory contract sent to him by Saccard, signs away his financial gains to him. In this sense, Hamelin is not only going blind, but is doubly impaired in his inability to 'see' the world as represented by financial flow.

L'Argent ultimately distils the totality of market events into a grudge match between Saccard and Gundermann while Hamelin is left out in the cold and presented as the victim of their war. At the end of the film, it is revealed that Gundermann had been abreast of Saccard's scheme all along and, by routing funds through stock exchanges around the world, deceived Saccard by buying up the majority of Banque Universelle shares. Hamelin's 'old-fashioned' mobility was no match for Saccard's power over the flow of information, but Gundermann trumps them both due to his superior access to global capital markets. Thus, the film shows how both Gundermann and Saccard are representative of a new form of liquid masculinity that wages battles outside of the realm of the physical and across the communications networks of financial markets.

Reactionary Modernism and Finance Capital

The Image of Northern German Industry in *Hanseaten*

Histories of the Weimar Republic frequently label the years between 1924 and 1929 as the 'period of stabilization' initiated by the recovery of the mark and an injection of foreign aid money in the form of the Dawes Plan.[39] Because of the external source of aid, the relative return of some semblance of economic stability to the republic posed a new challenge to any narrative of post-war recovery for the nation. This period was also marked by the emergence of the aesthetic of the *Neue Sachlichkeit*, which was defined in 1923 by Gustav Hartlaub in relation to painting as 'the return to objective realism in the aftermath of Expressionism and Dada.'[40] *Neue Sachlichkeit* has been defined with varying degrees of clarity across different media. In architecture, it was epitomized in 1923 by Mies van der Rohe and the 'G Group,' who rejected formalist and expressionist tendencies in favour of 'a house of work [...] of organization, of clarity, of economy.'[41] Mies's comments make clear the importance of linking spatial notions of stability and efficiency with the economy itself, and the resuscitation of orderly labour and discipline. In the cinema, *Neue Sachlichkeit* has been somewhat unsatisfactorily defined. Siegfried Kracauer claims that the films produced in relation to this idea subjected reality to a detached cynicism and that 'reality is portrayed not so as to make facts yield their implications, but to drown all implications in an ocean of facts, as in the UFA *Kulturfilme*.'[42] Otherwise, Kracauer's chapter on 'the stabilized period' in *From Caligari to Hitler* makes reference only to the films of G. W. Pabst as demonstrative of the 'New Realism.' Lotte Eisner makes almost no mention of it at all in *The Haunted Screen*, which is unsurprising given the foregrounding of expressionist theatre in her classic study of the films of the period. Richard McCormick has pointed out the specific links between the emergence of this aesthetic and key aspects of the construction of masculinity at this time. In 1929, Kurt Pinthus published an essay entitled 'Männliche Literatur,' in which he defined *Neue Sachlichkeit* tendencies in post-expressionist literature as 'masculine' and 'mature.'[43] The construction of Weimar masculinity is 'closely connected to the *Neue Sachlichkeit*' and its various attempts to establish a 'strong-again

39 See the section entitled "The phase of relative stabilization, 1924–9" in Eberhard Kolb, *The Weimar Republic* (London: Routledge, 2008). For a critical historiographical approach to this pervasive narrative of the republic, see the section "Deceptive Stability" in Detlev Peukert, *The Weimar Republic* (New York: Hill and Wang, 1993). Siegfried Kracauer also adopts the term 'The Stabilized Period' in Siegfried Kracauer, *From Caligari to Hitler: A Psychological History of the German Film* (Princeton, NJ: Princeton University Press, 2004).

40 Richard W. McCormick, "Private Anxieties/Public Projections: 'New Objectivity,' Male Subjectivity, and Weimar Cinema," *Women in German Yearbook* 10 (1994): 4.

41 Mies van der Rohe quoted in William J. R. Curtis, *Modern Architecture since 1900* (London: Phaidon, 2001), 190.

42 Kracauer, *Caligari*, 166.

43 McCormick, "Private Anxieties," 6.

Figure 15. The stern Karl Twersten (left) and Theodor Bramberg, his *Raffke*-like rival (right) in *Hanseaten* (Gerhard Lamprecht, 1925). Photo: Deutsche Kinemathek.

masculinity,' in the form of what Helmut Lethen dubbed the detached *kalte persona* ('cool-headed persona').[44]

I will turn now to an example of a *Neue Sachlichkeit* film that is set in the world of international trade and mobilizes the tropes of water and shipping, but that exemplifies a reactionary vision of capitalism and patriarchy that is particular to its milieux. Released in the same year as *Die freudlose Gasse*, Gerhard Lamprecht's little-known second film, *Hanseaten* (1925), survives in the form of a very clean 35 mm print at the Deutsche Kinemathek in Berlin.[45] As the film is not widely available for viewing at the time of writing, I will describe its plot in some detail. It portrays two established old Hanseatic families – the *Reeder* ('ship builder' or 'ship owner') Karl Twersten, and the *Spediteur* ('shipper') Martin Vanheil, as well as the drama that develops around their business dealings. A third figure, Theodor Bramberg, is introduced as an indifferent investor from the city to the south – another embodiment of the *Raffke* (Figure 15). *Hanseaten* defines the various ideologies of its three male figures through their various costumes; Karl is reserved, severe and stiff, in a wool overcoat, while bumbling Martin Vanheil is marked by his wire-rim glasses and *Kaiserwilhelmbart* (a beard in the style of Kaiser Wilhelm II) as a remnant of another era. Bramberg by contrast, is chic and fat, with slicked back hair, the sunken eyes of a night owl, wearing stylish suits, and sporting ostentatious pocket squares, white gloves, and a bowler hat. He primps and preens in the film and is thoroughly feminized throughout, in one scene having a servant apply a cloud of perfume while he looks at himself in the mirror. His wife Ingeborg, by contrast, is a shrewd and wise businesswoman, dressed in outmoded but opulent attire. As the brains behind Bramberg's business ventures, she catches the eye of Karl Twersten, and a love affair develops between them. The costuming in the film seems to conflate two time periods – that of the late nineteenth century and the contemporary moment of 1925 – and this confusion of periodization will be returned to.

Many of the films under discussion here have presented the disruptive space of finance capital as threatening to 'stable' categories of gender and nation. *Hanseaten* actively promotes an alternative order that responds to this threat by presenting a vision of Northern German patriarchal capitalism. Significantly, the reactionary narrative of this film takes place at the

44 Mihaela Petrescu, "Billy Wilder's Work as Eintänzer in Weimar Berlin," *New German Critique* 40, no. 3 120 (September 21, 2013): 66.

45 Thanks to Philipp Stiasny for his enthusiasm and insight in discussing some of the more obscure points of this understated film with me.

Hamburg harbour, in a place of intense international commercial 'flow' and trade. As we shall see, the film attempts to reconcile nautical international trade in Germany with a stabilized idea of German industrial capitalism. At the same time, it attempts to redeem notions of the patriarchal family unit and a stable national identity.

Another love interest develops in the film between Robert Twersten, son of the harbour master, and Martin's daughter Marga Vanheil, of the rival yet friendly old-money family that has fallen on hard times in recent years. Robert's very young Brazilian mother, Angela, played by the celebrity ballerina Tamara Karsavina, tries to gain more influence by suggesting that her husband Karl take the family business public so that her son, 'Bob' (Robert), can oversee the selling of shares. Significantly, Twersten refuses, saying that he will not divide his company into a joint-stock corporation so that 'a hundred indifferent donkeys might make a profit from it.'[46] Robert seeks the approval of his severe father, and the film portrays his coming of age through his handling of the family business.

After the argument, Twersten's wife Angela leaves for Rio de Janeiro and news of trouble caused by her reckless gambling later reaches Germany. Twersten then throws his economic and paternal might into a plan to both reclaim his wife and make a large profit for the company. He attempts to enlist the finances of the Vanheil family, but old Vanheil does not have the stomach for the risky venture. In response to Vanheil's hesitation, Twersten teases that he has become *altfränkisch* in his business dealings, a loaded reference to the medieval Franks that signifies Vanheil is quaint and old-fashioned, and Vanheil then agrees to join the venture.[47] Twersten entrusts his son Robert to oversee the business venture, as well as bring his mother home. On the way, Fritz Vanheil, brother of Marga and friend of Robert Twersten, is discovered as a stow-away and proceeds to join the venture. Here the plot seamlessly fuses the interests of industrial capital with the maintenance of familial order. When in Rio, Robert discovers that his mother is having an affair with someone who she introduces as his 'cousin José' – a revelation that throws the family into crisis. José is a one-dimensional, racially stereotypical villain and is played as a lustful, slimy, and vicious interloper. A *Film-Kurier* reviewer dismisses this minor character as generically 'other,' stating that Angela 'takes some Spaniard,

46 Intertitle: 'Was soll ich? Eine Aktiengesellschaft?! Aus meinemWerk für hundert gleichgültige Esel Gewinn herauswurtschaften?'

47 Intertitle: 'Ich glaube, dein Geschäft hat ein Aufmunterung nötig. Es ist altfränkisch geworden, Martin.'

Italian or some other rogue with a nut-brown tint and Gallic downwardly brushed moustache, as her lover.[48] José and Angela's indiscretions are discovered in the middle of the night by Fritz Vanheil, who is subsequently stabbed by José during a brief scuffle. Fritz lives, but his right arm is maimed, and Angela's story is never explicitly resolved as she does not appear again after this point.

Meanwhile, back in Hamburg, it turns out that Marga Vanheil, upon hearing of her father's unwillingness to enter into the venture, had approached Robert Twersten with her *Sparbuch* ('savings book'). After she produces this money Twersten calls her a 'real Hamburg girl' who he 'wishes was his daughter' – a gesture that gives paternal approval to the budding romance and aligns business and familial relations.[49] Upon Robert Twersten's return, he and Marga Vanheil are married, thus joining the firms Twersten and Vanheil and renewing the prospects of the Vanheil family. Conveniently, the *Raffke* character, Theodor Bramberg, drops dead near the end of the film while drinking and dancing at a lively nightclub, thus leaving no obstacle for the budding romance between his wife Ingeborg with Karl Twersten. The film ends with Robert and Marga's embrace, the implication that Karl and Ingeborg marry, a return to narrative equilibrium, and profits for all.

Significantly, at the crisis point of the film, after Fritz has been stabbed and the elder Vanheil passes away, the Vanheil family finds itself in a precarious financial position in which Karl Twersten has control of their invested capital in the transatlantic venture. Karl has the opportunity to profit at the expense of the Vanheil family but instead decides to help the family back to its feet in a show of old-world camaraderie that reifies the central ideology of the film – that the 'Hanseatic' business elite operate on a code of honour that trumps pure profit alone. Released on the heels of the period of hyperinflation that devastated Weimar Germany, the film distances the Hanseatic business elite from the image of the post-war profiteer or speculator. As such, the film presents a very different picture from the dominant archetypical representations of finance and economy in the Weimar Republic.

Hanseaten operates on a central binary opposition, portraying a world of propriety, honour, and the promotion of 'productive' capital of the privately held company, while rejecting the 'speculative' capitalist notion of 'going public' and offering shares on the open market. It suggests that there is a clear boundary between legitimate venture capital and illegitimate financial

48 "Hanseaten," *Film-Kurier*, December 22, 1925.

49 Intertitle: 'Sie sind ein echtes Hamburger Mädel. Ich wollte, Sie wären meine Tochter.'

brinkmanship. This aporia at the centre of capitalism – that was later so ruthlessly highlighted in the propaganda of National Socialism, as well as by the Marxist left – can still be found in the present-day conversation on the use and abuse of financial markets in the form of the popular notions of the 'vampiric' or 'parasitic' role of finance capital to the *real* sector of the economy. As such, the film can be read negatively as a conservative tribute to a romantic vision of national economy that was driven by a mythos that spans back to the mediaeval roots of the Hanseatic league. This reading is also in keeping with Jeffrey Herf's idea of 'reactionary modernism,' as the film is not so much a rejection of capitalism or modernity in general, as it is of a threatening non-German form of it.

Hanseaten's nationalism and *völkisch* motifs stem from its source material – the 1909 novel of the same name by Rudolf Herzog. Now forgotten, and dismissed in high cultural circles in his time as a non-serious writer, Herzog was nonetheless one of the most widely read novelists of the first decades of the twentieth century in Germany.[50] Herzog, whose career spanned from 1900 to 1938, was a major writer of *Zuckerwasserromane* ('light fiction,' literally 'fresh-water fiction'), feuilletons, and conservative journalism, as well as National Socialist literature later in his career.[51] His oeuvre is marked by his constant framing of narratives around a central male figure who surpasses all others in his leadership capacity.[52] In addition, a full third of all his protagonists were *Fabrikherr* ('factory owners,' or 'entrepreneurs'), while another fifth were military.[53] However, he avoided depictions of the *Junkertum* ('nobility'), preferring 'self-made' businessmen and entrepreneurs.[54]

Hanseaten was adapted to the screen by Luise Heilborn-Kärlitz, who also wrote the script for Lamprecht's *Die Verrufenen* (1925). The film was glowingly reviewed in *Film-Kurier* upon its release in 1925, even if reviews were quick to point out the similarities in the setting to Thomas Mann's *Buddenbrooks* (1901). Willy Haas noted that the plot was 'such a typical Thomas Mann topic,

50 For further discussion of National Socialism and Rudolf Herzog see Pascal Jardin, "Aux sources du national-socialisme. Les romans de Rudolf Herzog et la culture politique allemande," *Vingtième Siècle. Revue d'histoire*, no. 43 (July 1, 1994): 43–54.

51 A review of the film from 1925 refers to the book as 'einem der meistgelesenen deutschen Romane' ('one of the most well-read German novels'). *Kinematograph*, no. 983/84.

52 Jardin, "Herzog," 48.

53 Ibid.

54 Herzog has an extensive entry in Jürgen Hillesheim and Elisabeth Michael, *Lexikon nationalsozialistischer Dichter: Biographien, Analysen, Bibliographien* (Würzburg: Königshausen & Neumann, 1993), 238.

that one is astounded to read another author's name in the program.'[55] In fact, Lamprecht had brought *Buddenbrooks* to the screen two years earlier in an overly stagey and plodding adaptation that rigidly followed Mann's novel. Available in an archival print at the Deutsche Kinemathek in Berlin, this film is a much lower-budget production in which Lamprecht had not yet found his directorial voice. It contains none of the formal innovations or contemporary historical details that make *Hanseaten* so interesting for the German cultural landscape in 1925. *Hanseaten* updates some of the central concerns of *Buddenbrooks*, including its depiction of the decline of the Hanseatic city state and the fall of a wealthy family in the face of the rise of the new metropolis of Berlin. It moves through similar terrain in terms of its depiction of anxieties surrounding German nationalism and the inversion of traditional social hierarchies as well as gender roles. The film can be seen as a reactionary throwback to the idealized notion of a paternalistic capitalism in the face of the shifting terrain of the modern work force. Although the film features several strong female characters, their actions ultimately support the conservative romantic coupling that the film promotes in the end.

Angela Twersten's Brazilian origins also echo Mann's own biography and his Brazilian-German mother, Júlia da Silva Bruhns. Though *Buddenbrooks* paints a sympathetic portrait of the German upper classes based on Mann's own upbringing in Lübeck and status as a 'Hanse' himself, it seems fair to say that Mann would not have approved of the reactionary modernist exceptionalism of *Hanseaten*. Mann was overtly critical of the emergence of this tendency in his time, writing in *Deutschland und die Deutschen* (1938–45) that 'the really characteristic and dangerous aspect of National Socialism was its mixture of robust modernity and an affirmative stance towards progress combined with dreams of the past: a highly technological romanticism.'[56] Mann remained acutely aware of the problematic combination of romanticism with modern economic, industrial, and social processes, which features so centrally in *Hanseaten*.

The film provides a narrative space to contain the inherent tensions at work in the idea of reactionary modernism, even though they threaten to dissolve its internal logic. In *Hanseaten*, the excess of signifiers of the nation threaten to collapse under their own weight, and a closer examination of their symbolic content exposes cracks within the film's foundations. Like

55 Willy Haas, "Hanseaten" *Film-Kurier*, December 22, 1925.

56 Translation from Brian Wilson Aldiss and David Wingrove, *Trillion Year Spree: The History of Science Fiction* (New York: Atheneum, 1973), 175.

Buddenbrooks the film is centred around the intermarriage of the Hanseatic *Besitzbürgertum* ('haute bourgeoisie'), but its inclusion of non-European characters such as Angela gives it an added transnational dimension. In one *Film-Kurier* review, Angela is described as an exotic *Halberotin* – literally a demigod of *eros* – while her son is '*Halb Rio, halb Waterkant*' ('Half Rio, half *Waterkant*') – a *Plattdeutsch* ('low-German') substantive identifying people born on the North Sea coast – who is 'conflicted as to which of his two heritages will win out.'[57] *Waterkant* or in High German *Wasserkant*, meaning water's edge or waterside, denotes both a historical marker of national identity, closely tied to the Nordic-Germanic imaginary, and conversely, the peripheral and transient position of the inhabitants of the German port cities. Bolstering the stabilizing use of this term, one contemporary reviewer explicitly confirms the film's alignment of the North Sea locale with notions of the importance of elemental nature and of the connection to the rustic turf and soil itself:

> The air in this film is good. It is a fragrant, cool sea breeze, with grandfatherly cosy rooms, that smell of turf, and people who in this air believe, and who in this air belong.[58]

This closing off of *Wasserkant* as a signifier of the local – and with *völkisch* overtones of connection to the soil itself – defines the unspoken ideology at work in the construction of identity in the film. At the same time, this construction glosses over a central contradiction inherent in any such definition of place and locale as markers of stability. *Place* matters to the construction of origin in the film in more ways than one, and ports are essential to a national economy, but they are also sites of migration and *portals* to the *space* of the international market. In this destabilizing sense, we can begin to read the location and subject matter of the film obliquely – as itself straining to establish yet ultimately undermining a simple equation of nation with productive capital and a Germanic mythological structure.

In the novel, Karl Twersten is portrayed as a 'veritable Teutonic knight of modern times,'[59] and the film certainly supports this reading as well. His son Robert is torn between two national identities – as exemplified by the contrast between the severe sobriety of his German father and the fiery recklessness of his Brazilian mother – making him as much a child

57 Willy Haas, "Hanseaten" *Film-Kurier*, December 22, 1925. Author's translation.

58 Ibid.

59 Jardin, "Herzog," 49.

of international commerce as of Germany. If we consider also that 'twer' is a middle German precedent for the high German 'quer' – which means 'across' or 'transverse' – the resonance of Karl Twersten's directive to his son – 'you are carrying my name into the world, now show that you are a Twersten'[60] – changes somewhat. In this sense, the name Twersten, functions *both* as an anchor of paternal stability as well as being indicative of the tension and categorical slippage that undermines the film's attempt to (literally) arrange a marriage between the notion of a liquid international market and the local propriety of a national economy based on relations between members of an established upper class. This symbolic slippage within the name of the central family of the film stands in for the aporia of national identity in the transnational world that the film takes place.

Hanseaten in the Context of *Die Verrufenen*

Gerhard Lamprecht's *Hanseaten* was released in 1925, the same year as his better-known *Die Verrufenen: die fünfte Stand* (literally 'The Notorious: The Fifth Class' but commonly known as 'Slums of Berlin') – a film that is often discussed as a prime example of *Neue Sachlichkeit* filmmaking. *Die Verrufenen* is a tragic portrayal of abject poverty and the lives of Germany's underclass that was hailed for its brutal realism. It tells the story of Robert Kramer (played by Bernhard Goetzke, who also played State Prosecutor Wenk in *Dr. Mabuse*). A trained engineer, he has recently been released from prison after being convicted of perjury. Upon his return to Berlin, he struggles to find employment and – a significant detail not usually discussed in commentary on this film – finds his former fiancé married to a stockbroker. When Kramer visits, the broker briefly greets him, but excuses himself to return to his seat by the radio to listen to *Börsennachrichten* ('stock market news'). This detail, though brief, is another document of the everyday presence of financial news which, in this case, permeates the private sphere of a Berlin apartment through the new medium of the radio. It serves to juxtapose this abstract realm with the realist portrayal of the mean streets that follow in the film, but also to bind them together in a similar manner as in Pabst's *Die freudlose Gasse*, and anticipates the aesthetic of the *Querschnitt* ('cross section') that will be discussed in chapter 5.

The film opens with a signed intertitle identifying the well-known satirical cartoonist Heinrich Zille, who then appears in the frame himself,

60 Intertitle: 'Du führst meinen Namen hinaus in die Welt. Nun zeige, daß Du ein Twersten bist.'

staring into the camera before proceeding to draw in his characteristic style. A dissolve transitions from the cartoon to a bar scene that opens the film. Full of local character and intertitles inflected by north-German slang, *Die Verrufenen* was a landmark film of *Neue Sachlichkeit* realism and the first true 'Zille Film.'[61] This was a form of *proletärische Film* ('proletarian film') or *Aufklärungsfilm* that, in keeping with the caricatures of Zille himself, 'confronted the bourgeoisie with the results of their class domination and cast blame, not through pathos, but rather through jokes, whose cynical punchlines concealed their inherent outrage.'[62]

After being cast out by his bourgeois father in *Die Verrufenen*, Robert Kramer proceeds to work a series of odd jobs, all while remaining a paragon of nobility in poverty and never turning to crime, although the temptation is all around him. His hard work eventually pays off when he impresses the owner of a factory in which he is employed by repairing a broken-down machine and revealing both his skill set as well as his previous (and, we may infer, inherent) class standing. Any reading of *Die Verrufenen* as a leftist condemnation of a class conflict must be tempered by the fact that the film only provides a way out of the slums for its 'fallen' bourgeois protagonist, while the secondary characters he encounters along the way remain condemned to their lot and the prostitute Emma who befriends him dies in the end. It is partly due to this pessimism that *Die Verrufenen* was hailed as an unflinching portrayal of the brutality of urban living at the time. Heinz Michaelis wrote in *Film-Kurier* in 1925:

> The name Zille, which looms above this film, is programmatic. [Zille] stands for the depiction of the proletarian psyche by way of art. This art does not judge. It pictures the proletarian as the product of his surroundings [...] It presents a slice of the real world and is content to say: this is how it is. Its simple portrayal of reality amounts to harsher criticism of the status quo than any of the published diatribes [...] Gerhard Lamprecht has managed to evoke the atmosphere of his world in a believable way. The characters become exponents of the milieu in which they live [...]

61 *Die Verrufenen* was the first of this subcategory of *proletärische Filme*, according to Bruce Arthur Murray, *Film and the German Left in the Weimar Republic: From Caligari to Kuhle Wampe* (Austin: University of Texas Press, 1990), 82. Other examples of this category include *Jenseits der Strasse* (Leo Mittler, 1929), the incredibly tragic *Mutter Krausens Fahrt ins Glück* (Piel Jutzi, 1929), and *Lohnbuchhalter Kremke* (Marie Harder, 1930). These three examples were part of a concerted effort at producing films with a progressive and socialist political message.

62 Georg Piltz, *Geschichte der Europäischen Karikatur* (Berlin: VEB Deutscher Verlag der Wissenschaften, 1976), 265. Author's translation.

> Lamprecht has achieved what is ultimately the goal of every film [...] namely that the world it pictures comes alive for the viewer.[63]

While also hailed for its realism, Lamprecht's *Hanseaten* portrays the world of the *haute bourgeoisie* of 1920s Hamburg, however, it contains almost none of the characteristics of the *Zille-Film*. Instead, *Hanseaten* attempts to hold together several central yet unstable binary oppositions: those of space vs. place, productive vs. non-productive capital, and the gendering of interior vs. exterior space. The film is notable for its resistance to classification in terms of the established genre discourses of Weimar cinema – partly because those genres are based on a small number of canonical films in which it was not included. It resembles a *Kammerspiel* drama at times, with its claustrophobic sets and large amount of interior action, but it lacks psychological depth or expressionist touches, such as the spatial vocabulary of stairs and courtyards, and is overly reliant on intertitles to advance its plot. More specifically, the spatial composition of the film – the function of public and private space – is not easily classifiable according to what Bruce Murray has identified as the spatial binary at work in many films of this era:

> While developing their claim to authenticity, street films portrayed urban environments as inherently dangerous, evil places, dominated by prostitutes, pimps, criminals, and alcoholics. They juxtaposed the evil public sphere of the street with a virtuous private sphere of lower-middle to middle-class families and developed their plots around dissatisfied daughters, sons, and sometimes husbands. These characters abandoned domestic security, suffered misfortune in the street, and returned to these families cleansed of discontent.[64]

In addition, Murray claims that these more typical films, though often formally innovative, can still be seen as re-inscribing reactionary politics and established gender roles. In this Marxian reading, the documentary claims of the street film genre are undermined by the constant return of hegemonic value judgements. Additionally, in established readings of the *Kammerspiel* and the street film, interior domestic space is aligned with the female, while the public sphere of the urban street is presented as a

63 Heinz Michaelis, *Film-Kurier*, August 29, 1925. Translated by Ulrich Döge in Laurence Kardish and Museum of Modern Art (New York, N.Y.), eds., *Weimar Cinema, 1919-1933: Daydreams and Nightmares* (New York: Museum of Modern Art, 2010), 109.
64 Murray, *Film and the German Left*, 81–82.

realm of both danger and opportunity for the male protagonist. By contrast, the street is almost completely absent from *Hanseaten*, and the interior *places* of the film, in the form of sets for the family offices and homes, are dominated by the male businessmen while the anonymous location-based shots of the exterior *space* of the harbour and city are essentially stock footage, shot in wide angle and populated by nameless extras rather than the main characters. These exterior spaces, while still under the control of the fathers and sons, are significantly activated by women engaged in forms of economic exchange.

As in the films discussed in chapter 3, women in *Hanseaten* are linked to commerce and the space of international capital flow. The ship at the centre of the business venture is named after Ingeborg Bramberg, while Marga Vanheil's marriage to the young Robert Twersten is explicitly transactional and initiated by her. Money, something akin to a dowry even, changes hands in the aforementioned scene (in which Marga reveals her savings to Robert's father while riding in an uncovered carriage) as it is she who effectively pays for Robert with her own money. In other significant ways, the manner in which the women are associated with financial exchange differs from canonical examples of Weimar cinema. Unlike Lulu in *Die Büchse der Pandora*, or Grete in *Die freudlose Gasse*, transactions involving the female body in *Hanseaten* are not conducted under the sign of prostitution. Instead, women are divided in terms of their conformity to the two opposed forms of capital depicted in the film. Either they support Twersten in his paternalistic ventures, or they are aligned with the speculative capital of the open market.

Contemporary reviewers, as well as Wolfgang Jacobsen in his book on Lamprecht, confirm the film's status as a melodrama, calling it a 'a tear jerker'[65] as well as a *Reeder-Melodram*[66] (literally, 'ship owner's melodrama'). Certainly, its release at Christmas and its generally reassuring tenor and happy ending mark it as something of a feel-good holiday film. Luise Heilborn-Kärlitz, who wrote *Hanseaten* and collaborated with Lamprecht on *Die Verrufenen*, applied similar melodramatic touches to the love stories in both films. It is unclear whether the film conforms to the well-established binary that Petro sets out – i.e., in contrast to how the street film appeals to a male audience, the melodrama is concerned more with the everyday and anticipates female spectatorship – and the unique way in which the film mobilizes several established clichés deserves to be explored further. Angela

65 Willy Haas, "Hanseaten" *Film-Kurier*, December 22, 1925.

66 Wolfgang Jacobsen, *Zeit und Welt*, (Munich: Edition Text + Kritik, 2013), 37.

Twersten is most interesting in this regard in that she is central to the film and motivates the plot and, as the gambler and source of both familial and financial conflict, aligns herself with speculative capital when she suggests that her husband sell shares in the company. Speculation is furthermore associated with destabilization of the family identity in the film – and by extension the conservative family-business-territory nexus that the film evokes. A contemporary *Film-Kurier* review explicitly links the volatility of gambling and vice with Angela's ethnicity, and her destabilizing identity in the film's narrative:

> She plays a South American, who is uprooted to northern Germany through her marriage to a Hamburg industrialist. The southern temperament comes into conflict with this completely different environment. A passion for gambling is awakened in her. She hopes to satisfy her *Daseinshunger* ['existential angst'] with this supplemental diversion. Even with the repeated warnings of her husband, she cannot stop her overindulgence in this vice.[67]

Here Angela is understood as somehow ill-prepared for the 'civilized' world she is thrown into, reacting as if against her own volition to the overwhelming pressure of the modern. Representative of the exotic 'outside' world, she is coded and clad in the garments of the new woman, smokes cigarettes, and embodies a *liquid* and destabilizing mobility. In the binary of productive vs. non-productive capital, Angela Twersten represents irrationality associated with gambling and illegitimate speculation. As before, the male figure of Karl Twersten is tasked with taming the 'irrational' *Kauflust* of the female character. However, in *Hanseaten* this problem is resolved differently in that Karl represents a fantasy of independence from speculative capital, as if the Hamburg *Reeder* can avoid the corrupting forces of the global market. Karl does not 'master' the rules of speculation, but rather avoids them altogether and replaces the metaphoric female representative of speculation with a more conservative surrogate in Frau Bamberg.

Going Public vs. Private Capital

In contrast to *Die Veruffenen*, the public space of the street is largely absent from *Hanseaten*, and the main exterior space of the film is the Hamburg harbour – a space of industrial capital and international commerce. The

67 *Film-Kurier*. "Glashaus," October 21, 1925.

action of the film primarily takes place in claustrophobic interior offices and houses of the families, while shots of the harbour and its workers are anonymous and abstracted. The proletariat of Hamburg appear in only one brief scene in which Robert and Fritz travel to the 'Niedernstrasse' – a street (likely a set rather than location shooting) in the working-class St. Pauli district of Hamburg. Serving as comic relief, the brief scene depicts the inhabitants of the neighbourhood engaged in a massive brawl and quarrelling over the dinner table. The triteness of this scene was not lost on some contemporary reviewers who remarked that it 'had nothing to do with the plot' and 'should have been avoided at all costs in a manuscript for a director with the reputation of *Verrufenen*.'[68] As has been shown here, however, this dismissive portrayal of the lumpenproletariat in *Hanseaten* may not have been as out of keeping with *Die Verrufenen*'s message after all. *Die Verrufenen* may have provided the illusion of class consciousness, but *Hanseaten* jettisons any pretension to it.

Hanseaten features many establishing shots of the harbour and its surroundings, including some of winter ice floes. One contemporary article on the production of the film noted the novelty of depicting the Hamburg harbour itself, as well as the fact that this was the first time the launching of a ship had been shown on film.[69] Shots of the dockyard are often abstracted, and depict starkly contrasting iron and steel formwork against the sky, reminiscent in their composition to the photography of Moholy-Nagy. In this sense, human figures – the workers and inhabitants of the area – are evacuated and replaced by the concentration on industry and the business of the propertied classes. The harbour exists only as a gateway for the business of the families, in both the personal and the economic sense of the term, but this abstraction also has the feel of documentary footage that is entirely separate from the plot of the film (Figure 16).

Documentary footage of a real ship launch, intercut with the diegetic world of the film, blurs the boundary between fiction and industry. The depiction of the launch was a novelty for many viewers of the time and functions as another way in which film could depict the economy to viewers. This conflation of fiction and historical detail also occurs when mention in the film is made of a real ship of historical significance. When Angela Twersten departs for Brazil she sends a 'radiogram' to Karl that states she is sailing aboard the 'Kap. Polonio.' This was an actual German ship, but reference to it only serves to further confuse the timeframe of the film. This

68 *Lichtbildbuhne*, December 22, 1925.

69 *Film-Kurier*, "Eine Weinachtspremiere," November 25, 1925.

Figure 16. The Hamburg harbour and the launching of the *Jngeborg* in *Hanseaten* (Gerhard Lamprecht, 1925). Photo: Deutsche Kinemathek.

ship, which was initially built in Hamburg by Blohm & Voss as an ocean liner, was in fact refitted and served in the German navy in the First World War. After the war, it was confiscated as part of the war reparations, and its appearance in the intertitles is anachronistic but also perhaps symptomatic of the perceived loss of German industrial and naval power. In a similarly confusing sense, *Hanseaten* feels like a relic of the nineteenth century due to the heavy influence of *Buddenbrooks* and the stodgy appearance of Martin Vanheil, Karl Twersten, and Ingeborg Bramberg, but characters like Theodor Bramberg and Angela Twersten dress in the fashion of 1925 and use modern technologies like the radiogram.

The importance of the ship-launch scene to the film's production is demonstrated by the exceptional amount of resources used to capture it. One contemporary review notes that no fewer than six cameras were used.[70] The fascination with capturing this event was also reflected in

70 "Der Stapellauf der Ingeborg," *Reichsfilmblatt*, November 28, 1925.

reviews of the film, several of which devoted as much column space to it as to discussion of the plot or actors. The *Reichsfilmblatt* reported the film as a cinematic event sure to 'go down in the history of cinematography,' and went on to describe the launch in great detail.[71] This fascination with shipbuilding was particularly poignant in 1925, as Hamburg had lost much of its former industrial might after the First World War. The connection between the loss of German sea power and the loss of German overseas colonies should also not be forgotten. It is especially relevant to the film's nationalistic tenor and the decision to adapt a novel published during the heyday of, and which made specific reference to, shipping concerns such as the Hamburg-Amerikanische Packetfahrt-Aktien-Gesellschaft (HAPAG)[72] and its significance to German sea power and international presence. Again, this points to a slippage at work in determining the period in which the film is set and evokes an image of progress mixed with nostalgia that seems to efface the contemporary reality of the post-inflation situation.

Although the established binary of public and private urban space in Weimar cinema is conspicuously absent from *Hanseaten*, a parallel spatial binary is at work in the film that contrasts the private with an alternative idea of 'public' that will be unpacked here. In stark contrast to *Die Verrufenen*, Lamprecht portrays a working-class neighbourhood in only one brief and problematic scene. In the absence of a portrayal of the actual public space of the street, the film operates on an alternative notion of what constitutes its public sphere. As has been outlined in the introduction, markets, news services, and communications networks are historically interdependent. The development of telegraphic networks was funded in the first place by the demand for financial quotations, and only secondarily developed into the newswire services of the late nineteenth century. Thus, the development of communications networks for market information was intimately connected with the development of mass media and the publication of news. This entanglement of market information with the spatial ideal of 'the public' created a new market-based definition of the public itself. The 'public' space of markets consists of the information that is widely available to all participants. For a company to 'go public' it sells shares on the open market and in turn registers the trades of insiders (employees and management) in order to promote the image of transparency and down-play any conception of anti-competitive behaviour. This financial definition of

71 *Reichsfilmblatt*, November 28, 1925.

72 Established in 1847, and often referred to as the 'Hamburg-America Line,' it suffered great losses to its fleet during the First World War.

the term 'public' differs from how the 'public sphere' is usually understood, but it is worth revisiting this definition in relation to the spatial binary that is set up in *Hanseaten*. In *Hanseaten*, the idea of the 'public' information of the market has replaced the spatio-social Habermasian concept as well as the intuitive notion of the public sphere that exists in the exterior spaces of the city. In terms of the production of an international market *space* under discussion in this book, this categorial shift is of central importance. The rise of mass media in the nineteenth century sealed the fate of the public sphere, and the same forces that created the public sphere (bourgeois capitalism) were responsible for its downfall as market forces led to property centralization and a greater disparity in wealth distribution. What was essentially an idealized spatial practice – the 'public life' which occurred in the market place (agora) – was mapped onto an informational space based on communications technology and *publicity*. In turn, the market of public information became a surrogate for the displaced space outside the private realm. In this arrangement, the control of flows of information determines what is essentially hidden (inside) and public (outside) in what has become a symbolic rather than proximate arrangement.

To illustrate how this financial reformulation of the idea of the 'public' is mobilized in the film, consider the following scene. Karl Twersten's seemingly flippant remark that he does not want his company to go public and be subject to the whims of the 'profiteering of indifferent donkeys' deserves further analysis. Though glossed over as a humorous aside, the joke itself reveals the central ideology of the film. Namely, it promotes a view of industry as being better off in the hands of private old money, rather than being accessible to a liberal ideal of market participation. Accordingly, Twersten's position can be read as a type of corrective or bulwark against the many depictions of finance capital as a destructive threat in Weimar cinema. As such, this brief moment of humour illuminates how the public/private binary, so often discussed in relation to melodramas of this time, is *atypically* deployed in *Hanseaten*. Twersten and Vanheil's power (and potential ruthlessness) is downplayed in the film in stark contrast to other lasting portrayals of the heads of business organizations from the time, such as Joh Fredersen in *Metropolis* (1927), Saccard in L'Herbier's *L'Argent* (1929), Dr. Mabuse, Haghi in Lang's *Spione* ('Spies,' 1928), or even Mackie Messer's short stint as a criminal-cum-bank director in Brecht and Weil's *Die Dreigroschenoper* ('The Threepenny Opera,' 1928).

The central tension that drives the narrative of *Hanseaten* stems from Angela Twersten's suggestion that the family firm 'go public' and expose itself to the only 'public' that the film offers to its viewers – that of the publicly traded company. It is important to note that since the private sphere of the family is so closely bound to its business ventures, the external threat of allowing the influence of the public market becomes a threat to dissolve the family itself. In the film, what is essentially a *domestic* drama plays out on the global market before being resolved in the private realm. In this sense, any notion in the film of a real public space has been replaced by the suggestion that there are only two spheres – the private sphere of productive capital and the ersatz-public sphere of non-productive finance capital. In relation to the central theme of this chapter, combatting the rupture of the 'public' market is aligned with a reaffirmation of traditional gender roles in the film and a reestablishment of the 'stable' patriarchal family itself. In aesthetic terms, the film proposes the static traditional interior spaces, unmoving camera, and stiff antiquated courtship as an antidote to scenes of liquidity so often adopted in depictions of finance capital on screen.

I have argued in chapter 2 that liminal figures like Mabuse stand in for access to the *spectral* realm of international finance. By this I mean that these figures function as fictional manifestations of anxieties surrounding the production of national identity and subjectivity by embodying the insubstantial and liquid nature of the market apparatus in the form of the modern-day spectre. Mabuse, in his multiple forms, represents a dissolution of the body and its reconstitution as the economic and liberal subject (*homo economicus*). He is a master of disguise whose identity is never fixed and, like the modern corporation, remains faceless and non-localizable within society.[73] By contrast, *Hanseaten*'s capitalists *do* have faces and names that the film struggles to tie to stable locations, even as the very category of 'Hanseatic' implies an extra-territorial alliance. The German Hanseatic cities – Bremen, Lübeck, and Hamburg – have been known since the Congress of Vienna in 1815 as *freie Hansastädte* ('free Hanseatic cities') and the city states of Hamburg and Bremen are examples of the retention of this distinction to this day. As such the term '*Hanseaten*' resonates as a marker of class distinction that sets the families apart from their surroundings. The alignment of markers of distinction, rooted in familial bonds and connection to the specific places in the film, as well as the nationalist overtones, is in tension with the extra-territorial allegiance implied by the history of the Hanseatic League which was a forerunner of post-national corporatism and globalization. This arises as another central and unresolved tension in the film, especially given its uneasy depiction of race and its reliance

73 See Stefan Andriopoulos, *Possessed: Hypnotic Crimes, Corporate Fiction, and the Invention of Cinema*, Cinema and Modernity (Chicago: University of Chicago Press, 2008), 123.

on notions of 'real Hamburg girls' versus *Halberotin* Brazilian interlopers, or its suggestion of an inbuilt sense of honour bred into the merchant and industrialist class, derived from their roots in the seafaring regions. This tension bubbles to the surface in the scenes set in Brazil (not filmed on location, except for some establishing stock footage of Rio de Janeiro) which introduce a comedic character noted only as *eine Kreolin* ('a creole woman') in the credits. Played in blackface by Maria Forescu, she is Angela Twersten's Brazilian maid and is depicted as comically infatuated by Angela's German son and his friend Fritz – leering suggestively at them while they laugh at her condescendingly.

In terms of its representation of finance capital and the world economy, *Hanseaten* functions as a stabilizing narrative that recuperates this threatening realm in reactionary modernist terms. An illusion of a seamless continuity between a patriarchal family and an idea of nation is created and then supported by the genre conventions of the melodrama and love story, as well as the alignment of the success of the family business with the national economy itself. Meanwhile, its implicit rejection of the contemporary reality of financial forces in the German economy, specifically in the form of the public company, creates a fantasy of industry devoid of speculative forces – and this is at the core of the imaginary of the film. The solutions that the film proposes play on widespread moral indignation at the disinterestedness and destructiveness of speculative capital – as embodied by Theodor Bramberg who is symbolically killed off near the end. Ultimately, the film suggests that the excesses of the *Raffke* lead to his own demise while north-German pragmatism and a code of honour, which is tied to notions of origin and heritage, will prevail in re-establishing an ordering of the home and, by extension, the economy.

By resolving its narrative within this 'reactionary modernist' framework, *Hanseaten* also can be seen as an attempt to symbolically solve the crisis of masculinity that films like *Die freudlose Gasse* introduced to Weimar audiences. By neatly excluding the disruptive figure of Angela Twersten from the conclusion of the narrative, the film attempts to smooth over its inherent conflicts concerning gender roles, race, nation, and the threat of finance capital to the notion of productive industrial capital. The film attempts this highly problematic symbolic manoeuvre, all the while mobilizing imagery of international trade, flows of capital, and literal movement of commercial products across the ocean. It portrays a 'reactionary modernist' vision of economic autarky that would later be taken up as Germany's economic policy. All of the main developments of the narrative take place around the port, or in the space across the sea, which evoke an international stage, yet the its resolution attempts to create an image with a stable signifier of *Heimat* ('homeland'). As such, the film is deeply invested at a symbolic level with the representation of capital flow and liquidity itself. At the same time, it attempts to resolve the threat of extraterritorial space by means of a restabilizing, reterritorializing, and shoring up of subjectivity that hearkens back to an earlier age of bounded tradition – an imaginary in which neither the boundaries of the masculine nor those of the nation state were under siege.

5. The Aggregate Image and the World Economy

Abstract: Chapter 5 turns to the emergence of the 'aggregate image' in the cinema and economic discourse of the Weimar Republic. It discusses Eisenstein's plans for a film based on Marx's *Das Kapital* and Brecht's unfinished play *Jae Fleischhacker in Chikago* (1924), which attempted to dramatize the grain market. Discovered fragments of Balázs's *K 13 513: Die Abenteuer eines Zehnmarkscheins* ('Adventures of a Ten Mark Note' or 'Uneasy Money,' 1926) – the first 'cross-section film' – are discussed along with *Kuhle Wampe, oder: Wem gehört die Welt?* ('Kuhle Wampe, or: Who Owns the World?,' 1932). The visual convention of the *Querschnitt* ('cross-section'), a radical montage aesthetic, was emptied of its political content in the creation of a corporate vision of the world economy in *Melodie der Welt* ('Melody of the World,' 1929). The cinematic 'aggregate image' of the world is placed alongside parallel developments in economics that were used to create an image of the world economy.

Keywords: World Economy, Financial Image, Montage, Statistics, Sergei Eisenstein, Bela Balázs

Macroeconomic Visions

Introduction

In this chapter, I address several key critical representations of finance capital. I am primarily concerned here with filmmakers who adopted montage as a central means to lay bare the inequality of capitalism, as well as the ways in which montage was used to present a new awareness of the global economy. I discuss examples of Soviet montage, both completed and abandoned, including Sergei Eisenstein's plan (begun in the early 1920s) to create a film based on Karl Marx's *Das Kapital*, Béla Balázs and Bertold Viertel's *K 13 513: Die Abenteuer eines Zehnmarkscheins* (1926),

Lyons, O., *Finance and the World Economy in Weimar Cinema*. Taylor & Francis Group, 2023.
DOI 10.5117/9789463727136_CH05

Bertolt Brecht and Slatan Dudow's *Kuhle Wampe* (1932), as well as Brecht's unfinished play *Jae Fleischhacker in Chikago* (1924). I will contextualize these works within larger image-making practices of the Weimar Republic that mobilized the idea of the *Querschnitt* ('cross-section') – which had taken hold in Weimar culture across a variety of media – to create an aggregate image. The use of the cross-section in the illustrated press, for example in the illustrated magazine *Querschnitt* itself, was, as Bela Bálazs states, an attempt to 'not focus only on a single image of the world, but rather show numerous simultaneous phenomena' and 'attempt to produce a cosmic impression, a total image of the world.'[1] In this chapter, I discuss the use of the *Querschnitt* alongside the use of montage, tracing the ways in which the initially radical montage aesthetic gave way to a more apolitical version in the form of Walter Ruttmann's *Berlin Sinfonie* (1927) and then to the creation of a corporate vision of the world economy in Ruttmann's *Melodie der Welt* (1929). This depoliticization of the cinematic aggregate image will be discussed alongside parallel developments in the sphere of economics and statistics. Ultimately, I aim to show how the manifestation of the aggregate in the sphere of popular media mirrored the mobilization of new statistical techniques for the representation of the economy.

Representations of the Economy and the Critique of Capitalism: Soviet Montage

As was discussed in chapter 4, the ostensible critique of capitalism that seems to be a feature of many films of the *Neue Sachlichkeit* style, vanishes under closure scrutiny. For example, Lamprecht's *Die Verrufenen* paints a fatalistic picture of class immobility but it does not lay bare the destitution of the Berlin slums that it portrays and allows a redemptive narrative for its 'fallen' upper middle-class lead. These depictions of the effects of finance and the economy are demonstrative of how the *Neue Sachlichkeit* style narrativized economic crisis, however, at a formal level they do not explicitly deal with the question of the representation of the de-individualized mass that is inherent in the idea of the economy. Films like *Die Verrufenen* and *Hanseaten* only reveal the everyday workings of economic forces symptomatically and through the actions of individual characters. After the so called 'period of stabilization,' the relative economic calm of the middle years of the Weimar

1 Béla Balázs, quoted in Michael Cowan, "Cutting through the Archive: Querschnitt Montage and Images of the World in Weimar Visual Culture," *New German Critique* 40, no. 3 120 (September 21, 2013): 2–3.

Republic seemed to promise that the fledgling republic's experiment with democracy might be a success after all. The republic's origin in the social democratic political sphere was accordingly reconfirmed with the electoral victory of the leftist parties in 1928. Out of a total of 491 seats and nine parties on the ballot, the Sozialdemokratische Partei Deutschlands (SPD) won 153 seats, the Kommunistische Partei Deutschlands (KPD, formally the revolutionary Spartakusbund) 54, and the left-liberal Deutsche Demokratische Partei (DDP) 25.[2] At the same time, and according to Siegfried Kracauer, the serialized publication of Erich Maria Remarque's *Im Westen nichts Neues* ('All Quiet on the Western Front,' November to December 1928) in the DDP-associated *Vossische Zeitung*, marked a new appreciation amongst the public for 'social criticism' and the disclosure of 'reactionary manoeuvres.'[3] Siegfried Kracauer remained unimpressed by the small number of truly 'socialist' films to appear, and he lamented the lack of an emergence of a radical film politics, similar to that of the Soviet cinema. Referencing melancholic films such as the devastating *Mutter Krausens Fahrt ins Glück* ('Mother Krausen's Journey to Happiness,' Piel Jutzi, 1929), *So ist das Leben* ('Such is Life,' Carl Junghans, 1929), and *Jenseits der Strasse* ('Beyond the Street,' Leo Mittler, 1929), Kracauer questioned their critical potential, claiming that 'their underlying revolutionary inclinations are secondary attitudes rather than primary impulses' and that 'all three seem to originate in a mind that is not too seriously concerned with emancipation.'[4]

Similarly, Kracauer was mercilessly critical of the 'colourless neutrality' of *Neue Sachlichkeit* filmmaking, but offered analyses of a few choice films that he considered formally innovative. One such film is Ernö Metzner's experimental short *Polizeibericht Überfall* ('Police Report of a Mugging,'1928). The film opens with the image of a coin lying in the street. A passing man attempts to pick up the coin but is run down by a car, after which the coin rolls into a gutter and is found by the film's unnamed protagonist. This chance find sets in motion a series of unfortunate events. After multiplying his good fortune by successfully gambling in a dice game with the found coin, the protagonist draws the attention of some local thugs. He is lured into a nearby house by a prostitute who is working with the thugs and they promptly assault him and steal his money. After regaining consciousness in

2 Dieter Nohlen and Philip Stöver, *Elections in Europe: A Data Handbook* (Baden-Baden: Nomos, 2010), 762.

3 Siegfried Kracauer, *From Caligari to Hitler: A Psychological History of the German Film* (Princeton, NJ: Princeton University Press, 2004), 190.

4 Ibid., 198.

a hospital bed, the protagonist is questioned by the police as to the identity of his attackers. When asked if he is strong enough to identify them, the film fades from his face to a close-up image of a large spinning one-mark coin. The question 'who is guilty?' is answered with an image of money itself.

Kracauer praised this film for 'debunking those street films of the stabilized period,' in that it 'neither glorifies the petty bourgeois as a rebel nor transforms the chaotic street into a haven for genuine love.'[5] He also claimed that the film's experimental photography and its use of distorting mirrors and trick photography to portray the moment of the attack marked the film as 'a protest against deep-rooted conventions,'[6] but he does not discuss the conclusion of the film and its ultimate assignment of blame to the circulation of money. Accordingly, German censors called *Polizeibericht Überfall* a 'criminal film' that does not frame its violence with 'an equal artistic equivalent to induce milder interpretation' and banned it 'because of its brutal and demoralizing effect.'[7] As Kracauer suggests, the film's 'demoralizing effect' was likely the result of its laying bare the unstable conditions of employment and fortune, in addition to the brutal violence portrayed. What made the film's violence unacceptable to censors was the lack of a framing gesture and the visual violence inflicted on the image itself in the scene of the assault – another clear example of a cinematic moment of liquidity. When the unnamed man is assaulted in the street, the image dissolves and distorts wildly, seeming to rend his face apart (Figure 17). His distorted face disappears into blackness and is replaced by a liquefied image of dice, then a spinning one-mark coin, and finally, distorted images of men gambling and hands exchanging coins. The protagonist is shown again in several shots in which his body appears as if fused with that of others, including the prostitute's. The film thus aligns the violence of street life with the dissolution of the image in order to reveal the underlying symbolic violence of the money economy itself and the existential threat of precarious economic conditions on the human subject. Its final image confirms the centrality of money to its message.

As in the examples discussed in the previous chapter, *Überfall* relies on the formal dissolution of the frame to represent the intersection of the money economy with the modern male subject. In so doing, the film

5 Ibid., 195.

6 Ibid.

7 Censor's letter to *Deutscher Werkfilm*, in "German Censor's Incomprehensible Bank," *Close up* 4, no. 5 (May 1929): 14. Translated by Ulrich Döge in Laurence Kardish and Museum of Modern Art (New York, N.Y.), eds., *Weimar Cinema, 1919-1933: Daydreams and Nightmares* (New York: Museum of Modern Art, 2010), 218.

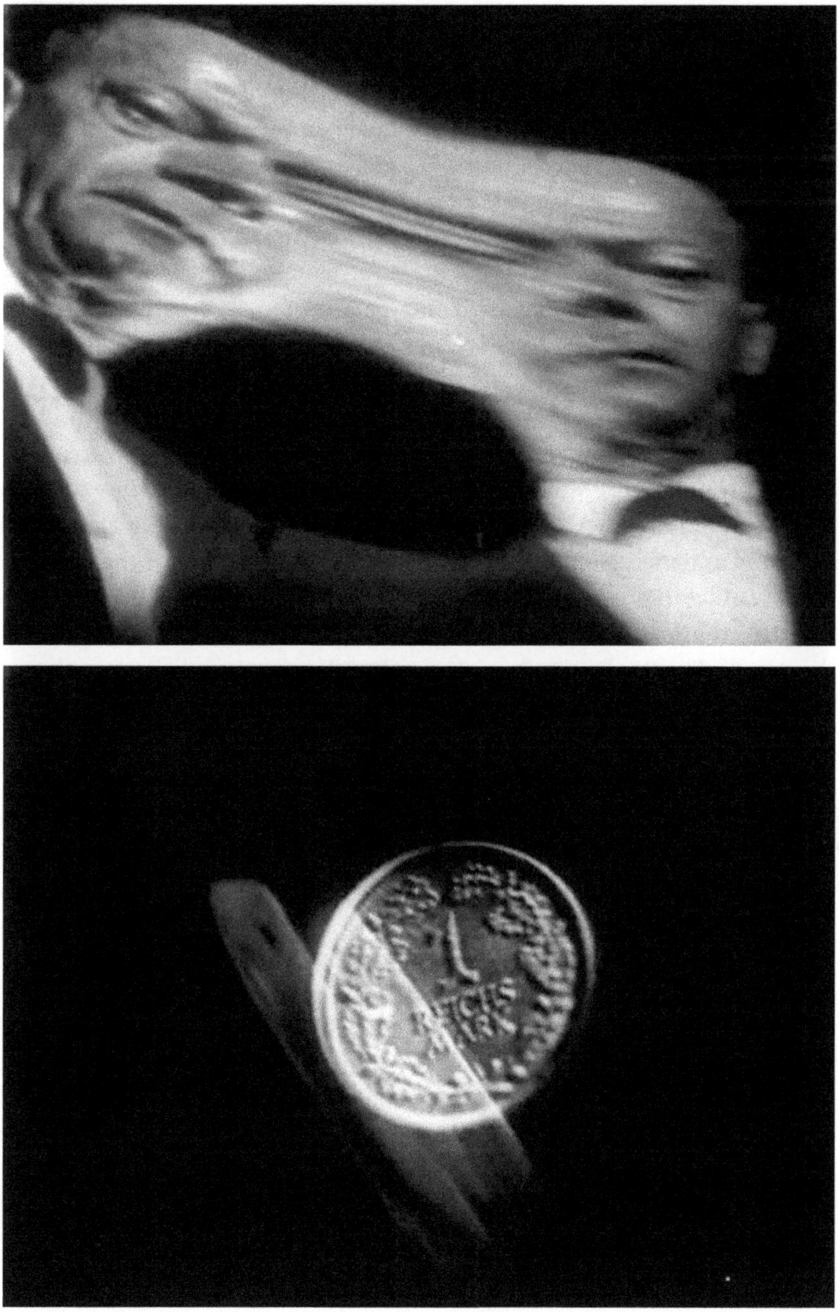

Figure 17. Dissolves and liquefaction join these two images in *Polizeibericht Überfall* (Ernö Metzner, 1928).

replicates the cynical demeanour of its time. It is comparable to *Dr. Mabuse* in the nihilistic portrait it paints and is similarly constructed around the logic of happenstance, though it lacks the vision of omnipotent control that Lang's film suggests. *Überfall*'s reliance on the trope of liquidity also recalls both anxieties surrounding the construction of masculine identity and the threat of invasion and border crossing that infuses so many fictions of finance capital. Ultimately, the film locates these threats once again in the figure of the individual.

After the provocation of Soviet cinema, German progressive filmmakers were faced with the challenge of not merely attacking capital on the grounds of the threat to the individual – in terms of the disruption of stable ideals of gender, class, and nation – but of also reconciling the fluidity and constant acceleration of industrial capitalism with an awareness of the interconnected masses of the world and a progressive vision of international order. A materialist approach to representing the world economy and its effects would have to somehow account for the masses, with a coinciding appeal to an aggregate image of their multitude. After Eisenstein's *Battleship Potemkin*'s Berlin premiere on April 29, 1926 at the Apollo Theatre, it ran for six months.[8] The film made it clear that a new visual language had been introduced that relied less on individually composed images, or individual characters, and more on creating meaning out of the collision of images. *Battleship Potemkin* downplayed the role of individuals and instead developed film conventions more suitable to the representation of mass effects. At the same time, Soviet montage techniques revealed the power of reassembling imagery and repurposing documentary footage.

Esfir Schub's 1927 *Fall of the Romanov Dynasty* most clearly demonstrated the potential power of the montage of documentary images by turning stock footage of the deposed tsarist regime against its original purpose. Schub's demonstration that the juxtaposition of documentary footage – images taken from reality – could create convincing new meaning would have powerful ramifications for the development of moving image propaganda. This further de-emphasized the denotative role of the central human subject and favoured the power of aggregate imagery and combinatory techniques, such as the famous example of the Kuleshov effect. Schub was influenced by the early *Kino-Pravda* work of Dziga Vertov and pioneered the documentary genre

8 Denise Hartsough, "Soviet Film Distribution and Exhibition in Germany, 1921–1933," *Historical Journal of Film, Radio and Television* 5, no. 2 (1985): 137.

known as the compilation film.[9] This form of documentary filmmaking emphasized cool detachment from the presentation of 'facts,' and is similar to a contemporaneous trend in German popular image making that manifested in illustrated magazines like *Der Querschnitt*, which will be returned to.

Eisenstein learned to assemble film under Schub's tutelage while assisting in the editing and subtitling of films imported into the Soviet Union. The first pieces of film that he reportedly assembled were from Fritz Lang's *Dr. Mabuse der Spieler.*[10] Schub and Eisenstein reassembled the German film to be more in line with Soviet ideals and changed its title to *Pozolpchennaya gnil*, which is variously translated as 'Gilded Mould,' 'Gilded Rot,' or 'Golden Putrefaction.'[11] Their edit of the film added a long intertitle to its opening: 'The international war brought imperialist Germany to division and capitalist crash [...] The men who did not participate in the war avoided experiencing its horrors, and during the war led empty lives, full of speculation and adventures.'[12] Eisenstein was fascinated with *Dr. Mabuse* and the experience of re-editing it would have a lasting effect on his style and influence his future projects.[13] Though presumed to be lost today, the surviving description of Schub and Eisenstein's version show it to be a critical re-editing of a film that, as has been shown, had a complicated relationship with capitalism and that can be seen as both a critique and, at times, an endorsement of its transformative power.

Eisenstein also wanted to return to the question of the direct depiction of capital in his never-realized adaptation of Marx's *Das Kapital*, for which he left extensive notes in his diaries from 1927 and 1928. He saw in Marx's original 'script' of *Das Kapital* an opportunity to adopt the author's 'ironic style' to his montage technique. Drawing on his admiration for the films of Charlie Chaplin, and Chaplin's ability to synthesize complex meaning in everyday objects – for example, how the image of the tramp silently eating his own boiled shoe tragically and humorously summarized his social standing – Eisenstein intended to find the satire and ironic humour in

9 Vlada Petric, "Esfir Shub: Film as a Historical Discourse," in *"Show Us Life": Toward a History and Aesthetics of the Committed Documentary*, ed. Thomas Waugh (Lanham, MD: Scarecrow Press, 1984), 22.

10 Sergei Eisenstein, *Film Form: Essays in Film Theory* (San Diego: Harvest/HBJ, 2014), 11.

11 Petric, "Esfir Shub," 26; David Kalat refers to it as 'Golden Putrifaction' in David Kalat, *The Strange Case of Dr. Mabuse: A Study of the Twelve Films and Five Novels* (Jefferson, N.C: McFarland, 2001), 60.

12 Petric, "Esfir Shub," 26.

13 Lotte H. Eisner, *The Haunted Screen: Expressionism in the German Cinema and the Influence of Max Reinhardt* (Berkeley: University of California Press, 2008), 245.

Marx's voluminous text.[14] Instead of showing the workings of capital markets directly, as in *Dr. Mabuse*'s stock market scenes, Eisenstein envisioned the filmic adaptation of *Das Kapital* as a study of everyday effects and the banality of 'a day in a man's life'[15] – but it is important to note that this 'man' is not intended to be anyone in particular. He likened his approach to James Joyce's *Ulysses* (1922). Just as Joyce had transposed the Homeric myth, Eisenstein intended to use Marx's text as his source material.[16] Banal commodities, such as silk stockings, were to be utilized to introduce the complexity of material and labour relations that lay behind their production. Unlike *Dr. Mabuse*, his film was to present financial markets not as 'a stock exchange, but as a thousand tiny details' rendered as a 'genre painting' and for which he took Zola's *L'Argent* (1890) as a model.[17]

Eisenstein's plans for *Das Kapital* were never realized, but in his notes he recognized the need for film to show the global reach of the cause-and-effect relations of industrial development and a globally connected capitalist market. For example, he describes in hurried images a scene in which the 'themes of textile machines and machine-wreckers should collide,' and the 'electric streetcar in Shanghai and thousands of coolies thereby deprived of bread, [lie] down on the tracks – to die.'[18] In another he describes linking the commodity form of silk stockings to the 'Indian women forced to incubate the silk cocoon by carrying them in their armpits!'[19] Eisenstein realized the montage aesthetic's unique ability not only to represent the workings of the capitalist world economy, but also to replicate its interconnected world of networks. For Eisenstein, montage could make the financial markets of the world visible, as it had in *Dr. Mabuse* and L'Herbier's *L'Argent*, at the same time that it worked in harmony with the dialectic structure of Marx's original text.

D. W. Griffith's work directly informed Eisenstein's understanding of how to represent class and capitalism on screen. It was Griffith who first used montage to juxtapose the worlds of the upper and lower classes under the effects of capitalism. This was not surprising as Eisenstein believed of American cinema in general, and Griffith's cinema in particular, that 'American capitalism finds its sharpest and most expressive reflection in

14 Zdeněk Hudec, "Eisenstein's Das Kapital: Attempting a New Genre," *Estetika: The Central European Journal of Aesthetics*, 2 (2008): 192.

15 Sergei Eisenstein et al., "Notes for a Film of 'Capital,'" *October* 2 (July 1, 1976): 15.

16 Hudec, "Eisenstein," 186.

17 Eisenstein, "Capital," 7.

18 Ibid., 8.

19 Ibid., 25.

the American cinema.'[20] Eisenstein acknowledged and built upon Griffith's mastery of parallel montage, recognizing within it the 'structure of bourgeois society' itself, and the Dickensian juxtaposition of the 'haves and have-nots.'[21] This was demonstrated very early on in the history of cinema in Griffith's critical portrayal of the effects of the wheat futures market in *A Corner in Wheat* (1909). This film demonstrated the American mistrust of derivative markets in foodstuffs – similar to the same debate in Germany around the turn of the twentieth century. Griffith juxtaposed the wealthy feasting in an opulent setting with a dejected line of starving wheat farmers who are unable to purchase a loaf of bread made from their own wheat. As mentioned in chapter 1, speculation in derivatives in foodstuffs (futures contracts) bore the brunt of the public's ire towards the financial industry because it so directly juxtaposed the intangibility of finance with commodities that had easily recognizable use value as nourishment.[22] Futures contracts also challenged the traditional perception of the role of the farmer. In Griffith's moral parable, this tangibility made the subject matter all the more suitable to cinematic representation. Yet in spite of his enthusiasm and belief in the suitability of montage to the task, Eisenstein's adaptation of *Das Kapital* was never realized. At the same time, and not coincidentally, Bertolt Brecht would take up the same task of representing finance capital and would also broach the subject of commodities futures by attempting to use wheat as a way of understanding and representing the capitalist system.

Fictitious Capital and Brecht's Fictions of Finance

Right before his definitive turn to Marxism in 1926, Bertolt Brecht became interested in the problem of representing the world market of commodities. Similarly to Eisenstein, Brecht developed ideas on creating an 'adaptation' of Marx's writing, an impulse that would later result in his 1945 conversion of the *Communist Manifesto* into poetic verse.[23] Brecht's interest in the

20 Sergej M. Eisenstein "Dickens, Griffith, and the Film Today," in *Film Form: Essays in Film Theory*, ed. Jay Leyda (New York: Harcourt, Brace & World, 1977), 196.

21 Ibid., 234.

22 An attack on 'derivatives' and other 'exotic financial instruments' seems to be a historically reoccurring feature of the backlash that follows financial crashes. One need only think of the 'exotic mortgage-backed securities' of the 2008 crisis to see this logic at work. Disavowal of inherent contradiction and the creation of a narrative of 'non-orthodox' practice is a central survival mechanism of the financial sector. It protects capitalism as a whole from direct critique in times of crisis.

23 Loren Kruger, "'To Those Born Later': Brecht's Centenary and Other Commemorations," *Rethinking Marxism* 11, no. 2 (March 1, 1999): 68.

problem of how to represent the workings of the financial world itself began in 1924 with the unfinished play *Jae Fleischhacker in Chikago* – co-written with Elisabeth Hauptmann who collaborated on several plays with Brecht. She is also credited as the 'translator' or co-author of works such as *Die Dreigroschenoper* ('The Threepenny Opera', 1928).

Recognizing the narrative potential of historical tensions surrounding futures in foodstuffs, Brecht and Hauptmann set *Jae Fleischhacker* against the backdrop of the Chicago wheat exchange (in the Old Chicago Board of Trade Building). They drew upon *The Epic of Wheat*, an unfinished trilogy by American author Frank Norris, who completed only two of the three volumes before his death in 1902. *The Octopus* (1901) depicts the conflict between Californian wheat farmers and the Pacific and Southwestern Railroad, while *The Pit* (1903) is set in the trading pits of the Chicago Board of Trade Building, and the final novel of the trilogy, *The Wolf*, was to be concerned with Europe.[24] Norris's trilogy was organized around the transformation of wheat from California grain, through its commodity form in Chicago, and into bread on the dinner tables of Europe. Brecht and Hauptmann intended to create a portrait of the downfall of a family of four who unsuccessfully seek fortune in Chicago. The play was intended to show 'the multitudinous juxtaposition of people, information, and chains of events,' and was to 'feature the weather as a central agency.'[25] Biblical floods and hurricanes would take the place of melodramatic elements and, as in the Bible, the story was to be recounted from several viewpoints.[26] Brecht intended to create a 'loose network, in which everything could be connected,' including 'warehouses, railway companies, the press, weather, wheat, grain traders, and corner, were combined in an indefinite thicket, a true swamp,' however, according to Monika Dommann, the play's 'fragmentary nature made it unmanageable and its lack of a large meta-narrative is evidence of a failure to create a coherent meaning.'[27]

At the centre of the planned drama was to be the manoeuvre of 'the corner' itself,[28] and Brecht and Hauptmann began to research how 'cornering

24 Monika Dommann, "Bühnen des Kapitalismus: Der Getreidehandel als Wissensobjekt zwischen den Weltkriegen," *Berichte zur Wissenschaftsgeschichte* 37, no. 2 (2014): 115.

25 Ibid., 118. Author's translation.

26 Ibid., 119.

27 Ibid. Author's translation.

28 In 1919, Rudolf Hilferding gave a concise account of how this situation occurs: 'One of the dangers of futures trading lies in the possibility of "cornering." If the seller does not deliver the commodity on the specified date, the buyer has the right to buy it on the market itself, on the seller's account. If the available supply of the commodity does not meet the demand, because

a market' worked as well as to understand the larger context of the market's jargon and mechanics. To this end, Brecht consulted financial experts,[29] but began to doubt the *Darstellbarkeit* ('representability') of these 'modern processes.'[30] Hauptmann noted that Brecht recognized an alternate causal relationship that defied dramatization in the activities at the exchange:

> These things, said Brecht, are not dramatic in our sense of the term, and if you rework them then they are no longer true, and drama itself is no longer a thing in this sense. And when you see that our current world can no longer be dramatized, then Drama no longer fits in our world.[31]

Brecht's own dedication to reality was troubled by his inability to come to terms with this particular reality. But it was not only Brecht who failed to adequately represent or envision this world. Even those directly engaged in the activity of the market, like traders and brokers, were unable to adequately describe its workings to him.

> No one, whether a well-known financial writer or businessman, or a broker who had worked his whole life on the Chicago Exchange – I travelled from Berlin to Vienna and back – no one could adequately explain the goings-on of the wheat market to me. I got the impression that these procedures were simply inexplicable, and not graspable by reason, meaning they were essentially irrational. The manner in which the grain of the world was distributed was simply incomprehensible.[32]

It seems that Brecht quickly realized the deep aporia at the heart of the idea of the rational market that was ostensibly the domain of the rational figure of the *homo economicus*.

the buyer has previously had the available stock bought up, very high fictitious prices will result, determined entirely by the decisions of buyers, and the sellers are at their mercy. Cornering is all the easier the smaller the available stocks of the commodity. [...] Cornering is usually possible only in special circumstances and for brief periods; for example, when grain stocks are low just before the harvest, and most of the old supply has already been sold. [...] In general, even successful "corners" only involve the expropriation of groups of speculators who are outsiders, and they have only a slight effect on the actual commerce and the real prices.' Rudolph Hilferding, *Finance Capital: A Study of the Latest Phase of Capitalist Development* (London: Routledge, 2006), 160.

29 Domman, "Bühnen," 116.

30 Ibid., 116.

31 From the Diary of Elisabeth Hauptmann, July 26, 1926, quoted in: Domman, "Bühnen," 116. Author's translation.

32 Brecht, quoted in Domman, "Bühnen," 117. Author's translation.

Brecht also may have realized a fundamental shortcoming of applying the theatrical form to the content of communications and trading technologies. Perhaps the pits on the trading floor themselves, filled with traders furiously exchanging futures contracts, were unpresentable for another reason. The traders's activity in theses pits is usually completely unintelligible to outsiders in part because of the general din and the fact that they use a form of complex sign language called 'open outcry' to communicate. Thus, the 'drama' of the exchange of contracts is already bound up in several levels of abstraction and signification such that there is little left to represent through dramatization. As I have argued throughout this book, the activity of the stock exchange itself was already configured as a labour of representation that was sophisticated in its mimetic power, reflexive, and engaged in its own self-representation. Brecht and Hauptmann were confronted with this closed loop of representational activity and abandoned the project as unfeasible. Brecht claims that it was shortly after this experience of bafflement that he began to 'read Marx in earnest.'[33]

Marx himself recognized the fact that financial systems were also systems of representation when he used the term 'fictitious capital' to refer to processes of 'capitalization' that relied on the collection of future earnings, such as stocks and bonds, or interest-bearing capital. For Marx, the stock market was a 'market for fictitious capital' and the notion of fictitious capital itself was an extension of the Marxist critique of the alienation of the process of production.[34] Fictitious capital as capitalist property appears on the stock exchange 'in its pure form, as a title to the yield, and the relation of exploitation,' and 'the appropriation of surplus labour, upon which it rests, becomes conceptually lost.'[35] In the Marxist discourse of the 1920s, this conceptualization of 'loss' was often an easy entry point into the pervasive discourse of authenticity. The revelation of the fictitious nature of capital markets and their propensity to create 'money out of thin air' evoked anxieties around the loss of essence and undercut non-monetary systems of value and morals. This fear was indebted as much to Marx as it was to works of literature like Goethe's *Faust* and its story of the derivation of wealth through a pact with arcane forces and an alchemical conjuring of value out of worthless paper. This discourse of a loss of authenticity, which arose from both ends of the political spectrum in the Weimar Republic, was a reaction to processes of modernization and the erosion of 'stable' categories

33 Ibid., 117.

34 David Harvey, *The Limits to Capital* (London: Verso, 2006), 276.

35 Hilferding, *Finance Capital*, 149.

of identity that have already been discussed in this study. At its heart, the discourse of authenticity revolved around a refusal to accept the world as *already represented*, as articulated by Heidegger and others in their rejection of modernity, and an insistence that access to the pure essence of things was possible. This disavowal of the shift from *sein* to *schein* ('being' to 'seeming') was thus part of the crisis at the heart of the republic itself.[36] It manifested along similar terms in relation to finance capital. Marxist critics insisted on a definitive categorial distinction between 'real' and 'fictitious' capital, which reactionary critics would reframe as a distinction between 'productive' and 'parasitic' sectors of the economy. At the same time, those initiated in the arcane jargon of the market, i.e., the *Angestellten* who accepted or at least were aware of the mediated nature of financial labour, were looked down on from the outside as lost to abstraction, while in reality, they were simply more engaged with the emergent discourse of this mediated and increasingly financialized world-as-picture. The scorn and criticism of both right- and left-wing attacks on new forms of post-industrial labour, and finance capital in general, exacerbated the conditions of 'spiritual homelessness' that Kracauer describes amongst these members of Weimar society.

A more nuanced Marxist approach recognized the problem of engaging with this discourse of authenticity. Austrian economist and politician Rudolf Hilferding, who in 1923 and 1928–29 served as the German finance minister, refined Marx's argument and conceded that finance capital was the 'supreme and most abstract expression' of capitalism.[37] At the same time, drawing on the metaphor of the 'inverted reflection' provided by Engels, Hilferding recognized that this abstraction, which at times 'seems to be independent' of industrial capital, was 'in reality its reflection.'[38] As Engels asserts, financial markets did not eliminate the causal relationship between use value and exchange value, but rather reversed or distorted it. Hilferding provides a historical example to illustrate this point: the introduction of a superior blend of coffee to the Berlin coffee market and the reversal of common-sense practice that this seems to create. Rather than being sold as an improved product, it was 'adulterated by adding black beans, kernels, etc.' in order for it to match the lower quality coffee on the Hamburg market.[39] This matching of quality was an ontological requirement of the commodity form itself, since, in order to be traded on

36 See Ward, *Weimar Surfaces*.

37 Hilferding, *Finance Capital*, 21.

38 Ibid., 21.

39 Ibid., 167.

the market, all coffee required the characteristic of 'fungibility' – meaning that any one standard unit of coffee must be exchangeable with any other on the market. This incident completely denies the use value of coffee and reverses the causal logic of creating a superior product for the consumer. Hilferding discusses the example of the commodities market, and the German historical resistance to the trading of futures in commodities, as the battleground for this debate. It is in these commodities transactions that the very nature of the commodity itself comes most distinctly into the fore.

Brecht would return to the question of the critique of capitalism in many of his later works, but ultimately never managed to create the image of the market of commodities promised by *Jae Fleischhacker*. He continued to explore the topic, however, and his subsequent plays, such as *Aufstieg und Fall der Stadt Mahagonny* ('Rise and Fall of the City of Mahagonny,' 1930) and *Die heilige Johanna der Schlachthöfe* ('Saint Joan of the Stock Yards,' 1931), maintained American commodities markets as their settings. But Brecht treated financial markets at a distance from their specific workings, choosing instead to show their material effects on the proletariat. His reliance on the theatrical form, even when collaborating on cinematic productions, precluded him from exploring the formal match between the medium of film and the space of capital markets promised by Eisenstein's intuitions, and so effectively exploited in films like *Dr. Mabuse der Spieler* and *L'Argent*. When he did return to overt representations of market forces, Brecht maintained his characteristic *Verfremdungseffekt* ('alienation effect' or 'estrangement effect') from the material at hand. This is most apparent in the final scenes of *Kuhle Wampe oder: Wem gehört die Welt?* – his collaboration with Slatan Dudow. Directed by Dudow and Brecht in 1932 as a 'last gasp' of the left at the end of the republic, *Kuhle Wampe* was initially censored, then edited and released in a limited number of theatres to a somewhat less than enthusiastic reception. It relies on a utopian conception of communal space from which the film obtains its title – the camp on the outskirts of Berlin, to which many unemployed and homeless workers fled the hardships of city life during the period. The film is a document of the political landscape of the era, and it was an important, though overdue, attempt to produce a Marxist cinematic intervention. It also represents Brecht's final attempt in Germany to create a critical representation of the world economy before he was forced into exile.

The narrative revolves around the plight of the impoverished Bönike family, who cling to the last vestiges of an imagined respectability characteristic of a petit bourgeois household. During a pivotal early scene depicting an argument around a dinner table, the father loudly berates his son for his inability to find a job while the mother frets over the possibility that they might be overheard by the neighbours. This scene is significant to the plot as well as the film's central critique of the bourgeois mentality as it implies the father's culpability in his son's subsequent suicide. Kracauer cautiously praised aspects of the film, although he was ultimately critical of it. He remarked on the rarity of seeing 'the intangible spirit of an epoch crystalized in such clear-cut images' that gave 'a concise idea of what German life was like during the crucial pre-Hitler days.'[40] However, he scolds Brecht and Dudow for their 'lack of flair and experience on the political plane,' especially in regards to what he saw as a counter-productive attack on the petite bourgeoisie at this critical point in time.[41]

The film portrays the economy of post-crash Germany and the rampant unemployment of the early 1930s. Scenes of masses of men looking for work and the lack of a central protagonist rhyme with the film's Marxist politics and display the state of the economy as embodied in workers who are de-individualized, decentralized, and unemployed. The film makes the effects of the economic crisis clearly visible in the domestic sphere by focusing on everyday details and hardships. For example, a central scene shows mother and father Bönike at home sitting across a small table from one another. Father Bönike reads a sensationalist newspaper article about Mata Hari out loud, which describes her body, opulent clothing, and jewellery in minute detail.[42] Engrossed in the details of the exotic intrigue, Father Bönike is oblivious to his wife working on the household finances across the table from him. His voice, still reading the story, is juxtaposed over shots of food and daily amenities, with prices attached, creating a typically Brechtian alienation effect, that forces the unsubtle point that he is more interested in this 'current event' than his own son's recent demise or his immanent impoverishment. The gesture overtly contrasts the father's unrealistic fascination in the fantastic story with the mother's concern for the workings of the real economy of the home. Shortly thereafter, they are evicted from their apartment and go to live in the Kuhle Wampe commune on the periphery of Berlin. This scene is typical of the film in its emphasis on commodities with high use value (food) and in its blunt portrayal of the crisis of the capitalist system. Quotations from Hegel, which are read aloud by a young man later in the film, are evidence of a similarly direct strategy.

Another representation of market forces in the film occurs near its end, and was reportedly scripted by Brecht himself. A man on the crowded

40 Kracauer, *Caligari*, 245.

41 Ibid., 246.

42 For a detailed discussion of this scene see Murray, *Film and the German Left*, 221–22.

S-Bahn is heading back into the city and announces to the occupants of the car that in Brazil 'they burned 24 million pounds of coffee' in order to eliminate a surplus that would have reduced the price of coffee on the world market. An argument between the occupants in the car breaks out, and various voices join in the discussion of the irrationality of the world economic system. Significantly, coffee, the same consumable commodity used by Hilferding to exemplify the workings of finance capital, serves here to stand in as a representation of the market as a whole. Hilferding had described the importance of the tangibility of commodities in his own reflections on commodity exchanges, as well as the historical hold-over of the *Börsengesetz* of 1896, which had banned the futures market in grains until 1931. For him, the stark contrast between the everyday understanding of commodities, which recognizes the absurdity of destroying them, and the perspective of the business owners themselves, to whom the act of destruction is perfectly reasonable, demonstrated how the logic of finance capital effectively turned common sense on its head. Using specifically Kantian language, Hilferding notes the separation of this financialized worldview from the everyday and the 'profane,' stating that 'it is business-in-itself, from which the profane phenomenal form of value – the use value – has been abstracted.' Accordingly, 'it is only natural that this economic thing-in-itself should appear as something transcendental to non-capitalist epistemologists who, in their anger, describe it as a swindle.'[43] Further, the capitalist sees all transactions as 'equal' regardless of their basis in reality, and ignores 'the fact that the circulation of securities is quite immaterial to the metabolism of society, whereas the circulation of commodities is its lifeblood.'[44] In the S-Bahn scene in *Kuhle Wampe*, the example of the absurdity of seeing coffee as a 'thing-in-itself' and not a thing with use value at the phenomenal level unites the opinion of the crowd, even as they argue about cause-and-effect relationships and express a range of political opinions. Though not phenomenally present – the coffee only exists in this abstract and mediated form as a news item, especially in the unimaginable quantity of 24 million pounds – the distinction between coffee's use value and the fungible nature of coffee on the world market, its *noumenal* image, is clearly understood by the crowd, and they seize on the apparent absurdity of this inversion of values and causal relationships.

Brecht and Hilferding's descriptions of the double perception of commodities on the exchanges are perfectly in line with Engels's claim that the

43 Hilferding, *Finance Capital*, 167.

44 Ibid., 167.

market represents the world as 'turned on its head' with causal relationships are reversed. By describing the division of market activity and reality in this way, this conception of finance also recapitulates the terms of the debate on the loss of authenticity. The S-Bahn scene presents a cross-section of the population – a sampling of class memberships. Accordingly, each of the individuals on the train expresses their dissatisfaction with the news that corresponds to their own political position. One well-dressed older gentleman announces his militaristic and autarkic position that Germany should not have to rely on the world market: 'if we still had a fleet, we would still have colonies; and if we still had colonies, we would have coffee!' Another older man attempts to rationalize the news by calculating the worth of the 24 million pounds of coffee, but this devolves into an argument about how much a pound of coffee costs in stores. A woman announces that 'something fishy is going on' since she wonders how her neighbours who are on welfare can afford to 'drink coffee by the pound.' Almost lost in the rapid exchange is a one man's assertion that 'coffee is a luxury good' and that 'people never used to drink coffee before.' The argument devolves into a generational conflict and almost comes to blows when the older, well-dressed gentleman takes exception to the leftist politics of a younger man – a friend of Annie Bönike's. Trying to calm the situation, another man stands and asks the seemingly apolitical question 'what is it to you what happens to the price of coffee in Brazil?' But Brecht's script does not let the luxury status of coffee blur the political message. The young man, now agitated, turns to the subject of wheat: 'if you're not interested in coffee, you still eat bread, right? How do you feel about the wheat they are using in America to fuel their boilers?' Annie Bönike then chimes in 'and the cotton!' The scene closes on the question of 'who will change the world,' to which Annie answers 'those of us who are not satisfied with it!' Brecht and Hanns Eisler's *Solidaritätslied* ('solidarity song') then plays over a shot of the backs of the crowd now walking through the tunnel of the train station.

Although the responses to the issue of destroying coffee are divided along political lines, everyone on the train is united in their condemnation of the event on some level. The film's title *Kuhle Wampe, oder: Wem Gehört die Welt?* ('Kuhle Wampe, or: Who owns the World?') demands that the answer to the problem of capitalism be acted out not only at the local level of the film's setting, but on a world stage, as evidenced by the following verse of Brecht and Eisler's *Solidaritätslied*:

We saw the sun shine,
on the road and on the field.

But we could never imagine,
that this would be our real world.[45]

Thus, the film ultimately advocates overcoming the divide between the world of commodification created by finance capital and a return to the 'real' unmediated world of things before commodification. Coming at the end of the Weimar Republic, the film appealed to its audience's sense of the loss of authenticity in a newly financialized world. Although the message relied upon an appeal to an ideal of authenticity that was a common feature of anti-capitalist rhetoric on both sides of the political spectrum, this appeal was ultimately used with much greater success by the right. As will be shown, the montage aesthetic that held so much promise for revealing the inherent contradictions of finance capital would ultimately be reterritorialized, one could say normalized, and put to use in the creation of another form of aggregate image.

The Cross-Sectional Aesthetic

When working on *Jae Fleishhacker* in 1924, Brecht and Hauptmann recognized the importance of the wheat market in the popular imaginary of global markets. They also touched on a central aspect of a watershed moment in economic theory and policy making around the globe. Brecht and Hauptmann wondered how they might represent the world wheat market, a question that was being asked in similar terms by economists and politicians attempting to understand a paradoxical situation in the world grain market. In 1924, global wheat production reached record levels, and the result was low wheat prices. Yet German and Soviet citizens still suffered shortages in grain.[46] In the same year, the American Food Research Institute, established in 1921, began publishing *Wheat Studies,* its collection of statistics on global wheat stocks, ten times annually.[47] This publication was part of a new gathering and interpreting of official economic statistics. Estimates of national income, for example, began to be published by the Soviet Union and Canada in 1925, and Germany in

45 'Sahen wir auf die Sonne scheinen,
Auf die Strasse, auf das Feld,
Konnten wir doch niemals meinen,
Dies sei unsere wahre Welt.'
Hans Eisler and Bertolt Brecht, "Solidaritätslied," 1932.

46 Dommann, "Bühnen," 127.

47 Ibid., 126.

1929.[48] In Britain, John Maynard Keynes and John Wilkinson Foster Rowe, acting in their capacity as representatives of the Royal Economic Society, officially recognized *Wheat Studies* as a 'complete summary' of global wheat stocks.[49] Keynes's contribution to macroeconomic theory, and his study of econometrics, would later definitively emerge in the form of *The General Theory of Employment Interest and Money* in 1936. Macroeconomic theory is characterized by a focus on the aggregate, and the emergence of methods of representing and quantifying the global economy as an interconnected and inter-reliant system. The *General Theory* is regarded as the key text of macroeconomics but, as Adam Tooze has convincingly demonstrated, similar aggregate approaches to economic activity had already emerged in Germany. In *Statistics and the German State, 1900–1945: The Making of Modern Economic Knowledge*, Tooze claims that the emphasis on British economists' role in formalizing this theory has resulted in less attention being paid to the emergence of aggregate approaches to the measurement of economic activity in Germany. He writes that 'Keynes's work must be situated within a broad sweep of new macroeconomic theorizing that can be traced back to the 1870s.'[50] Tooze points specifically to the role of Ernst Wagemann, president of the Statistisches Reichsamt ('National Statistical Office' – formerly the Wilhelmine Reichswirtschaftsministerium, 'Ministry of National Economy'), which had already been working on gathering statistical information on the German economy for some time. Over the course of the 1920s, Wagemann's Statistisches Reichsamt reshaped German official statistics 'into a recognizably modern form of economic knowledge' through early forms of macroeconomic modelling and policies that served to create statistically normalized types that replaced the idea of the individual.[51] At this time in Germany, a far more sophisticated aggregate image of the economy was created than anywhere else and the effect of thinking in aggregates and through forms of statistical samples and collections was also mirrored in non-economic representations.

The concept of the aggregate image was not limited to the sphere of economic theory. The cut-up aesthetic and montage, as formal organizational principles, were central features of modernism. Within the Weimar context, however, the aesthetic manifested itself in specific ways, often

48 Adam Tooze, *Statistics and the German State, 1900–1945: The Making of Modern Economic Knowledge*, (New York: Cambridge University Press, 2001), 8.

49 Dommann, "Bühnen," 126.

50 Tooze, *Statistics*, 12.

51 Ibid., 80.

Die Spitze der Londoner Börse

Der Stein an der Themse bei Putney, von wo jährlich das Bootsrennen Oxford—Cambridge gestartet wird

Fot. Sport & General Press, London

Der Schneider in Eton, der nach Beginn der Ferien die Hosen der Eton-boys zur Reparatur abholt

Figure 18. For example, this composition from the final issue of *Der Querschnitt* magazine. Clockwise from the top left, the captions translate as: 'The spire of the London stock exchange'; 'The stone on the Thames at Putney, where the yearly rowing race between Oxford and Cambridge begins'; 'The tailor in Eton who gathers the clothes of the Eton boys, in order to repair them after they leave for vacation.' *Der Querschnitt*, 16.1936, H.10, October: arthistoricum.net.

being employed in representations of finance capital and speculation, such as in the use of juxtaposition on the cover of the first issue of *Der Dada* magazine of 1919 that was discussed in chapter 2. Mixing stock quotations with religious symbols and other signifiers, Dada artists suggested the nonsensical logic at the core of financial markets.[52] In this sense, the Dadaist combinatorial method was both an adoption of a way of representing data as well as a parody of the statistical method, in that it sought to create a breakdown of signification, rather than the unification of parts into a greater meaning.

The aggregate aesthetic manifested itself in other forms, such as the *Querschnitt* ('cross-section'), which was popularized by the illustrated magazine of that name, *Der Querschnitt*, which was founded in 1921 and banned by the state in 1936. This magazine was known for its innovative illustrations and photography and, in particular, the sometimes-controversial practice of juxtaposing multiple images, usually based on a graphic match between them (Figure 18). From the middle to end of the 1920s, the phenomenon of the cross-section appeared as an organizing metaphor across a variety of media, including a large number of printed compilations that presented an overview of a wide variety of subjects of 'popular knowledge.'[53]

In Weimar cinema, the first references to the 'cross-sectional film' denoted a particular type of *Kulturfilm* created by UFA using footage from its rapidly expanding archive.[54] These were largely educational and formally conventional uses of the technique. It was only later that more innovative examples of the genre would begin to be labelled as such. Michael Cowan has interpreted this impulse as 'an effort to come to terms with' the proliferation of archives of filmic and photographic imagery at this time.[55] The form also coincided with the broader move across social sciences like economics to understand the world through statistical methods. Significantly, the concept of the cross section was first applied to the cinema by Béla Balázs, whose own cross-sectional film would use it to create a direct

52 By 1928 the inclusion of a stock market and business section was a feature of all German daily newspapers. See Fulda, *Press and Politics*, 34.

53 For an extensive list of these see Michael Cowan, "Archive," 8.

54 These included *Henny Porten: Leben und Laufbahn einer Filmkünstlerin* ('Henny Porten: Life and Career of a Film Actress,' 1928), *Rund um die Liebe: Ein Querschnittsfilm* ('All about Love: A CrossSection Film,' 1929), *Von der Wundertrommel bis zum Werbetonfilm: Ein Querschnitt durch 20 Jahre Pinschewerfilm* ('From the Zoetrope to Sound Advertising Film: A Cross-Section through Twenty Years of Pinschewer Productions,' 1929), *Wasser und Wogen: Ein Querschnittfilm* ('Water and Waves: A Cross-Section Film,' 1929), *Quer durch den Sport* ('Cross Section through Sports,' 1929), and *Die Wunder der Welt* ('The Wonders of the World,' 1930). See Cowan, "Archive," 6.

55 Cowan, "Archive," 4.

representation of the circulation of money in society – clearly demonstrating the prevalence of the economic underpinnings of the form. Of the form itself, Balázs wrote that:

> [Simultaneism] is based on the same idea: namely, that the representation should not focus only on a single image of the world, but rather show numerous simultaneous phenomena, even if these bear no causal relationship to one another or to the main element. Such sequences, by offering a cross section of life as a whole, attempt to produce a cosmic impression, a total image of the world.[56]

Balázs's script for the now lost film *K 13 513: Die Abenteuer eines Zehnmarkscheins* (Bertold Viertel, 1926), was intended to provide such a cross-sectional image. In particular, it explicitly links the cross-sectional aesthetic back to the question of the money economy itself. This film, the title of which translates as 'The Adventures of a Ten-Mark Note,' used the structuring logic of the circulation of money to bind together its episodes, following a ten-Rentenmark note as it changes hands. While no full print of this film remains today, a fragment of it exists in the form of an extended trailer at Filmarchiv Austria in Vienna (approximately 2 minutes, 40 seconds in length). This fragment, or trailer, appears to be assembled linearly as a condensed version of the overall film and, as such, gives us some idea of the overall structure. It shows the note at the beginning of the film – a hand-drawn facsimile of a ten-Rentenmark note – the serial number of which lends the film its title (Figure 19). The fragment depicts the film's star, Mary Nolan, and her discovery of the note at the beginning of the film, which sets the plot in motion. The short scenes that unfold depict a changing cast of characters and the structure of the film is clearly organized around the exchange of the money (at that time a fairly respectable sum). The film appears to depict a cross section of situations and social milieux connected only by the structuring effect of the circulating currency. The film was set during the inflation period and links unrelated episodes set in 'a factory, a night café, a pawnshop, the music room of a profiteer, an employment agency, a rag-picker's den and a hospital.'[57] It drew on Griffith's *Isn't Life Wonderful?* (1924), and pre-empted the plot of *Kuhle Wampe* (1932), by showing a pair of lovers in the film retiring to 'one of

56 Béla Balázs, *Der sichtbare Mensch* (Frankfurt am Main: Suhrkamp, 2008), 89. Originally published in 1924. Translated in Cowan, "Archive," 3.
57 Kracauer, *Caligari*, 181.

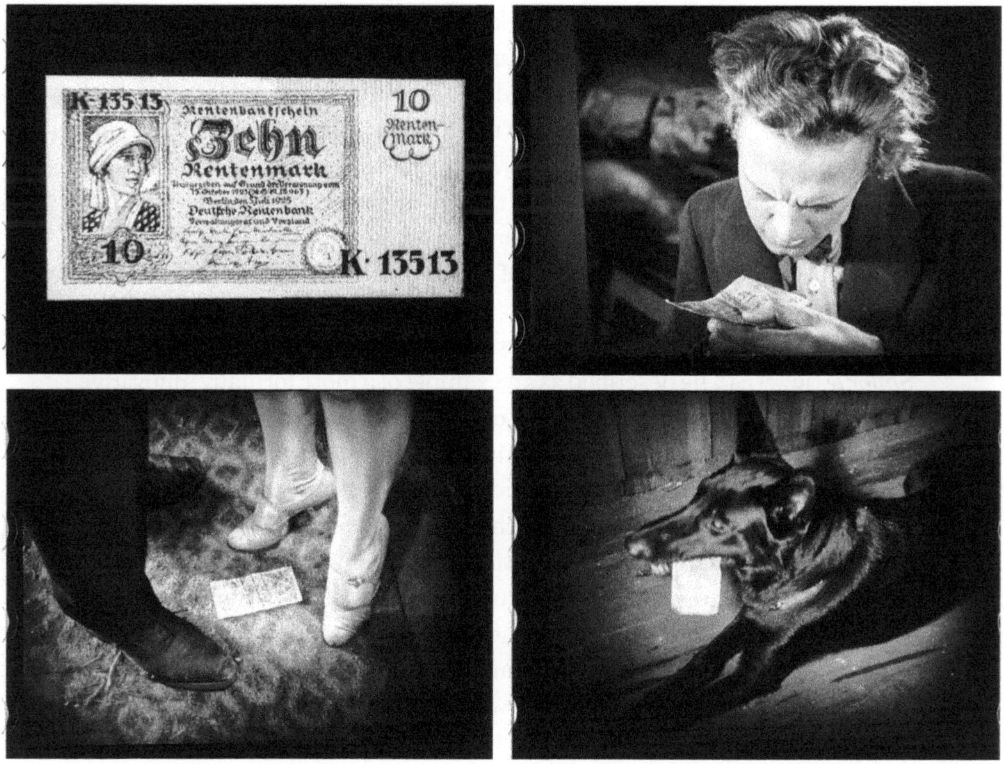

Figure 19. Stills from *K 13 513: Die Abenteuer eines Zehnmarkscheins*, (fragment, Berthold Viertel, 1926). Photo: Filmarchiv Austria.

those wooden cabins that spread (sic.) all over the outskirts of Berlin.'[58] In his description of the film, Kracauer claimed that the ten-mark note returns to the lovers, providing a happy ending, but in the fragment of the film that still exists, a final scene shows the note being devoured by a black dog (Figure 19), and we can only speculate as to whether the ending was thus tragic, ironic, or, perhaps, a commentary on the couple not needing money for their happiness.

Kracauer also confirms that Balázs was the first to use the term 'cross section' in the context of film, and it is significant that this first example of the type was explicitly linked to financial exchange.[59] The structural logic of the film follows from Simmel's *Philosophie des Geldes*, which states that 'most relationships between people can be interpreted as forms of exchange,' and that 'exchange is the purest and most developed kind of interaction,

58 Ibid.
59 Ibid.

which shapes human life when it seeks to acquire substance and content.'[60] While the film is lost, it is clear from this fragment that it showed how money functioned to connect individuals across spatial and class divisions – for example, connecting rag-picker to profiteer. This formal arrangement, as Cowan points out, mirrored the way in which Simmel's text 'cuts one cross-section after another through the social and individual life of people in the age of a highly developed money economy,' and further bring 'into consciousness the interwovenness of all the pieces of the world manifold.'[61]

Like *Die Abenteur eines Zehnmarkscheines*, Walther Ruttmann's *Berlin Sinfonie* (1927) can be described as an example of a more formally innovative cross-sectional film. It has, however, often been criticized for its superficiality. Kracauer's negative response to the film stemmed from his recognition that it made use of the montage principle of Soviet cinema, but shirked the '"duty" of social commentary' that the form demanded.[62] He disapproved of the film's claim to be a sort of 'optical music,' which he considered to be 'a music that, whatever else it tried to impart, marked an utter withdrawal from the world.'[63] Kracauer also criticized the film for its formalism, its refusal 'to go beneath the surface,' and its depiction of society as a 'harsh mechanical process.'[64] However, I would like to suggest another way of reading this apparent superficiality. Whereas in the previous chapter I argued for the centrality of economic concerns to the crisis moment of *Berlin Sinfonie* – at the point when the woman's suicide is conflated with the idea of 'liquidity' – here I suggest that the supposed 'superficiality' of this film's structural logic can be read in another light, as a cinematic representation of the economic ordering of the city that is in accordance with the emergent aggregate image of the economy.

Ruttmann captures a day in the life of Berlin and the film begins with a shot of the dark and slowly undulating surface of a body of water. This initial image connects what follows back to the idea of the liquid flows of capital in the interconnected *Weltstadt* ('world city' or 'cosmopolitan city'). This shot dissolves into the only animated sequence of the film, a composition

60 Georg Simmel, *The Philosophy of Money*, ed. David Frisby, 3rd ed. (London: Routledge, 2004), 79.

61 Cowan, "Archive," 14.

62 David Macrae, "Ruttmann, Rhythm, and 'Reality': A Response to Siegfried Kracauer's Interpretation of *Berlin. The Symphony of a Great City*," in *Expressionist Film: New Perspectives*, ed. Dietrich Scheunemann (Rochester, NY: Camden House, 2006), 251.

63 Kracauer, *Caligari*, 68.

64 Ibid., 186.

of similarly undulating horizontal lines. The movement of the animation gradually increases in speed, and images of a circle and a rectangle alternate in entering the frame from the bottom right and arching over to the far left. The images are non-representational at first, though the repeated movement of the circle recalls the motion of the sun through the sky and the passing of days. As the movement increases, the images begin to resemble a rotating camshaft or other industrial mechanisms, and this is confirmed when the accelerated animation fades into a photographic image of a speeding train. Images taken from the train show Berlin slowly rising from the countryside to the factories in the industrial outskirts to the city centre, at the Anhalter Bahnhof. The train travels along a literal cross-section of the city in the film's opening minutes. While *Berlin Sinfonie* attempts a comprehensive portrait of all activities in the city, it is organized entirely around the rhythm of the work day itself. It begins in the early dawn in its depiction of factory workers heading to work and then clerks and white-collar workers. The early sequences focus heavily on portraying the mechanisms and machinery of both industrial and post-industrial labour.

Berlin Sinfonie's musical and rhythmic form was not only a result of Ruttmann's careful use of metric and rhythmic montage, but also borrowed from the movements of the machines captured within the images. Shots from the train of factories are interrupted by the staccato flickering of a passing iron bridge that introduces a counterpoint to the overall rhythm of the cutting. One quick montage at the end of act two shows office machinery at work, quickly cutting between images of typewriters, tabulation equipment, telephones, and switchboards. As the movement reaches a frenzied pace, an image of a screaming monkey is intercut, followed promptly by an image of fighting dogs. Far from superficial in his treatment of the material, Ruttmann here edits with an explicitly critical intent: to illuminate the inherent rhythm and patterns all around him. Referring to his earlier animation work, he states:

> During the long years of my production of films from abstract materials I could not rid myself of the desire to construct something from living materials, to create a film symphony from the millions of actual and already existing sources of motion energy animating the organism of the modern city.[65]

65 Ruttmann quoted in Walter Schobert, "On German Avant-Garde Films of the 1920s" in *Expressionist Film: New Perspectives*, ed. Dietrich Scheunemann (Rochester, NY: Camden House, 2006), 244.

But it is this formalist impulse in Ruttmann's work that separates his depiction of labour and capital from examples such as *Die Verrufenen* or other *Kulturfilme*. *Sinfonie* relies on eliminating the story of any individual – in fact, the only personal story that it depicts is of the elimination of an individual through suicide. It is Ruttmann's willingness to see the 'actual and already existing sources of motion energy animating the organism of the modern city' – i.e., the material conditions of the city – as interchangeable with his previous experiments with abstract geometry that is key here. This is the city reduced to the metrics of economy and trade and reassembled to the standardized time of industry.

The cross section became a common organizing principle of Weimar popular media and created a new aggregate form that assembled individual and sometimes dissimilar images into a new whole. As mentioned, it was at this same time that statistical methods applied to the gathering of information on trade, productivity, employment, and resources were being used to create comprehensive aggregate images of the economy in the form of major indices and concepts, such as the gross domestic product of a nation state. Though these concepts would only become widely known in the macroeconomic theories of the 1930s, by the 1920s in Germany it became possible, as Adam Tooze explains, to 'picture the economy, in statistical terms, as a self-contained "circular flow" of production, income, and expenditure.'[66] This understanding of the economy was possible through the efforts of organizations like the Statistisches Reichsamt, which in the 1920s had been 'reinvented as a clearing house of information.'[67] Furthermore, the assembly of these statistics was made possible through the use of tabulation machines, originally designed for the sorting and cataloguing of data within the financial industry, which created a 'statistical revolution' through the 'mechanization of data' – early precursors to the datafication of the world that we experience today. The image of the world economy that was emerging in economic discourse was directly indebted to the mechanisms of visualization that arose in the financial market itself and in visual forms such as the cinema. As discussed in chapter 1, a media-archaeological approach to these representational technologies reveals the connection between the spaces of finance, the stock ticker, and the quantized time of Edison's Kinetoscope. In this sense, *Sinfonie* brings together the impulse to describe the economy of the city as a cross section of all economic activity, with the formal mechanism of the cinema itself. The opening sequence of the film,

66 Tooze, *Statistics*, 9.

67 Ibid., 24.

which rhymes optical animation with the most abstract of referential footage (undulating black water) drives home this connection. Ruttmann's formal experiments with light and colour, which reduce the world of movement to its bare essentials, resemble two-dimensional Cartesian space of the graph and chart. At the same time, the link to actual footage of water returns this abstract association to the concrete manifestation of capital flow, trade, and currency in the figure of the body of water.

Awareness of the emergence of these new methods of social profiling and measurement also appears in key films outside of the cross-sectional genre. In Pabst's adaptation of Brecht and Hauptmann's *Die Dreigroschenoper* (1931), for example, the rationalization of the work force through the gathering of statistics is parodied in the scenes introducing the empire of the 'beggar king,' Peachum, who surveils his team by demanding that they purchase one of his 'beggar licenses' and keep a precise account of the daily take of their earnings. Beggars are required to wear costumes that correspond to a normalized 'five basic types of misery guaranteed to move the human heart,' such as the 'young man from a good family who has fallen on hard times,' amongst others. Fritz Lang provided an almost identical image in *M* (1931), released a few months later. In *M*, a version of the stock market itself is shown in the form a 'beggar's exchange.' In this parody of a commodities exchange, the price of discarded pieces of food is continually updated on a blackboard on the wall (Figure 20), and the vagaries of the recent crash on the real exchange is lampooned by an off-camera voice that exclaims '*schwarzer Freitag ins Braten*' ('black Friday for roast meat').[68] *M* produces an image of the city of Berlin as ruled by the emergent practice of surveillance and information gathering, and the eventual capture of the murderer is achieved by a coordinated effort of two highly hierarchical and ordered systems of surveillance – the police and the criminal underworld.[69] Similarly, the rise of statistical profiling in the 1920s was far from a politically neutral process and, in the 1930s, the statisticians of the Statistisches Reichsamt 'began to imagine themselves at the centre of the state-controlled economy.' Later, 'a radical faction within the Statistical Office sought to reconstruct German official statistics as a seamless system of surveillance.'[70] The presentation

68 'Black Friday' in the German context would have referred to the stock market crash that occurred before the *Weltwirtschaftskrise* on Friday, May 13, 1927, when the Aktienindex des Statistischen Reichsamtes fell by over 30 per cent. See Hans-Joachim Voth, "With a Bang, Not a Whimper: Pricking Germany's 'Stock Market Bubble' in 1927 and the Slide into Depression," *The Journal of Economic History* 63, no. 1 (March 2003): 65–99.

69 See Anton Kaes, *M*, BFI Film Classics (London: BFI, 2000).

70 Tooze, *Statistics*, 24.

of the city in *M* can be read as a dystopian holdover of the structuring logic of earlier representations such as Ruttmann's *Berlin Sinfonie*, where the novelty of the 'visibility' of the aggregate image of the city has given way to the realpolitik of the surveillance state. Clearly, and as many critics have noted, the film is an important document of modern forms of surveillance. In reading the film as such, it is worth pointing out that *M* specifically mobilizes the method of statistical tracking to determine the identity of the murderer. Significantly, the killer is not identified by his visual appearance in the end, but rather, the blind beggar who listens to the passers-by in the street everyday identifies him by recognizing a pattern of behaviour (his whistling) that cannot be seen. It is the recognition of this pattern, this repetitive and compulsive behaviour, that causes the individual identity of the murderer to emerge from the background noise of the crowd in the street.

This new statistical method of representing the world has parallels in both the cross-sectional film and the increasingly prevalent photographic media that sought to reproduce the world in the pages of popular illustrated magazines. Siegfried Kracauer wrote that 'the aim of such journals is the complete reproduction of the world as accessible to the photographic apparatus.'[71] While Kracauer is selective in his assignment of praise to certain films that adopted this aesthetic, he harshly criticized Ruttmann's efforts in *Berlin Sinfonie*, as we have seen.[72] Kracauer favoured films that could overcome his suspicion of 'spatial impressions' through a dialectical approach and a Marxist aesthetics. On the other hand, he saw those films that did not adopt such an approach as 'a threat to the more authentic temporal experience of memory.'[73] Kracauer's dilemma, and the crux of his argument for or against the validity of the cross-sectional aesthetic, relied on the establishment of criteria for the determination of the authenticity of the image. In this sense, he articulated the central difference between a capitalist and non-capitalist application of the aggregate as a category of knowledge. Both systems of economic organization rely on the assemblage of an image of the economy as abstracted from the individual, but arrive at different conclusions as to its utility and worth. In what follows, the mobilization of a cross-sectional aesthetic completely emptied of any authentic temporal experience or

71 Kracuaer "On Photography," quoted in Cowan, "Archive," 20.

72 Kracauer's criticism of Ruttmann, in contrast to his praise of Hans Richter, was also influenced by the fact that Ruttmann remained in Germany working within the film industry under the Third Reich while Richter became a fellow exile. See Walter Schobert, "On German Avant-Garde Films of the 1920s" in *Expressionist Film: New Perspectives*, ed. Dietrich Scheunemann (Rochester, NY: Camden House, 2006), 238.

73 Cowan, "Archive," 20.

Figure 20. The 'Beggar's Exchange' in *M* (Fritz Lang, 1931). Photo: Praesens-Film.

Marxist dialectic will be examined, in an example that represents the nadir of what Kracauer considered contemptible in these films.

Corporate Visions of the World in *Melodie der Welt*

In 1929, Walter Ruttmann was commissioned to make an ambitious film by Tobis Film and the HAPAG shipping conglomerate. Eager to use Ruttmann's avant-garde aesthetic in their own publicity efforts, HAPAG employed him to create *Melodie der Welt*. Based in Hamburg, HAPAG, often referred to as the *Hamburg America Line*, was a symbol of resurgent German economic might. After half its fleet had been destroyed in the First World War, its leader Albert Ballin was intent on its reestablishment as a global corporate power in the shipping industry. The film was shot not by Ruttmann himself but by a team of cinematographers during a round-the-world trip on the HAPAG ship *Resolute*.[74] This resulted in approximately 16,000 metres of

74 Karl Brodmerkel, Paul Holzki, Adolf Jansen, and Reimar Kuntze were responsible for the cinematography, and Ruttmann did not accompany them on the voyage.

footage.[75] *Melodie der Welt*'s opening on March 12, 1929 was a major event because of the recent success of *Berlin Sinfonie*, as well as by the publicity efforts of the corporate interests behind the film. It was billed as the first German synchronized sound film and the premiere was 'comparable to the biggest premieres in Weimar film culture' because of the 'intersection of politics, the economy, and art.' HAPAG president and former Reichskanzler (1922–23) Wilhelm Cuno attended the event and introduced the film.[76] This conflation of corporate and state pedigree was reinforced in the opening title of the film, which claimed endorsement by the governments of all the territories through which the *Resolute* had sailed.

The film is organized rhythmically as a 'symphony' and Ruttmann's eye for details and graphic matches dictates the editing strategy. Any concept of verisimilitude with the vast distance travelled is eliminated in the editing, which matches architectural and formal details from different countries, such as the intercutting of street scenes from India with scenes shot in London. Similarly, culturally and religiously specific architectural features of places of worship are cut together to create a montage of faiths that seeks to eliminate or minimize signifiers of difference. As one reviewer noted:

> With startling objectivity Walther Ruttmann exposes the rhythmic repetition of the same customs in people's lives: work, commerce, sports, war, theater – a series of juxtaposed motifs of movement that have been pursued from New York to Tokyo, from Berlin to Ceylon, around the whole world, and composed in the manner of a symphony.[77]

The ostensible aim of the film was to prove the similarity between all cultures in the world by collecting and displaying matching details from each for the audience. In effect, however, the film enacted what Stefan Zweig had decried in 1925 as the 'monotonization of the world,' through the levelling of all forms of cultural expression.[78] This massive project of enlightenment by montage was summed up in the film's opening quotation from Oscar Wilde's *The Picture of Dorian Gray* (1891): 'The true mystery of the world is the visible, not the invisible.' Taken from a longer passage in *Dorian*

75 Malte Hagener, *Moving Forward, Looking Back: The European Avant-Garde and the Invention of Film Culture, 1919–1939* (Amsterdam: Amsterdam University Press, 2007), 207.
76 Ibid., 230.
77 Hans Sahle, *Der Montag Morgen*, March 18, 1929. Quoted in Kardish, *Weimar*, 151.
78 First published as "Die Monotonisierung der Welt," *Berliner Börsen-Courier* (February 1, 1925). Translated in Anton Kaes, Martin Jay, and Edward Dimendberg, eds., *The Weimar Republic Sourcebook* (Berkeley: University of California Press, 1995), 397.

Gray on the value of superficial judgment and beauty in youth, the quote seems almost intended to defend the superficiality of the film's project.[79]

In its utopian projection of global harmony, the *Melodie der Welt* also taps into the contemporaneous debate that arose around the invention of the sound film: the question of whether film could be understood as a universally decipherable visual language. Defending the silent cinema, Béla Balázs suggested that it 'seems to hold out the promise of redemption from the curse of Babel,' and that 'the screens of the world are now starting to project the first *international language*.'[80] Similarly, Dziga Vertov's *Man with a Movie Camera* (1929) exclaims in its opening titles that its intention is to create 'a truly international language of cinema.' This utopian vision of a universal language would be explored in Victor Trivas's film *Niemandsland* ('Hell on Earth,' 1931), which depicted a group of soldiers from rival nations trapped together in a trench. The soldiers eventually begin to be able to communicate across the language barrier, and the pacifist message of the film supports the unity of all human cultures through open communication. As Hannes Meyer wrote in 1926: 'The fatherland fades away. We learn Esperanto. *We become citizens of the world*.'[81] In *Melodie*, there is no such pacifist moral, but rather, the unity of the world is held together by the global reach of the HAPAG corporation while all markers of previous forms of imperialism or colonialism are effaced. Furthermore, the cross-sectional aesthetic posited a unity no longer present in representations of the world – 'a "total image of the world" – that would reduce the threat of contingency by locating elements within a paradigmatic system.'[82] One of HAPAG's businesses, the transportation of people around the world, was intimately connected to this 'total image of the world,' since the tourism industry promised members of the world's leading economies voyages to the world's beautiful, yet impoverished, locales and the opportunity of returning home with a collection of photographic snapshots.

79 In the novel, Dorian Gray states: 'People say sometimes that Beauty is only superficial. That may be so. But at least it is not so superficial as Thought is. To me, Beauty is the wonder of wonders. It is only shallow people who do not judge by appearances. The true mystery of the world is the visible, not the invisible... Yes, Mr. Gray, the gods have been good to you. But what the gods give they quickly take away.' Oscar Wilde, *The Picture of Dorian Gray* (Leipzig: Bernhard Tauchnitz, 1908), 34.

80 Béla Balázs from his 1924 book *Der sichtbare Mensch oder die Kultur des Films*. Translated in Marc Furstenau, ed., *The Film Theory Reader: Debates and Arguments* (London: Routledge, 2010), 71.

81 First published as "Die neue Welt," *Das Werk* 13, no. 7 (1926), 205–24. Translated in Kaes et al., *Sourcebook*, 445.

82 Ibid.

Melodie der Welt was another major example of Weimar filmic representations of the world economy that relied on the trope of liquidity and the mechanism of the sea voyage. In comparison to *Hanseaten*, *Melodie* shares many of the same themes, but contains no appeal to the idea of autarky, the matrix of nationalism and patriarchy, nor any appeals to a reactionary modernism. Instead, *Melodie* replaces the individual narrative and presents a corporate vision of the world. The film portrays no central characters beyond the unnamed sailor, who appears a few times wearing the HAPAG logo on his hat, and his female partner, who sees him off in the beginning. The protagonist of the film is in effect the aggregate corporate legal entity itself. Though derived from the seed of a radically critical aesthetic in Soviet montage, *Melodie* effectively mobilizes this aesthetic to promote the opposite of what it was intended for. The film harnesses the power of the montage aesthetic, assimilates it into its capitalist structure, and evacuates it of any revolutionary potential.

While *Mabuse* and *Melodie* make use of some of the same formal techniques, the economic contexts in which they premiered were very different. *Mabuse*, released in the midst of the inflation and only shortly after the end of the war, was much more paranoid and pessimistic in tone, whereas *Melodie*, released at the height of the short-lived economic recovery of the period of stabilization and right before the collapse that would arrive in October 1929, was optimistic and outward-looking, recalling Gustav Stresemann's declaration before the birth of the republic that politics is 'today first of all the politics of the world economy.'[83] By the time Stresemann became chancellor of the Weimar Republic (1923), and subsequently its foreign minister (1923–29), Germany's national economic policies were increasingly turning towards the global market, and international cooperation. *Melodie*'s image of a liberal, corporatist order was in line with the prevailing official policy of the time. It also tapped into the idea of a world of nations, a concept that had been showcased in its modern form for the first time in the Amsterdam Summer Olympics of 1928, which featured the now standard parade of nations for the first time. At exactly this time, the fascination with the *Weltrundfahrt* ('round-the-world voyage') was also bolstered by the highly publicized voyages of the Graf Zeppelin, which first completed the circuit in 1929.

As a representation of an ideal of the global economy, *Melodie* provides powerful and evocative images at its beginning and end. The film opens

83 Quoted in Adam Tooze, *The Wages of Destruction: The Making and Breaking of the Nazi Economy* (London: Allen Lane, 2006), 3.

with an image of planets lit with spotlights against the darkness of space. These studio-built models present the planets of the solar system as ideal Platonic forms. At the same time, they are illuminated by multiple spotlights and not the single source of the sun, which connects the image not to the celestial but rather to the illuminating power of human technologies of vision. Though an extra-terrestrial perspective, the opening of *Melodie* immediately recalls the terrestrial abstractions of the opening of *Berlin Sinfonie*, in that this brief abstract image of the earth and other planets is immediately followed by an indexical image of water. The soundtrack then announces the presence of the HAPAG ship *Resolute*, and its smoke stack is shown belching smoke as it sounds its horn. Images of waves on a shore cut to the undulating form of an accordion, thus beginning the chain of graphic matches that dominates the film and introducing the centrality of musical composition. An exuberant image of neo-liberal order is created that is reliant on this distant perspective to smooth over the irregularities of culture and geography. The ship's voyage thus becomes a conquest of space itself. The image of the earth in its entirety combines with the cross-sectional aesthetic to render an aggregate image of the world in its totality. In Heideggerian terms it is a perfect example of the *Weltbild* ('world picture') of the modern era:

> The fundamental event of the modern age is the conquest of the world as picture. The word 'picture' [*Bild*] now means the structured image [*Gebild*] that is the creature of man's producing which represents and sets before. In such producing man contends for the position in which he can be that particular being who gives the measure and draws up the guidelines for everything that is.[84]

At this moment in the history of the Weimar Republic, integration into this corporatist image of the global economy was presented as a possible path for the German nation. But reactionary figures such as Heidegger had already begun to demonstrate their dissatisfaction with this particular world picture. The increasingly mediated image of the world along with the de-individualization of aggregate systems of knowledge-making were reconfiguring the concept of the sublime, or in his terms the 'gigantic,' away from previous conceptions based in religion or nature, and towards the quantitative. Heidegger wrote that the concept of 'the gigantic' was

84 Martin Heidegger, *The Question Concerning Technology, and Other Essays* (New York: Harper & Row, 1977), 134.

appearing 'everywhere and in the most varied forms and sizes,' and he criticized the acceptance of the gigantic in the 'endlessly extended emptiness of the purely quantitative,' in the 'annihilation of great distances by the airplane,' or the 'setting before us of foreign and remote worlds in their everydayness.'[85] Fundamentally, Heidegger's criticism stemmed from a sense of loss of essence in the endless reproduction of the world-as-picture. He remained fixated on the redemption of an authentic pre-mediated reality and the insistence on the primacy of the 'aura.' Thus, the suggestion of stepping into this aggregate image of world trade was problematic to the reactionary mindset in two ways. First, it was antithetical to a fixed notion of national identity, and second, it posed a threat to the idea of the existence of an ontologically authentic reality.

Released on the eve of the *Weltwirtschaftskrise* ('The Great Depression'), *Melodie der Welt* lives up to the Faustian roots of its opening quotation from *The Picture of Dorian Gray*. The fragile democracy of the Weimar Republic had struck a bargain with the 'magician' of the world economy. The spectacular crash that soon came would ultimately lead to the reactionary backlash that brought the republic to an end. After 1929, 'the interdependence of foreign policy and economic expansion backfired' and 'inter-state conflict mounted as each country tried to salvage what it could.' The liberalization of world trade was replaced by a 'rush into national and regional autarky.'[86] In its utilization of the image of the ship as representative of the transnational space of the market, *Melodie* directly challenged the national imaginary. As I have written elsewhere – in particular of the two post-Weimar films *Gold* (Karl Hartl, 1934) and *Der Kaiser von Kalifornien* ('The Kaiser of California,' Luis Trenker, 1936) – the cinema of the Third Reich would attempt to re-appropriate this imagery by attaching it to older mythical representations of bodies of water and liquid and the essence of gold itself.[87]

Melodie was a corporatist appropriation of a cinematic aesthetic that arose within the revolutionary dialectical forms of Soviet filmmakers like Esfir Schub, Sergei Eisenstein, and Dziga Vertov. It also appropriated the formal match between the construction of the space of finance capital and the representation of the corporation in *Dr. Mabuse der Spieler* to the purpose of representing the actual corporation of HAPAG. As has been

85 Ibid., 135.

86 Detlev Peukert, *The Weimar Republic* (New York: Hill and Wang, 1993), 198.

87 See Owen Lyons, "'Denn Gold ist Glück und Fluch dieser Welt:' Examining the Trope of Gold in 'Gold' (1934) and 'Der Kaiser von Kalifornien' (1936)," in *Continuity and Crisis in German Cinema 1928–36*, eds. Barbara Hales, Mihaela Petrescu, and Valerie Weinstein (Rochester: Camden House, 2016).

argued throughout this study, financial markets are at their core labours of representation that seek to create an image of the world economy. This film is an early example of an aesthetic practice that would become commonplace throughout the later twentieth-century history of corporate self-representation. The promotion of the image of a 'global' presence is a central concern of multinational corporations, who rely on the image of the global to bolster their claim to pre-eminence in their sector, and the power at their command, whether true or not.[88] HAPAG sought to project the image of itself as a corporation with global reach, and turned to the cinematic convention of the cross section that had already been utilized to represent finance capital and the world market in Weimar cinema. At the same time, its use of montage rhymed perfectly with the economic models that were emerging at the time of its release. These models would further expand the reach of economic theory and enhance the representational power of financial models.

88 For a discussion of the importance of the image of the 'global' versus the reality of the 'embeddedness' of corporations within established financial centres see Saskia Sassen, *The Global City: New York, London, Tokyo* (Princeton, N.J: Princeton University Press, 2001).

Epilogue

Fungibility and Authenticity

The end of the Weimar Republic was marked by a series of increasingly severe and devastating financial crises. The Berlin stock exchange crash – *Schwarz Freitag* – Friday, May 13, 1927 marked the beginning of the end of Weimar Republic's most stable period and ended its only true stock market boom.[1] Just over two years later, on Black Tuesday, October 29, 1929, the panic at the New York stock exchange marked the beginning of the *Weltwirtschaftskrise* ('Great Depression' – literally 'Global Economic Crisis'). For German liberals like Gustav Stresemann, the former Reichskanzler (1923) and highly influential foreign minister (1923–29), who had placed their faith in the world economy, this was a devastating blow. The brief economic boom of the period of stabilization was entirely 'dependent on Germany's integration into the world economy.'[2] Any possibility of recovery was rapidly destroyed in May 1931 when the Austrian Creditanstalt and German Danat Bank collapsed, leading to a run on banks in Berlin and long lines of people in the streets hurrying to withdraw their savings.[3] These banking collapses were connected to the wider European banking crisis of 1931 that exacerbated the global crisis and led to the closure of the Berliner Börse in September of that year (see cover image). The collapse of the world economy led to the 'disastrous mass unemployment between 1930 and 1933' that was so clearly captured in *Kuhle Wampe*. The Weimar Republic would not recover from this combination of economic collapse and crisis of political legitimacy.

The rise of the Nationalsozialistische Deutsche Arbeiterpartei ('National Socialist German Workers's Party') at this time was characterized by a superficial performance of suspicion towards finance capital as inherently 'parasitical' and 'Jewish,' however, the fascist realpolitik made the Nazis friendly to German

1 See Hans-Joachim Voth, "With a Bang, Not a Whimper: Pricking Germany's 'Stock Market Bubble' in 1927 and the Slide into Depression," *The Journal of Economic History* 63, no. 1 (March 2003): 65–99.

2 Detlev Peukert, *The Weimar Republic* (New York: Hill and Wang, 1993), 197.

3 Alexandra Richie, *Faust's Metropolis: A History of Berlin*, (New York: Carroll & Graf, 1998), 396.

Lyons, O., *Finance and the World Economy in Weimar Cinema*. Taylor & Francis Group, 2023.
DOI 10.5117/9789463727136_EPI

big business when it suited their purposes.[4] While there are many examples of representations of finance and 'non-productive' capital in the cinema of the Third Reich,[5] an examination of them is beyond the scope of this study. Instead, I would like to return to the central question of the idea of 'productive' and 'non-productive' capital in order to discuss how this prevalent binary informs the discourse on authenticity that marked this period.

Chapter 5 showed that the appearance of the cinematic aggregate image at the same time as the cultural phenomenon of the *Querschnitt* corresponded with the rise of the idea of the aggregate as a mode of measurement in economics.[6] Adam Tooze has mapped the gradual increase in Germany of the use of statistics and indices to track and record the components of the German economy such as unemployment numbers, the trade balance between countries, and price information. Though the rise of econometrics is often associated with the British economist John Maynard Keynes, Britain did not begin to account for its economy using these methods until after the Second World War. According to Tooze, the League of Nations 'began to compile estimates of the balance of payments for the leading nations in the 1920s' with 1926 marking the year that the United States 'issued the first official estimates of the US foreign account' and with Germany following suit 'later in the decade.'[7] The rise of the aggregate image of the German and world economies corresponds with a de-individualization of both people and things that posed a threat to the concept of authenticity. In Heideggerian terms, that which was considered a thing in itself before – such as a mountain or forest – was now reduced to a mere representation of 'standing reserve' of natural 'resources' (*Bestande*) – for example, coal or lumber – that could be extracted from it. Heidegger's observations that the 'fundamental event of the modern age is the conquest of the world as picture' comes at the same time that the image of the global economy looms into view. Heidegger's fear of a 'loss' of authentic identity is echoed in the formulation of 'fungibility' in the commodity form on the market. In the

4 See: Adam Tooze, *The Wages of Destruction: The Making and Breaking of the Nazi Economy* (London: Allen Lane, 2006).

5 For examples, see depictions of Jews and finance in *Der ewige Jude* (Fritz Hippler, 1940), *Jud Süß* (Veit Harlan, 1940), and *Die Rothschilds* (Erich Waschneck, 1940).

6 'Between the 1840s and 1880, 24 countries established reliable trade statistics. By 1913 this number had increased to 33 and by the 1920s the trade between 90 countries could be monitored in statistical terms. The international economy was thus defined as a space of trading relationships between more or less clearly defined national economic units tied together by the well-monitored movements of goods.' Adam Tooze, *Statistics and the German State, 1900–1945: The Making of Modern Economic Knowledge*, (New York: Cambridge University Press, 2001), 5.

7 Ibid., 7.

present study, the cases that have repeatedly arisen are coffee, wheat, and other essential foodstuffs, which must be interchangeable with any other unit, thereby losing any semblance of inherent essence as unique substances. Shortly after the demise of the Weimar Republic, Walter Benjamin would publish his well-known essay that examined the loss of 'aura' that occurred when this precise process of mechanical reproduction and exchangeability was applied to the work of art. In the cinema of the Weimar Republic, tensions concerning the opposition of the authentic and inauthentic – here previously referred to as the opposition of a culture of *sein* ('being') versus *schein* ('seeming') – can be found everywhere. I would like to suggest a few of the ways that this opposition can be traced back explicitly to fundamental questions concerning the money economy and the issue of the aggregate image and dissolution of the individual subject.

As I have shown, the idea of fungibility, and the related term 'liquidity,' are central to representations of finance and economy in the Weimar Republic. As Martin Jay and Theodor Adorno have discussed, these terms are also at the heart of the crisis of authenticity that marked the final years of the republic. The degree to which a commodity can be reduced from its use value to the fungible and liquid form of the commodity in circulation also marks the degree to which the commodity itself has been abstracted from any semblance of authenticity. During the inflation years of the Weimar Republic, this abstract financial concept was experienced as a very real phenomenon as the circulation of ersatz commodities – sometimes outright forgeries or substitutions – threatened notions of the reliability of the fungible commodity in circulation. For example, much of the unsavoury gains made by the *Raffke* and *Schieber* figures discussed at length in chapter two were the result of their trade in adulterated goods. Wilhelm Dieterle's 1929 silent film *Durch's Brandenburger Tor* ('Through the Brandenburg Gate'), set in 1923, is evidence of the endurance of these figures in Weimar popular culture and the deep-seated threat to the idea of the 'authentic' that they pose. The film makes light of the substitution of goods in a key scene where a street urchin sells a customer a sandwich but substitutes boot polish for mustard. In the regional dialect written into an intertitle, he subsequently exclaims '*Oh, pardon, beinah hätt ick mir einer kleinen Schiebung schuldich jemacht!*' ('Oh sorry! I nearly ripped you off [*Schiebung*] by accident!'). The sale of adulterated goods and foodstuffs was a well-documented scam perpetuated by the *Schieber* of the post-war inflationary period. But this act of substitution also posed a categorical threat to the idea of the fungible commodity more generally, that demanded an increased attention to what it meant for a substance to be considered 'pure.'

The period of inflation revealed a striking relativity in the relationship between things, commodities, and people and its effects remained in the German cultural memory long after. Though only experienced over this brief period, these obvious adulterations of common foodstuffs lived on in the cultural imagination of the republic and played upon fears concerning authenticity that can be traced back to discourses surrounding productive and non-productive capital – of ill-gotten gains as opposed to 'honest' work – and are at the source of what Peter Sloterdijk has labelled the rise of modern cynicism.[8] Bernd Widdig quotes directly from the period in Paul Ufermann's 1924 *Könige der Inflation* ('Kings of Inflation'), a collection of biographies of ten well-known *Raffke* and *Schieber*:

> Even more than war, its daughter 'inflation' upset all notions of loyalty and trust, of ethics and morals, of love and patriotism. They were superseded by brutal violence, naked arbitrariness, and cold calculation — a madness of numbers and zeros, that drowned everything that could have been seen as a sign of human civilization into a sea of deceit and brutality.

The official economic reaction to the memory of the instability of inflationary paper money was a resurgence of interest in the gold standard – a feature of the German currency that had been abandoned in 1914. After the period of rampant inflation, the Rentenmark that was introduced in November 1923 was backed by bonds denominated in US dollars.[9] By September 1924, the gold standard was reintroduced in Germany as well as several other major national economies.[10] Writing in *The Stabilisation of the Mark* at the time, Reichsbank President Hjalmar Schacht noted that 'the theory of metallic currency is now stronger and not weaker, than it ever was' and that 'nothing showed the superiority of gold so much as the war.'[11] For it was gold, and gold only, that could conceptually shore up the damage caused by the twin threats to the purity of money and commodities – caused by the inflation and the profiteers, respectively.

As Martin Jay and Theodor Adorno have argued, gold, as a representative of a 'genuine' store of value and a fundamentally incorruptible substance,

8 See Peter Sloterdijk, *Critique of Cynical Reason* (Minnesota: Minnesota University Press, 1988).

9 R.G.H., "Review of *The Stabilisation of the Mark* by Hjalmar Schacht," *Journal of the Royal Statistical Society* 91, no. 1 (January 1, 1928): 100–102.

10 Barry Eichengreen and Peter Temin, "The Gold Standard and the Great Depression," *Contemporary European History* 9, no. 2 (July 1, 2000): 187.

11 R.G.H. "Review," 102.

is closely tied to a metaphysics of presence and authenticity. Jay writes that, 'like believers in the intrinsic value of gold, devotees of authenticity think that they can isolate a standard of value before the onset of the exchange principle, which reduces everything to a fungible counter in a circulation without end.'[12] However, Jay and Adorno agree that gold, along with other ideas of the authentic and genuine article that exists outside of systems of exchange, is an illusion that creates a cult of origins. Throughout history, periods of economic or political turmoil have often corresponded with the lionization of the gold standard, or a return to it, as a source of fiscal stability. But, as Jay writes, 'gold as an absolute standard of value is thus no antidote to the empty circulation of exchange but rather its fetishistic complement.'[13] For Jay, the concept of the 'authentic' only arises 'against the backdrop of reproducibility' and further, is connected to reactionary and fascistic notions of 'being-in-the-world' in an unmediated sense of the term, or, as Jay summarizes Adorno's thoughts on the topic, the idea of the authentic 'provides a hollow substitute for lost religious belief in ultimate values; it is based on a mistaken search for proprietary origins that establish rights of the earliest settlers; it rests on a dubious ideal of self-possession and integrity, which fails to credit the mimetic moment in the creation of selfhood.'[14] In other words, the idea of the purity of gold promotes not only the fiction of the self-made individual, but also obscures the fundamental act of mimesis – Nietzsche's idea of the donning of a mask – that marks selfhood in modernity. It is important to point out that the 'mimetic moment' essential in the presentation of the self as an individual that Adorno claims in *Negative Dialectics* is denied in this 'jargon of authenticity' is explicitly related to the mimetic gesture inherent in the creation of the fungible commodity in circulation on the market. Adorno writes that:

> The discourse of genuineness as a last bulwark of individualistic ethics is a reflection of mass-production. Only when countless standardized commodities project, for the sake of profit, the illusion of being unique, does the idea take shape, as their antithesis yet in keeping with the same criteria, that the non-reproducible is the truly genuine.[15]

12 Martin Jay, "Taking on the Stigma of Inauthenticity: Adorno's Critique of Genuineness," *New German Critique*, no. 97 (January 1, 2006): 20.

13 Ibid., 23.

14 Ibid., 25.

15 Adorno, *Minima Moralia*, 155. Quoted in Jay, "Stigma," 22.

Gold then becomes the authentic commodity par excellence, but the idea of its uniqueness and non-reproducibility is paradoxical to the very essence of the fungible and exchangeable commodity. Modern forms of exchange in gold require no 'real' gold to change hands, merely the certificates of 'authenticity' that are guaranteed to be redeemable in gold. Thus, gold stands for a perfect paradox of the commodity form – both unadulterated and pure while infinitely interchangeable with any other standardized unit.

I have written about the resonance of the idea of the gold standard and of gold's association with the 'genuine' and as an antidote to the 'problem' of authenticity that can clearly be read in the reactionary politics and cinema of the Third Reich – particularly in Karl Hartl's *Gold* (1934) and Luis Trenker's *Der Kaiser von Kalifornien* (1936), for gold truly maintained a ritual value in these films that placed it beyond the realm of 'use' and connected back to the mythology of the *Rheingold* – an object of value that transcended economic exchange.[16] As an idealized substance, it has been used in the history of monetary policy as an antidote to the 'flotation' of currencies on the global market[17] and a flight to the 'safety' of gold has been a common feature of economic crises throughout history. Paradoxically again, it is a substance that has historically suggested stability and immutability but is also a reminder of the boom and bust cycles of the world economy.

Reinhart Koselleck has shown that the concept of 'crisis' in the economic sense of the term appeared in Germany between the 1840s and 1860s.[18] As discussed in chapter 1, this period is marked by both the boom in *Aktiengesellschaften* ('joint stock companies'), as well as the economic collapse that followed the California Gold Rush (1848–55), which Koselleck claims was the first global crisis that was locatable 'everywhere and nowhere' at the same time.[19] The emergence of crisis as a concept in this sense was directly related to the drastic consequences of newly mobilized 'flows of capital' that drove Germany's rapid transition into modernity. Yet the concept of 'flow' itself should be interrogated and is a central trope in language and imagery that represents capital and the world economy. As Augustine Sedgewick has

16 See Owen Lyons, "'Denn Gold ist Glück und Fluch dieser Welt:' Examining the Trope of Gold in 'Gold' (1934) and 'Der Kaiser von Kalifornien' (1936)," in *Continuity and Crisis in German Cinema 1928–36*, eds. Barbara Hales, Mihaela Petrescu, and Valerie Weinstein (Rochester: Camden House, 2016). For a discussion of the importance of the image of the 'global' versus the reality of the 'embeddedness' of corporations within established financial centres see Saskia Sassen, *The Global City: New York, London, Tokyo* (Princeton, N.J: Princeton University Press, 2001).

17 For example, the Bretton Woods system of fixed currencies tied to the value of gold.

18 R. Koselleck and M. W Richter, "Crisis," *Journal of the History of Ideas* 67, no. 2 (2006): 391.

19 Ibid., 392–93.

shown, in the late nineteenth century, the concept of flow replaced earlier models of production as labour and work with an image of fast-moving currents and effortless flux. 'Flow' appeared as 'an instrumentality' that was 'developed and deployed by vested interests to smooth out, and in so doing legitimate and win increased power over, the process by which people and things move through space and time.'[20] Further, he contends that this 'submersion of work in the flows metaphor' promotes a particular worldview in which 'everyone and everything is already liquid, already money.' Sedgewick points out that this naturalizing discourse of flow and liquidity 'effaces deadly serious struggles over who moves, what moves, and how' in the emergent notion of an interconnected world economy.[21] I argue that, in the face of the crushing forces of finance capital that shaped the era, the cinema of the Weimar Republic still promoted a fantasy of power and mobility in the form of super-human individuals – such as Dr. Mabuse – and that these figures introduced new ways of being in and amongst these forces.

In this study, I have repeatedly returned to the concept of 'liquidity,' in order to reveal and discuss its frequent appearance in the films of the Weimar Republic. At its heart, the concept of liquidity is closely related to that of the crisis of authenticity since it demands the overturning of fixed categories and identities, and relies on expansion across boundaries of territories. For example, in chapter 4, I have shown how the concept of a 'liquid masculinity' driven by finance capital destabilizes the idea of a traditional notion of physical power. Key films of the Weimar Republic reproduced the influential application of this metaphor across all forms of engagement with the financial sphere. These films reproduced an image of money and economy that rhymed closely with Georg Simmel's influential study *Philosophie des Geldes*, in which he states that:

> It is significant that we term money in circulation 'liquid' money: like a liquid it lacks internal limits and accepts without resistance external limits that are offered by any solid surroundings. Thus, money is the most decisive and completely indifferent means for transposing the supra-individual rhythm in the conditions of life into the harmony and stability that allow a freer, more individual and more objective confirmation of our personal energies and interests.[22]

20 Augustine Sedgewick, "Against Flows," *History of the Present* 4, no. 2 (November 1, 2014): 143.
21 Ibid.
22 Georg Simmel, *The Philosophy of Money*, ed. David Frisby, 3rd edition (London: Routledge, 2004), 500.

It is important to reiterate, however, that this naturalizing metaphor of flows and liquidity is part of the discourse of financial markets that obscures the relationship of finance capital to its particular mode of objective 'reality' – or as I have suggested, following Engels, creates and 'inverted reflection' of the world itself. These metaphors provide 'not merely a way of seeing, but also the threshold to a way of inquiring' and are 'a way of investigating the relation of the parts to the whole, of evaluating and valuing, and of telling stories about change over time in a language that, as the career of the flows metaphor suggests, has as much power to remake the world as to reflect it.'[23] For the film-going public of the Weimar years, beset on all sides by crisis after crisis, the metaphor of flow – of being liquid, of going with the flow, of mastering the currents of economic crisis – would serve as a powerful fantasy that played out in specific visual codes that have been discussed here.

Throughout the Weimar Republic, the cinema of the era both reflected and mirrored an image of speculation, finance, and the economy to its audience – the *homo economicus* who 'looks to film for the satisfaction of his spiritual needs.'[24] Here I have shown the variety of ways that these representations intersected with central discourses of modernity including gender, authenticity, the space of the city, the boundaries of the nation state, and the emergence of a statistically informed aggregate image of the economy. In so doing, it has been my hope to reposition the pervasive and everyday experience of finance capital as central to the experience of modernity in the Weimar Republic. In the early years of the Weimar Republic, a large body of films explored the theme of speculation and profiteering – a fact of life of the inflationary period – reflecting back this everyday reality. At the same time, these films increasingly reflected the experience of a new class of salaried financial workers, producing narratives that could stand in for the complex vagaries of the market itself. I have identified the central tropes and types that emerged at this time, and that remained central to representations of finance capital throughout Weimar Republic. At the same time, I have shown how figures like Dr. Mabuse could function both as representative of conspiratorial forces as well as anti-heroes who appear to master the emergent flows and liquidity of this newly financialized reality.

23 Sedgewick, "Against Flows," 166.

24 Karl Demeter, "The Sociological Foundations of the Cinema Industry," first published as "Die soziologischen Grundlagen des Kinowesens," in *Deutsche Rundschau* 52 (July 1926). Translation by Michael Cowan. See: Anton Kaes, Nicholas Baer, and Michael Cowan, *The Promise of Cinema: German Film Theory, 1907–1933* (University of California Press, 2016), 174.

This powerful fiction of mastery still resonates today for it describes an idealized yet central type of modernity, the rational speculator and financier who is able, seemingly through the power of his (almost always his) reason alone, to come out ahead of the tide of destruction and change that financial flows often leave in their wake. As is illustrated in *Der letzte Mann* and *L'Argent*, the invention of this idealized *homo economicus* threatened established categories of masculinity – reconfiguring the performance of masculinity in face of the random chance of market forces. At the same time, and as was illustrated by *Die Börsenkönigin*, the rise of finance capital corresponded with radical changes for bourgeois women after the end of the First World War, however, outside of this exceptional example, representations of women and finance often positioned them as agents of destruction, in *Die freudlose Gasse* or *Metropolis*, rather than as rational masters of speculation. This gendering of finance capital in popular representations is one of the most lasting legacies of this time, for it reinforced the commonly held view of financial markets as the domain of men for decades to come, even though finance was a traditionally 'feminized' form of labour. To this day, the gender binaries and contradictions described in this study resonate with the performance of masculinity and femininity that characterizes the financial sector.

Towards the final years of the Weimar Republic, the contours of the world economy that had been described by German-speaking economists for decades began to become readily apparent in the popular productions of the time. Narratives and images of the world economy at this time reflected the statistical methods that revealed the world economy in their mobilization of montage. On the very brink of its collapse in 1929, the world economy appeared as a global aggregate image either in the form of the critique of Eisenstein and Brecht, or in its crystallized and smooth form, in the emptied-out imagery Ruttmann produced for the HAPAG corporation – 'powerful propaganda for the financial sector'[25] indeed. It is my hope that the centrality of finance and speculation to the cinema of the Weimar Republic has been demonstrated here. Though the Weimar Republic has been widely discussed in terms of its central role as a 'laboratory of modernity,' the role of finance capital – and the ways in which it cuts across so many of the key experiences of modernity – has been under-discussed. This book can be read as something of a corrective to that omission, but also within the larger discussion of the role that fictions of finance play in the production of not just an image of financial markets, but of the central tropes, types, practices, and assumptions that structure and guide them.

25 Ibid.

Appendix

'Raffke Couplet,' Kurt Tucholsky, 1922
(author's translation)[1]

Ick bin die allerneuste Zeiterscheinung,	I am the latest trend/scam,
Sie treffen mir an alle Orte an –	You meet me everywhere –
Ick pfeife uff die öffentliche Meinung,	I whistle at public opinion,
Weil ick als Raffke mir det leisten kann.	Because as a *Raffke*, I surely can.
Ick bin die feinste von die feinen Nummern,	I am the finest of the finest stock,
Ick steh schon in die Illustrierte drin;	Magazines – you'll find my picture in;
Denn ob Jeschäfte oder Sekt und Hummern:	Whether business or champagne and lobster:
Ick knie mir rin, ick knie mir richtig rin!	I dig in, I really dig in!
Meen Vata war ein kleener Weichenstella,	My father was a little railway operator,
Und meene Jugend, die war sehr bewecht –	And my youth was very rough –
Ick stand doch damals in' Jemisekella,	Then I was only in the vegetable cellar
Und habe mit die Jurken einjelecht.	With the cucumbers and other stuff.
Denn stieg ick uff. Und wurde richtig Raffke.	Then I grew up. And became a real *Raffke*.
Und steckt die janze Welt in' Dalles drin: –	And drove the whole world to poverty: –
Denn macht mir nischt, denn ick vadiene daffke.	Then I did nothing! And made good money.
Ick knie mir rin, ick knie mir richtig rin!	I dig in, I really dig in!
Von wejen Kunst un so – ick kenn Tosellin!	Because of art and all that – I know Tosellin!
Ick weeß, der Strauß, der geigt det hohe Fis.	I know Strauß who fiddles the high F sharp.
Nur weeß ick nischt Jenaus von B-b-boticellin,	But I don't know for sure if B-B-Boticelli,
Ob det nun'n Cognak oder'n Keese is,	Is a cognac or a cheese,
'n Bild in Auftrag jeben tu ick imma,	I'm always commissioning paintings,

1 Kurt Tucholsky, "Raffke Couplet," in *Gesamtausgabe: Texte und Briefe*, vol. 5, ed. Roland Links and Elfriede Links (Reinbeck bei Hamburg: Rowohly, 1999). Special thanks to Philipp Stiasny for bringing this song to my attention.

Lyons, O., *Finance and the World Economy in Weimar Cinema*. Taylor & Francis Group, 2023.
DOI 10.5117/9789463727136_APP

Weil ick nu mal,' jawoll, Meezeene bin –	Because, by god, I'm a patron of the arts –
Jefällt mir't nisch, häng icks ins Badezimma:	If I don't like it, I'll hang it in the bathroom:
Ick knie mir rin, ick knie mir richtig rin!	I dig in, I really dig in!
In der Jeschäfte wüsten Lärm und Hasten	In business, noise and haste
Vajess ick ooch die süße Liebe nich.	I never forget the sweet life's taste.
Sie, meene Olle is valleicht 'n Kasten,	My woman is perhaps a crate,
Die hat so zweenhalb Zentner Schwerjewicht!	Who weighs two and a half hundredweight!
Aus meinen Schloss mit seine Silberputten,	Out of my castle with its silver putti,
Da mach ick raus, wenn ick alleene bin –	I do get out, when I'm alone –
Et jibt ja Jott sei Dank noch so viel Nutten –	I thank god for easy women,
Ick knie mir rin, ick knie mir richtig rin!	I dig in, I really dig in!
Wat Sie hier sehn an meine dicken Händen,	What you see on my fat hands,
Den janzen Perlen- und Brillantsalat –	Is a pearl and diamond salad –
Sie, det sin allet meine Dividenden,	They are all the dividends,
Denn ick bin dreißigfacher Aufsichtsrat.	From the thirty directorships I've had.
Und in den alljemeinen Weltenkoller,	And in the general global madness,
Da schieb ick still zur Bank von England hin:	As I push towards the Bank of England:
Und macht ihrs doll – ick mache immer Dollar![1]	When you do well (doll) – I always make Dollars!
Ick knie mir rin, ick knie mir richtig rin!	I dig in, I really dig in!

1 This is a play on the German slang term *doller*, meaning 'stronger,' and the American 'dollar.' Literally: 'If you do well (doll), I do better (doller)!' (Thanks to Rob McFarland for help with this translation).

Bibliography

Adams, Carole Elizabeth. *Women Clerks in Wilhelmine Germany: Issues of Class and Gender.* Cambridge: Cambridge University Press, 1988.

Adorno, Theodor W., and E. F. N. Jephcott. *Minima Moralia: Reflections from Damaged Life.* New York: Verso, 2005.

Aldiss, Brian Wilson, and David Wingrove. *Trillion Year Spree: The History of Science Fiction.* New York: Atheneum, 1973.

Andriopoulos, Stefan. *Possessed: Hypnotic Crimes, Corporate Fiction, and the Invention of Cinema.* Chicago: University of Chicago Press, 2008.

Ankum, Katharina von, ed. *Women in the Metropolis: Gender and Modernity in Weimar Culture.* Berkeley: University of California Press, 1997.

Ashkenazi, Ofer. *Weimar Film and Modern Jewish Identity.* New York: Palgrave Macmillan, 2012.

Bauman, Zygmunt. *Liquid Modernity.* Malden, MA: Wiley-Blackwell, 2000.

Bauman, Zygmunt. *Modernity and Ambivalence.* Ithaca, NY: Cornell University Press, 1991.

Bellour, Raymond. "On Fritz Lang," *SubStance* 3, no. 9 (April 1, 1974): 25–34.

Benjamin, Walter. *One-Way Street, and Other Writings.* London: NLB, 1979.

Benjamin, Walter. *Understanding Brecht.* New York: Verso, 2003.

Benjamin, Walter, and Rolf Tiedemann. *The Arcades Project.* Cambridge, MA: Harvard University Press, 1999.

Berghoff, Hartmut. "Der Berliner Kapitalmarkt im Aufbruch (1830–1870)." In *Geschichte des Finanzplatzes Berlin.* Edited by Hans Pohl, 53–97. Frankfurt: Knapp, 2002.

Berlin und die Berliner. Whitefish, MT: Kessinger Publishing, 2010.

Berman, Marshall. *All That Is Solid Melts into Air: The Experience of Modernity.* New York: Viking Penguin, 1988.

Bersch, Julia, and Graciela L. Kaminsky. "Financial Globalization in the 19th-century: Germany as a Financial Center." September, 2008. https://home.gwu.edu/~graciela/HOME-PAGE/RESEARCH-WORK/WORKING-PAPERS/Germany-center.pdf.

Biro, Matthew. *The Dada Cyborg: Visions of the New Human in Weimar Berlin.* Minneapolis: University of Minnesota Press, 2009.

Blumenthal-Barby, Martin. "Faces of Evil: Fritz Lang's Dr. Mabuse, the Gambler." *Seminar: A Journal of Germanic Studies* 49, no. 3 (2013): 322–43.

Blumer, Ronald H. "The Camera as Snowball: France 1918–1927." *Cinema Journal* 9, no. 2 (April 1, 1970): 31–39.

Böhme, Helmut. *An Introduction to the Social and Economic History of Germany: Politics and Economic Change in the Nineteenth and Twentieth Centuries.* Oxford: B. Blackwell, 1978.

Borchardt, Knut. *Perspectives on Modern German Economic History and Policy.* Cambridge: Cambridge University Press, 1991.

Bourdieu, Jérôme, Johan Heilbron, and Bénédicte Reynaud. "Les structures sociales de la finance." *Actes de la recherche en sciences sociales* 146–147, no. 1 (March 1, 2003): 3–7.

Bramwell, Anna. *Blood and Soil: Richard Walther Darré and Hitler's "Green Party."* Abbotsbrook: Kensal Press, 1985.

Breckenridge, Keith. "'Money with Dignity': Migrants, Minelords and the Cultural Politics of the South African Gold Standard Crisis, 1920–33." *The Journal of African History* 36, no. 2 (January 1, 1995): 271–304.

Buck-Morss, Susan. "The Flaneur, the Sandwichman and the Whore: The Politics of Loitering." *New German Critique*, no. 39 (October 1, 1986): 99–140.

Buck-Morss, Susan. *The Dialectics of Seeing: Walter Benjamin and the Arcades Project*. Cambridge, MA: MIT Press, 1989.

Burch, Noël. *In and out of Synch: The Awakening of a Cine-Dreamer*. Aldershot: Scolar Press, 1991.

Burch, Noël. *Life to Those Shadows*. Berkeley: University of California Press, 1990.

Butler, Erik. "Dr. Mabuse: Terror and Deception of the Image." *The German Quarterly* 78, no. 4 (October 1, 2005): 481–95.

Campbell, Jan. *Film and Cinema Spectatorship: Melodrama and Mimesis*. Cambridge: Polity, 2005.

Canetti, Elias. *Crowds and Power*. New York: Farrar Straus Giroux, 1984.

Carter, E. J. "Breaking the Bank: Gambling Casinos, Finance Capitalism, and German Unification." *Central European History* 39, no. 02 (2006): 185–213.

Carter, E. J. "The Green Table: Gambling Casinos, Capitalist Culture, and Modernity in Nineteenth-Century Germany." PhD diss., University of Illinois at Urbana-Champaign, 2002.

Cassis, Youssef. *Capitals of Capital: A History of International Financial Centres, 1780–2005*. Cambridge: Cambridge University Press, 2006.

Cetina, Karin Knorr, and Alex Preda. *The Oxford Handbook of the Sociology of Finance*. Oxford: Oxford University Press, 2012.

Charney, Leo, and Vanessa R. Schwartz, eds. *Cinema and the Invention of Modern Life*. Berkeley: University of California Press, 1995.

CineGraph, Hamburgisches Centrum für Filmforschung., ed. *Film-Kurier Index*. Hamburg: Hamburgisches Centrum für Filmforschung, 1993).

Clark, Christopher M. *Iron Kingdom: The Rise and Downfall of Prussia, 1600–1947*. Cambridge, MA: Belknap Press of Harvard University Press, 2006.

Clarke, Simon. "The Globalisation of Capital, Crisis and Class Struggle." *Capital & Class* 25, no. 3 (October 1, 2001): 93–101.

Collins, Peter. *Changing Ideals in Modern Architecture, 1750-1950*. Montreal: McGill-Queens University Press, 1998.

Cowan, Michael. "Cutting through the Archive: Querschnitt Montage and Images of the World in Weimar Visual Culture." *New German Critique* 40, no. 3 120 (September 21, 2013): 1–40.

Cowan, Michael. *Cult of the Will: Nervousness and German Modernity*. University Park, PA: Pennsylvania State University Press, 2008.

Crary, Jonathan. *Suspensions of Perception: Attention, Spectacle, and Modern Culture*. Cambridge, MA: MIT Press, 1999.

Curtis, William J. R. *Modern Architecture since 1900*. London: Phaidon, 2001.

Debord, Guy. *The Society of the Spectacle*. Berkeley, CA: Bureau of Public Secrets, 2013.

Dimendberg, Edward. *Film Noir and the Spaces of Modernity*. Cambridge, MA: Harvard University Press, 2004.

Doane, Mary Ann. *The Emergence of Cinematic Time: Modernity, Contingency, the Archive*. Cambridge, MA: Harvard University Press, 2002.

Döblin, Alfred, and Eugène Jolas. *Berlin Alexanderplatz: The Story of Franz Biberkopf*. London: Continuum, 2004.

Dölle, Gilla. *Die (un)heimliche Macht des Geldes: Finanzierungsstrategien der Bürgerlichen Frauenbewegung in Deutschland zwischen 1865 und 1933*. Bd. 2. Frankfurt am Main: Dipa, 1997.

Dommann, Monika. "Bühnen des Kapitalismus: Der Getreidehandel als Wissensobjekt zwischen den Weltkriegen." *Berichte zur Wissenschaftsgeschichte* 37, no. 2 (2014): 112–31.

Dyer, Richard. *White*. London: Routledge, 1997.

Eichengreen, Barry, and Marc Flandreau. *Gold Standard in Theory and History*. London: Routledge, 1997.

Eisenlohr, C. J. *Ueber die Errichtung allgemeiner Komm-Scuhulden-Tilgungs-Kassen für einzelne Kreise und ganze Länder*. Karlsruhe: C.C. Müllerschen, 1818.

Eisenstein, Sergei. *Film Form: Essays in Film Theory*. Translated and edited by Jay Leyda. San Diego, CA: Harcourt, Brace & World, 2014.
Eisenstein, Sergei, Jay Leyda, Annette Michelson and Maciej Sliwowski. "Notes for a Film of 'Capital.'" *October* 2 (July 1, 1976): 3–26.
Eisner, Lotte H. *The Haunted Screen: Expressionism in the German Cinema and the Influence of Max Reinhardt*. Berkeley: University of California Press, 2008.
Elliott, John E. "Marx and Schumpeter on Capitalism's Creative Destruction: A Comparative Restatement." *The Quarterly Journal of Economics* 95, no. 1 (August 1, 1980): 45–68.
Elsaesser, Thomas. *Weimar Cinema and After: Germany's Historical Imaginary*. London: Routledge, 2000.
Elsaesser, Thomas, and Adam Barker, eds. *Early Cinema: Space, Frame, Narrative*. London: BFI Pub, 1990.
Elsaesser, Thomas, and Michael Wedel, eds. *A Second Life: German Cinema's First Decades*. Amsterdam: Amsterdam University Press, 1996.
Elsaesser, Thomas, and Michael Wedel, eds. *The BFI Companion to German Cinema*. London: BFI Pub, 1999.
Engels, Friedrich. *Briefe über den historischen Materialismus (1890–1895)*. Berlin: Dietz, 1979.
Engels, Friedrich. "Letter from Friedrich Engels to Conrad Schmidt in Berlin – Oct. 27, 1890." In *Marx and Engels Correspondence*. Translated by Donna Torr. New York: International Publishers, 1968.
Evans, Richard J., and W. Robert Lee, eds. *The German Family: Essays on the Social History of the Family in Nineteenth- and Twentieth-Century Germany*. London: Croom Helm, Barnes & Noble, 1981.
Fabian, Ann. *Card Sharps and Bucket Shops: Gambling in Nineteenth-Century America*. New York: Routledge, 1999.
Feder, Gottfried, and Adolf Hitler. *Kampf gegen die Hochfinanz*. Munich: Franz Eher Nachfolger, 1933.
Feldman, Gerald D. *The Great Disorder: Politics, Economics, and Society in the German Inflation, 1914–1924*. New York: Oxford University Press, 1993.
Ferguson, Niall. *High Financier: The Lives and Time of Siegmund Warburg*. New York: Penguin Press, 2010.
Ferguson, Niall. *Paper and Iron: Hamburg Business and German Politics in the Era of Inflation, 1897-1927*. Cambridge: Cambridge University Press, 1995.
Ferguson, Niall. *The House of Rothschild*. New York: Penguin, 1998.
Fergusson, Adam. *When Money Dies: The Nightmare of the Weimar Collapse*. London: Kimber, 1975.
Flanner, Janet. "The Swindling President – II." *The New Yorker*, August 26, 1939. http://www.newyorker.com/magazine/1939/09/02/the-swindling-president-ii.
Fohlin, Caroline. *Finance Capitalism and Germany's Rise to Industrial Power*. Cambridge: Cambridge University Press, 2007.
Fraser, Nancy. "Rethinking the Public Sphere: A Contribution to the Critique of Actually Existing Democracy." *Social Text*, no. 25/26 (January 1, 1990): 56–80.
Friedberg, Anne. *Window Shopping: Cinema and the Postmodern*. Berkeley: University of California Press, 1993.
Frölich, Margrit. "Playing the European Market: Marcel L'Herbier's *L'Argent* (1928), Ufa, and German-French Film Relations." In *Continuity and Crisis in German Cinema 1928–36*. Edited by Barbara Hales, Mihaela Petrescu, Valerie Weinstein. Rochester: Camden House, 2016.
Fulda, Bernhard. *Press and Politics in the Weimar Republic*. Oxford: Oxford University Press, 2009.
Furstenau, Marc. *The Film Theory Reader: Debates and Arguments*. London: Routledge, 2010.

Gabriel, Barbara, and Suzan Ilcan, eds. *Post-Modernism and the Ethical Subject*. Montreal: McGill-Queen's University Press, 2004.

Gay, Peter. *Weimar Culture: The Outsider as Insider*. New York: W.W. Norton, 2001.

Geisst, Charles R. *Wall Street: A History: From Its Beginnings to the Fall of Enron*. Oxford: Oxford University Press, 2004.

Gerschenkron, Alexander. *Continuity in History, and Other Essays*. Cambridge, MA: Belknap Press of Harvard University Press, 1968.

Gerschenkron, Alexander. *Economic Backwardness in Historical Perspective*. Cambridge: Belknap Press, 1962.

Giddens, Anthony. *The Consequences of Modernity*. Stanford: Stanford University Press, 1991.

Giedion, Sigfried. *Space, Time and Architecture: The Growth of a New Tradition*. Cambridge, MA.: Harvard University Press, 1967.

Gilman, Sander L. *The Jew's Body*. New York: Routledge, 1991.

Gömmel, Rainer. "Entstehung und Entwicklung der Effektenbörsen im 19. Jahrhundert bis 1914." In *Deutsche Börsengeschichte*. Edited by Hans Pohl, 135–207. Frankfurt: Knapp, 1992.

Goodbody, Axel, and Berbeli Wanning. *Wasser – Kultur – Ökologie: Beiträge zum Wandel im Umgang mit dem Wasser und zu seiner literarischen Imagination*. Göttingen: Vandenhoeck & Ruprecht, 2008.

Graeber, David. *Debt: The First 5,000 Years*. Brooklyn: Melville House, 2014.

Gunning, Tom. *The Films of Fritz Lang: Allegories of Vision and Modernity*. London: British Film Institute, 2000.

Gutwein, Daniel. "Jewish Financiers and Industry, 1890–1914: England and Germany." *Jewish History* 8, no. 1 (March 1, 1994): 177–89.

Habermas, Jürgen. *The Structural Transformation of the Public Sphere: An Inquiry into a Category of Bourgeois Society*. Cambridge, MA: MIT Press, 1991.

Hacking, Ian. *The Taming of Chance*. Cambridge: Cambridge University Press, 1990.

Hagener, Malte. *Moving Forward, Looking Back: The European Avant-Garde and the Invention of Film Culture, 1919–1939*. Amsterdam: Amsterdam University Press, 2007.

Hake, Sabine. *Passions and Deceptions: The Early Films of Ernst Lubitsch*. Princeton: Princeton University Press, 1992.

Hales, Barbara, Petrescu, Mihaela, and Weinstein, Valerie, eds. *Continuity and Crisis in German Cinema, 1928–1936*. Rochester, NY: Camden House, 2016.

Hales, Barbara, and Valerie Weinstein, eds. *Rethinking Jewishness in Weimar Cinema*. Film Europa: German Cinema in an International Context, vol. 24. New York: Berghahn Books, 2020.

Hall, Sara F. "Trading Places: 'Dr. Mabuse' and the Pleasure of Role Play." *German Quarterly* (2003): 381–97.

Hall, Sara F. "Inflation and Devaluation: Gender, Space and Economics in G. W. Pabst's *The Joyless Street* (1925). In *Weimar Cinema: An Essential Guide to Classic Films of the Era*. Edited by Noah Isenberg, 135–154. New York: Columbia University Press, 2009.

Halle, Randall, and Margaret McCarthy, eds. *Light Motives: German Popular Film in Perspective*. Detroit: Wayne State University Press, 2003.

Haller, Andrea. "Shadows in the Glasshouse: Film Novels in Imperial Germany, 1913–1917." *Film History: An International Journal* 20, no. 2 (2008): 164–80.

Hansen, Miriam. "The Mass Production of the Senses: Classical Cinema as Vernacular Modernism." *Modernism/modernity* 6, no. 2 (1999): 59–77.

Hansen, Miriam. *Babel and Babylon: Spectatorship in American Silent Film*. Cambridge: Harvard University Press, 1994.

Hartsough, Denise. "Soviet Film Distribution and Exhibition in Germany, 1921–1933." *Historical Journal of Film, Radio and Television* 5, no. 2 (1985): 131–48.

Harvey, David. *Paris, Capital of Modernity*. New York: Routledge, 2003.
Harvey, David. *The Limits to Capital*. London: Verso, 2006.
Hegel, Georg Wilhelm Friedrich. *Hegel's Philosophy of Right*. Translated by Thomas Malcolm Knox. London: Oxford at the Clarendon Press, 1967.
Heidegger, Martin. *The Question Concerning Technology, and Other Essays*. New York: Harper and Row, 1977.
Helleiner, Eric. "Economic Nationalism as a Challenge to Economic Liberalism? Lessons from the 19th Century." *International Studies Quarterly* 46, no. 3 (2002): 307–29.
Henry, Nancy, and Cannon Schmitt. Victorian Investments: New Perspectives on Finance and Culture. Bloomington: Indiana University Press, 2008.
Henning, Friedrich-Wilhelm. "Börsenkrisen und Börsengesetzgebung von 1914 bis 1945 in Deutschland." In *Deutsche Börsengeschichte*. Edited by Hans Pohl, 211–93. Frankfurt: Knapp, 1992
Herf, Jeffrey. *Reactionary Modernism: Technology, Culture, and Politics in Weimar and the Third Reich*. Cambridge: Cambridge University Press, 1984.
Herzfelde, Wieland, and Brigid Doherty. "Introduction to the First International Dada Fair." *October* 105 (July 2003): 93–104.
Herzog, Lisa. *Inventing the Market: Smith, Hegel, and Political Theory*. Oxford: Oxford University Press, 2013.
Hilferding, Rudolph. *Finance Capital: A Study of the Latest Phase of Capitalist Development*. London: Routledge, 2006.
Hillesheim, Jürgen, and Elisabeth Michael. *Lexikon nationalsozialistischer Dichter: Biographien, Analysen, Bibliographien*. Würzburg: Königshausen & Neumann, 1993.
Hirschstein, Hans, and Karl W. Scholz. "Commodity Exchanges in Germany." *Annals of the American Academy of Political and Social Science* 155 (May 1, 1931): 208–17.
Holtfrerich, Carl-Ludwig. *Frankfurt as a Financial Centre: From Medieval Trade Fair to European Banking Centre*. Munich: Beck, 1999.
Horak, Jan-Christopher. "Film History and Film Preservation: Reconstructing the Text of *The Joyless Street* (1925)." *Screening the Past*, no. 5 (1998).
H., R. G. "Review of *The Stabilisation of the Mark* by Hjalmar Schacht." *Journal of the Royal Statistical Society* 91, no. 1 (January 1, 1928): 100–102.
Hudec, Zdeněk. "Eisenstein's Das Kapital: Attempting a New Genre." *Estetika: The Central European Journal of Aesthetics*, 2 (2008): 184–197.
Huyssen, Andreas. *After the Great Divide: Modernism, Mass Culture, Postmodernism*. Bloomington: Indiana University Press, 1986.
Isenberg, Noah William, ed. *Weimar Cinema: An Essential Guide to Classic Films of the Era*. New York: Columbia University Press, 2009.
Jacobsen, Wolfgang, ed. *G.W. Pabst*. Berlin: Argon, 1997.
Jacobsen, Wolfgang. *Zeit und Welt*. Munich: Edition Text + Kritik, 2013.
Jacques, Norbert, and Günter Scholdt. *Dr. Mabuse, Der Spieler: Roman, Film, Dokumente*. St. Ingbert: W.J. Röhrig, 1987.
James, Harold. "Strukturwandel in Kriegs- und Krisenzeiten 1914–1945." In *Geschichte des Finanzplatzes Berlin*. Edited by Hans Pohl, 157–213. Frankfurt: Knapp, 2002.
Jameson, Fredric. "Culture and Finance Capital." *Critical Inquiry* 24, no. 1 (October 1, 1997): 246–65.
Jameson, Fredric. *Postmodernism, Or, The Cultural Logic of Late Capitalism*. Durham: Duke University Press, 1991.
Jameson, Fredric. "The Aesthetics of Singularity." *New Left Review*, no. 92 (April 2015): 101–32.
Jardin, Pascal. "Aux sources du national-socialisme. Les romans de Rudolf Herzog et la culture politique allemande." *Vingtième Siècle. Revue d'histoire*, no. 43 (July 1, 1994): 43–54.

Jauss, Hans Robert. *Toward an Aesthetic of Reception*. Vol. 2. Minneapolis: University of Minnesota Press, 1982.

Jay, Martin. "Taking On the Stigma of Inauthenticity: Adorno's Critique of Genuineness." *New German Critique*, no. 97 (January 1, 2006): 15–30.

Jelavich, Peter. *Berlin Cabaret*. Cambridge, MA: Harvard University Press, 1993.

Jensen, Erik Norman. *Body by Weimar: Athletes, Gender, and German Modernity*. Oxford: Oxford University Press, 2010.

Jonsson, Pernilla, and Silke Neunsinger. *Gendered Money: Financial Organization in Women's Movements, 1880–1933*. New York: Berghahn Books, 2012.

Kaes, Anton. *Shell Shock Cinema: Weimar Culture and the Wounds of War*. Princeton: Princeton University Press, 2009.

Kaes, Anton. *M*. BFI Film Classics. London: BFI, 2000.

Kaes, Anton, Nicholas Baer, and Michael Cowan, eds. *The Promise of Cinema: German Film Theory, 1907–1933*. Berkeley: University of California Press, 2016.

Kaes, Anton, Martin Jay, and Edward Dimendberg, eds. *The Weimar Republic Sourcebook*. Berkeley: University of California Press, 1995.

Kalat, David. *The Strange Case of Dr. Mabuse: A Study of the Twelve Films and Five Novels*. Jefferson, NC: McFarland, 2001.

Kapczynski, Jennifer M., and Michael David Richardson, eds. *A New History of German Cinema*. Rochester, NY: Camden House, 2012.

Kardish, Laurence, and Museum of Modern Art (New York, N.Y.), eds. *Weimar Cinema, 1919–1933: Daydreams and Nightmares*. New York: Museum of Modern Art, 2010.

Kern, Stephen. *The Culture of Time and Space, 1880–1918: With a New Preface*. Cambridge, MA: Harvard University Press, 2003.

Kindleberger, Charles Poor. *A Financial History of Western Europe*. London: Allen & Unwin, 1984.

Kitchen, Martin. *The Political Economy of Germany, 1815–1914*. London: Croom Helm, 1978.

Kleeberg, John M. "The Disconto-Gesellschaft and German Industrialization: A Critical Examination of the Career of a German Universal Bank, 1851–1914." PhD diss., Oxford University, 1988.

Kloss, Rudolf. "The Coal Supply of Austria after the Revolution of 1918." *Annals of the American Academy of Political and Social Science* 98 (November 1, 1921): 16–19.

Knorr-Cetina, Karin, and Alex Preda. *The Sociology of Financial Markets*. Oxford: Oxford University Press, 2006.

Koepnick, Lutz P. *The Dark Mirror: German Cinema between Hitler and Hollywood*. Berkeley: University of California Press, 2002.

Kolb, Eberhard. *The Weimar Republic*. London: Routledge, 2008.

Koselleck, R., and M. W Richter. "Crisis." *Journal of the History of Ideas* 67, no. 2 (2006): 357–400.

Kracauer, Siegfried. *From Caligari to Hitler: A Psychological History of the German Film*. Princeton, NJ: Princeton University Press, 2004.

Kracauer, Siegfried. *The Salaried Masses: Duty and Distraction in Weimar Germany*. London: Verso, 1998.

Kracauer, Siegfried. *The Mass Ornament: Weimar Essays*. Edited by Thomas Y. Levin. Cambridge, MA: Harvard University Press, 1995.

Kreimeier, Klaus. *The Ufa Story: A History of Germany's Greatest Film Company, 1918–1945*. Translated by Rita Kimber and Robert Kimber. Berkeley: University of California Press, 1999.

Kruger, Loren. "'To Those Born Later': Brecht's Centenary and Other Commemorations." *Rethinking Marxism* 11, no. 2 (March 1, 1999): 67–79.

Krugman, Paul. "The Capitalist; Dr. Mabuse Returns." *The New York Times*, November 8, 1998. http://www.nytimes.com/1998/11/08/magazine/the-capitalist-dr-mabuse-returns.html.

La Berge, Leigh Claire. "The Rules of Abstraction Methods and Discourses of Finance." *Radical History Review* 2014, no. 118 (December 21, 2014): 93–112.

Laurence, Anne, Josephine Maltby, and Janette Rutterford, eds. *Women and Their Money 1700–1950: Essays on Women and Finance*. 15. London: Routledge, 2009.

Lefebvre, Henri. *The Production of Space*. Malden, MA: Blackwell, 1991.

Lehmann-Hasemeyer, Sibylle, and Jochen Streb. "The Berlin Stock Exchange in Imperial Germany: A Market for New Technology?" *American Economic Review* 106, no. 11 (November 1, 2016): 3558–76.

Lerner, Gerda. "The Origin of Prostitution in Ancient Mesopotamia." *Signs: Journal of Women in Culture and Society* 11, no. 2 (January 1986): 236–54.

Lévi-Strauss, Claude. *The Elementary Structures of Kinship*. Translated by James Harle Bell, John Richard von Sturmer and Rodney Needham ed. Boston: Beacon Press, 1969.

Levy, Jonathan. *Freaks of Fortune: The Emerging World of Capitalism and Risk in America*. Cambridge, MA: Harvard University Press, 2012.

Lewin, Ellen, ed. *Feminist Anthropology: A Reader*. Malden, MA: Blackwell, 2006.

Light, Andrew, and Jonathan M. Smith, eds. *Philosophy and Geography*, II, *The Production of Public Space*. Lanham: Rowman & Littlefield Publishers, 1998.

Lovin, Clifford R. "Agricultural Reorganization in the Third Reich: The Reich Food Corporation (Reichsnährstand), 1933–1936." *Agricultural History* 43, no. 4 (October 1, 1969): 447–62.

Lovin, Clifford R. "Blut Und Boden: The Ideological Basis of the Nazi Agricultural Program." *Journal of the History of Ideas* 28, no. 2 (April 1, 1967): 279–88.

Lyons, Owen. "'Denn Gold ist Glück und Fluch dieser Welt:' Examining the Trope of Gold in 'Gold' (1934) and 'Der Kaiser von Kalifornien' (1936)." In *Continuity and Crisis in German Cinema 1928–36*, edited by Barbara Hales, Mihaela Petrescu, Valerie Weinstein, 92–110. Rochester: Camden House, 2016.

MacKenzie, Donald A. *An Engine, Not a Camera: How Financial Models Shape Markets*. Cambridge, MA: MIT Press, 2006.

Martin, Randy. *Financialization of Daily Life*. Philadelphia: Temple University Press, 2002.

Marx, Karl. *Capital: A Critique of Political Economy*. Vol. 1. London: Penguin Books, 1981.

Marx, Karl. *Marx: Early Political Writings*. Edited by Joseph J. O'Malley. Cambridge: Cambridge University Press, 1994.

Marx, Karl. *The Communist Manifesto: Annotated Text*. Edited by Fredric L. Bender. New York: W.W. Norton, 1988.

Matsuda, Matt K. *The Memory of the Modern*. New York: Oxford University Press, 1996.

Mayer, Bruno. *Die Effectenbörsen und ihre Geschäfte*. Vienna: A. Hölder, 1899.

McCormick, Richard W. *Gender and Sexuality in Weimar Modernity: Film, Literature, and "New Objectivity."* New York: Palgrave, 2001.

McCormick, Richard W. "Private Anxieties/Public Projections: 'New Objectivity,' Male Subjectivity, and Weimar Cinema." *Women in German Yearbook* 10 (1994): 1–18.

Michie, Ranald C. *The London Stock Exchange: A History*. Oxford: Oxford University Press, 2001.

Mieck, Ilja. "Berlins Aufstieg zum ersten preußischen Finanzplatz bis zur Industrialisierung." In *Geschichte des Finanzplatzes Berlin*. Edited by Hans Pohl, 1–52. Frankfurt: Knapp, 2002.

Muller, Jerry Z. *The Mind and the Market: Capitalism in Modern European Thought*. New York: Alfred A. Knopf, 2002.

Murray, Bruce Arthur. *Film and the German Left in the Weimar Republic: From Caligari to Kuhle Wampe*. Austin: University of Texas Press, 1990.

Nalbach, Alex. "'Poisoned at the Source'? Telegraphic News Services and Big Business in the Nineteenth Century." *The Business History Review* 77, no. 4 (December 1, 2003): 577–610.

Nasar, Sylvia. *Grand Pursuit: The Story of Economic Genius*. New York: Simon & Schuster, 2011.

Nohlen, Dieter, and Philip Stöver. *Elections in Europe: A Data Handbook*. Baden-Baden: Nomos, 2010.

O'Rourke, Kevin H. *Globalization and History: The Evolution of a Nineteenth-Century Atlantic Economy*. Cambridge, MA: MIT Press, 1999.

Otsuru, Atsushi. "Prisoners of War (Japan)." In 1914–1918 Online. International Encyclopedia of the First World War. Edited by Ute Daniel, Peter Gatrell, Oliver Janz, Heather Jones, Jennifer Keene, Alan Kramer, and Bill Nasson. Freie Universität, Berlin, 2014. https://encyclopedia.1914-1918-online.net/article/prisoners_of_war_japan.

Persky, Joseph. "Retrospectives: The Ethology of Homo Economicus." *The Journal of Economic Perspectives* 9, no. 2 (April 1, 1995): 221–31.

Petley, Julian. *Capital and Culture: German Cinema 1933–45*. London: British Film Institute, 1979.

Petrescu, Mihaela. "Billy Wilder's Work as Eintänzer in Weimar Berlin." *New German Critique* 40, no. 3 120 (September 21, 2013): 65–84.

Petro, Patrice. *Joyless Streets: Women and Melodramatic Representation in Weimar Germany*. Princeton, NJ: Princeton University Press, 1989.

Peukert, Detlev. *The Weimar Republic*. New York: Hill and Wang, 1993.

Pflanze, Otto. *Bismarck and the Development of Germany; the Period of Unification, 1815–1871*. Princeton, NJ: Princeton University Press, 1963.

Pierre Manigat, Matari. "Finance Capital and Financialization: A Comparative Reading of Marx and Hilferding." *OEconomia*, no. 10–4 (December 1, 2020): 687–710.

Pile, Steve. *Real Cities: Modernity, Space, and the Phantasmagorias of City Life*. London: Sage, 2005.

Piltz, Georg. *Geschichte der Europäischen Karikatur*. Berlin: VEB Deutscher Verlag der Wissenschaften, 1976.

Pohl, Hans. *Aufbruch der Weltwirtschaft: Geschichte der Weltwirtschaft von der Mitte des 19. Jahrhunderts bis zum Ersten Weltkrieg*. Stuttgart: F. Steiner Verlag Wiesbaden, 1989.

Pohl, Hans (ed.). *Geschichte des Finanzplatzes Berlin*. Frankfurt: Knapp, 2002.

Pomerance, Murray, ed. *Cinema and Modernity*. New Brunswick, NJ: Rutgers University Press, 2006.

Poovey, Mary. "Writing about Finance in Victorian England: Disclosure and Secrecy in the Culture of Investment." In *Victorian Investments: New Perspectives on Finance and Culture*. Edited by Nancy Henry and Cannon Schmitt, 39–57. Bloomington: Indiana University Press, 2009.

Preda, Alex. *Framing Finance: The Boundaries of Markets and Modern Capitalism*. Chicago: University of Chicago Press, 2009.

Presner, Todd Samuel. *Mobile Modernity: Germans, Jews, Trains*. New York: Columbia University Press, 2007.

Read, Donald. *The Power of News: The History of Reuters, 1849–1989*. Oxford: Oxford University Press, 1992.

Reisser, J. *The German Great Banks and Their Concentration in Connection with The Economic Development of Germany*. Vol. 4, Publications of the U.S. National Monetary Commission. Washington, DC: Government Printing Office, 1911.

Reith, Gerda. *The Age of Chance Gambling in Western Culture*. London: Routledge, 1999.

Rentschler, Eric, ed. *The Films of G.W. Pabst: An Extraterritorial Cinema*. New Brunswick: Rutgers University Press, 1990.

Rentschler, Eric. "There's No Place like Home: Luis Trenker's *The Prodigal Son* (1934)." *New German Critique*, no. 60 (October 1, 1993): 33–56.

Richie, Alexandra. *Faust's Metropolis: A History of Berlin*. New York: Carroll & Graf, 1998.

Robb, George. "Ladies of the Ticker: Women, Investment, and Fraud in England and America, 1850–1930." In *Victorian Investments: New Perspectives on Finance and Culture*. Edited by Nancy Henry and Cannon Schmitt, 120–42. Bloomington: Indiana University Press, 2009.

Robertson, Ritchie. *The "Jewish Question" in German Literature, 1749–1939: Emancipation and Its Discontents*. Oxford: Oxford University Press, 1999.

Rogowski, Christian. *The Many Faces of Weimar Cinema: Rediscovering Germany's Filmic Legacy*. Rochester, NY: Camden House, 2010.

Roske, Ralph J. "The World Impact of the California Gold Rush 1849–1857." *Arizona and the West* 5, no. 3 (October 1, 1963): 187–232.

Roth, Joseph, and Elie Wiesel. *Wandering Jews*. Translated by Michael Hofmann. New York: Norton, 2001.

Sassen, Saskia. *The Global City: New York, London, Tokyo*. Princeton, NJ: Princeton University Press, 2001.

Scheunemann, Dietrich. *Expressionist Film: New Perspectives*. Rochester, NY: Camden House, 2006.

Schivelbusch, Wolfgang. *The Culture of Defeat: On National Trauma, Mourning, and Recovery*. New York: Metropolitan Books, 2003.

Schivelbusch, Wolfgang. *The Railway Journey: The Industrialization of Time and Space in the 19th Century*. Berkeley: University of California Press, 1986.

Schulte-Sasse, Linda. *Entertaining the Third Reich: Illusions of Wholeness in Nazi Cinema*. Durham: Duke University Press, 1996.

Scott, A. O. "Michael Douglas Returns in Oliver Stone's Sequel." *The New York Times*, September 23, 2010.

Seibel, Alexandra. "Vienna, Girls, and Jewish Authorship: Topographies of a Cinematic City, 1920–40." PhD, New York University, 2008.

Shiller, Robert J. *Irrational Exuberance*. Princeton: Princeton University Press, 2015.

Simmel, Georg. *The Philosophy of Money*. Edited by David Frisby. London: Routledge, 2004.

Slobodian, Quinn. *Globalists: The End of Empire and the Birth of Neoliberalism*. Cambridge, MA: Harvard University Press, 2018.

Sloterdijk, Peter. *Critique of Cynical Reason*. Minnesota: Minnesota University Press, 1988.

Stäheli, Urs. *Spectacular Speculation: Thrills, the Economy, and Popular Discourse*. Stanford: Stanford University Press, 2013.

Stepelevich, Lawrence S., ed. *The Young Hegelians, an Anthology*. Cambridge: Cambridge University Press, 1983.

Stern, Fritz Richard. *Einstein's German World*. Princeton, NJ: Princeton University Press, 1999.

Stern, Fritz Richard. *Gold and Iron: Bismarck, Bleichröder, and the Building of the German Empire*. New York: Knopf, 1977.

Stiasny, Philipp. "Glück und Elend der Neureichen." *Filmblatt* 19, no. 55/56 (Winter 2014–15): 2–23.

Stiasny, Philipp. *Das Kino und der Krieg: Deutschland 1914–1929*. Munich: Edition Text + Kritik, 2009.

Stoetzler, Marcel. *The State, the Nation, and the Jews: Liberalism and the Antisemitism Dispute in Bismarck's Germany*. Lincoln: University of Nebraska Press, 2008.

Stratigakos, Despina. *A Women's Berlin: Building the Modern City*. Minneapolis: University of Minnesota Press, 2008.

Tatar, Maria. *Lustmord: Sexual Murder in Weimar Germany*. Princeton: Princeton University Press, 1995.

Theweleit, Klaus. *Male Fantasies*. Vol. 1, *Women, Floods, Bodies, History*. Translated by Stephen Conway, Erica Carter and Chris Turner. Minneapolis: University of Minnesota Press, 1989.

Theweleit, Klaus. *Male Fantasies*. Vol. 2, *Male Bodies: Psychoanalyzing the White Terror*. Translated by Stephen Conway, Erica Carter and Chris Turner. Minneapolis: University of Minnesota Press, 1989.

Thompson, John B. *Media and Modernity: A Social Theory of the Media*. Cambridge: Polity Press, 2013.

Tönnies, Ferdinand. *Community and Civil Society*. Cambridge: Cambridge University Press, 2001.

Tooze, Adam. *The Wages of Destruction: The Making and Breaking of the Nazi Economy*. London: Allen Lane, 2006.

Tooze, Adam. *Statistics and the German State, 1900–1945: The Making of Modern Economic Knowledge*. Cambridge: Cambridge University Press, 2001.

Torp, Cornelius. *The Challenges of Globalization: Economy and Politics in Germany, 1860–1914*. New York: Berghahn Books, 2014.

Tunstall, Graydon A. *Blood on the Snow: The Carpathian Winter War of 1915*. Lawrence, Kansas: University Press of Kansas, 2010.

Umbach, Maiken, and Bernd-Rüdiger Hüppauf, eds. *Vernacular Modernism: Heimat, Globalization, and the Built Environment*. Stanford: Stanford University Press, 2005.

Vidler, Anthony. "The Explosion of Space: Architecture and the Filmic Imaginary." *Assemblage*, no. 21 (1993): 45–59.

Voth, Hans-Joachim. "With a Bang, Not a Whimper: Pricking Germany's 'Stock Market Bubble' in 1927 and the Slide into Depression." *The Journal of Economic History* 63, no. 1 (March 2003): 65–99.

Ward, Janet. *Weimar Surfaces: Urban Visual Culture in 1920s Germany*. Berkeley: University of California Press, 2001.

Wasserman, Renata R. Mautner. "Financial Fictions: Émile Zola's *L'argent*, Frank Norris' *The Pit*, and Alfredo de Taunay's *O Encilhamento*." *Comparative Literature Studies* 38, no. 3 (2001): 193–214.

Waugh, Thomas. *"Show Us Life": Toward a History and Aesthetics of the Committed Documentary*. Lanham, MD: Scarecrow Press, Incorporated, 1984.

Weatherall, James Owen. *The Physics of Wall Street: A Brief History of Predicting the Unpredictable*. Boston: Houghton Mifflin Harcourt, 2013.

Weber, Max. *Börsenwesen: Schriften und Reden 1893–1898*. Edited by Knut Borchardt and Cornelia Meyer-Stoll. Tübingen: J.C.B. Mohr (Paul Siebeck), 1999.

Weber, Max "Stock and Commodity Exchanges 'Die Börse' (1894)." *Theory and Society* 29, no. 3 (June 1, 2000): 305–38.

Weinstein, Valerie. '(Un)Fashioning Identities: Ernst Lubitsch's Early Comedies of Mistaken Identity.' In *Visual Culture in Twentieth-Century Germany: Text as Spectacle*. Edited by Gail Finney. Bloomington: Indiana University Press, 2006. 120–133.

Whyte, Iain Boyd, and David Frisby, eds. *Metropolis Berlin: 1880–1940*. Berkeley: University of California Press, 2012.

Widdig, Bernd. *Culture and Inflation in Weimar Germany*. Berkeley: University of California Press, 2001.

Wiesen, S. Jonathan. *Creating the Nazi Marketplace: Commerce and Consumption in the Third Reich*. Cambridge: Cambridge University Press, 2011.

Wilde, Oscar. *The Picture of Dorian Gray*. Leipzig: Bernhard Tauchnitz, 1908.

Wolfe, Tom. *The Bonfire of the Vanities*. New York: Farrar, Straus Giroux, 1987.

Zschaler, Frank. "Erzwungene Reorientierung im Zeichen der deutschen Teilung (1945–1990)." In *Geschichte des Finanzplatzes Berlin*. Edited by Hans Pohl, 215–52. Frankfurt: Knapp, 2002.

Zweig, Stefan. *Sternstunden Der Menschheit*. Frankfurt: Fischer, 2013.

List of Films

A Corner in Wheat (D. W. Griffith, 1909)
Afgrunden (Urban Gad, 1910)
Battleship Potemkin (Sergei Eisenstein, 1926)
Berlin: Die Sinfonie der Großstadt (Walter Ruttmann, 1927)
Bräutigam auf Aktien (Viggo Larsen, 1918)
Café Elektric: Die Liebesbörse (Gustav Ucicky, 1927)
City Bank (Robert Scholz, 1921)
Das Geld auf der Strasse (Reinhold Schünzel, 1922)
Das Testament des Dr. Mabuse (Fritz Lang, 1933)
Der Kaiser von Kalifornien (Luis Trenker, 1936)
Der letzte Mann (F. W. Murnau, 1924)
Der Schieberkönig (Hubert Möst, 1920)
Der schwarze Montag (Robert Dietrich, 1922)
Die Börsenkönigin (Edmund Edel, 1918)
Die Büchse der Pandora (G. W. Pabst, 1929)
Die Austernprinzessin (Ernst Lubitsch, 1919)
Die Dame mit der Maske (Wilhelm Thiele, 1929)
Die Dreigroschenoper (G. W. Pabst, 1931)
Die Filmprimadonna (Urban Gad, 1913)
Die freudlose Gasse (G. W. Pabst, 1925)
Die Prostitution (Richard Oswald, 1919)
Die Stadt ohne Juden (Gustav Ucicky, 1924)
Die Verrufenen (Gerhard Lamprecht, 1925)
Dirnentragödie (Bruno Rahn, 1927)
Dr. Mabuse der Spieler (Fritz Lang, 1922)
Durch's Brandenburger Tor (Wilhelm Dieterle, 1929)
Eldorado (Marcel L'Herbier, 1921)
Fall of the Romanov Dynasty (Esfir Schub, 1927)
Fräulein Raffke (Richard Eichberg, 1923)
Gesindel (Martin Berger, 1921)
Hanseaten (Gerhard Lamprecht, 1925)
Inflationsbild (Hans Richter, 1928)
Intolerance (D. W. Griffith, 1916)
Jenseits der Strasse (Leo Mittler, 1929)
Kauft Mariett-Aktien (Alexander von Antalffy, 1922)
Kuhle Wampe, oder: Wem gehört die Welt? (Slatan Dudow, 1932)
L'Argent (Marcel L'Herbier, 1929)

L'Inhumaine (Marcel L'Herbier, 1924)
M (Fritz Lang, 1931)
Man with a Movie Camera (Dziga Vertov, 1929)
Margin Call (J. C. Chandor, 2011)
Melodie der Welt (Walter Ruttmann, 1929)
Metropolis (Fritz Lang, 1927)
Mutter Krausens Fahrt ins Glück (Piel Jutzi, 1929)
Niemandsland (Victor Trivas, 1931)
Planetenschieber (Reinhard Bruck, 1920)
Polizeibericht Überfall (Ernö Metzner, 1928)
So ist das Leben (Carl Junghans, 1929)
Spione (Fritz Lang, 1928)
Vier um die Frau (Fritz Lang, 1921)
Wall Street (Oliver Stone, 1987)
Wall Street: Money Never Sleeps (Oliver Stone, 2010)

Index

For Product Safety Concerns and Information please contact our EU
representative GPSR@taylorandfrancis.com
Taylor & Francis Verlag GmbH, Kaufingerstraße 24, 80331 München, Germany

www.ingramcontent.com/pod-product-compliance
Ingram Content Group UK Ltd.
Pitfield, Milton Keynes, MK11 3LW, UK
UKHW020012200926
475702UK00014B/1851

* 9 7 8 1 0 4 1 1 7 9 4 4 3 *